SOME NEWLY ESTABLISHED ASIAN STATES
AND
THE DEVELOPMENT OF INTERNATIONAL LAW

J. J. G. SYATAUW
J. S. D. (YALE)

SOME NEWLY ESTABLISHED ASIAN STATES AND THE DEVELOPMENT OF INTERNATIONAL LAW

THE HAGUE
MARTINUS NIJHOFF
1961

ISBN 978-94-015-0321-1 ISBN 978-94-015-0863-6 (eBook)
DOI 10.1007/978-94-015-0863-6

To
my Mother
and
the memory of my Father

ACKNOWLEDGEMENTS

It is with great pleasure that I acknowledge the debt that I owe to those who guided me in the preparation of this work.

I wish to express my sincere gratitude to the Yale Law School for permitting me to publish this book, and especially to Professor Myres S. McDougal whose stimulating ideas and kind encouragement have been of great value to me.

I am also much indebted to the London School of Economics and Political Science for the research facilities made available to me, and to Professor D. H. N. Johnson for his kind advice and help.

Finally, I would like to extend my sincere thanks to the University of Leiden for all the knowledge and experience that I have gained under its Faculty of Law.

The responsibility for the views expressed and the facts stated in the succeeding pages is, of course, mine alone.

November 1960. J. J. G. S.

TABLE OF CONTENTS

Maps

ABBREVIATIONS

A.J.I.L.	American Journal of International Law
Am. Pol. Sci. Rev.	American Political Science Review
B.Y.I.L.	British Year Book of International Law
Col. L.R.	Columbia Law Review
For. Aff.	Foreign Affairs
For. Pol. Bull.	Foreign Policy Bulletin
Hague Recueil	Recueil des Cours, Académie de Droit International de la Haye
I.C.J.	International Court of Justice
I.C.L.Q.	International and Comparative Law Quarterly
I.L.Q.	International Law Quarterly
IMTFE	International Military Tribunal for the Far East
India Q.	India Quarterly
Int. Aff.	International Affairs
Int. Org.	International Organization
I.Y.I.A.	Indian Year Book of International Affairs
J.A.I.L.	Japanese Annual of International Law
L.Q.R.	Law Quarterly Review
Mich. L.R.	Michigan Law Review
Neth. I.L.R.	Netherlands International Law Review
N.R.C.	Nieuwe Rotterdamse Courant
N.Y. Times	New York Times
Pac. Aff.	Pacific Affairs
P.C.I.J.	Permanent Court of International Justice
Pol. Studies	Political Studies
Tijdschrift Ind. T.L.V.	Tijdschrift voor Indische Taal-, Land- en Volkenkunde
Trans. Grot. Soc.	Transactions of the Grotius Society
U.N.	United Nations
U.N. Rev.	United Nations Review
Yale L.J.	Yale Law Journal
Y.B.W.A.	Year Book of World Affairs

CHAPTER I

THE PROBLEM

The world today is in a process of deep-rooted changes which is reshaping the global picture. In this connection one is accustomed to think in the first place of the technological achievements of mankind, and expressions like "atomic age," "nuclear age" and now "space age" have found their place in common speech.

These technological developments are not the only important changes which have come about in the last few decades. There are other events which, although perhaps of a less spectacular character, have equally affected the course of our history. The bipolarization of the world, the rise of nationalism, the decline of the colonial empires and the birth of new states are only a few examples to this effect.

It is a common phenomenon that significant changes in one field of human endeavour will ultimately affect other areas. International law is one example where the impact of world developments is very noticeable. The impact of the changing world is, indeed, strongly reflected in the field of international law which is consequently in a similar state of transition and the present state of international law has, therefore, become the growing concern of international jurists all over the world.[1] This book – as the title suggests – is intended to be a small contribution to the understanding of the significance of these changes for the development of international law, particularly from the viewpoint of some newly established Asian states.

Which are the new Asian states considered here?

The present map of Asia shows several countries which were not created until after World War II. This work will limit itself to four countries, namely India, Indonesia, Burma and Ceylon. For a justification of this selection several reasons can be given.

[1] Alvarez, Brierly, Eagleton, Fenwick, Jenks, Jessup, Keeton, Kunz, Lauterpacht, McDougal, Morgenthau, Quincy Wright, Röling, Rousseau, Stone, Schwarzenberger, De Visscher and Wilk are only a few of those whose writings deal frequently with the changing character of international law. The list could be supplemented with numerous authors from the same and other countries.

First of all, the chosen countries show a striking degree of similarity with regard to their past historical experiences, their present national development, and their expectations of the future. The similarity is clearly reflected in their domestic policy and – perhaps even more so – in the execution of their foreign policies.[2] Because of their particular brand of foreign policies, which tries to avoid any commitment to either of the two power blocs of the world, they are considered to belong to the "neutralist" or "non-committed" camp in which they indeed play a leading part.[3] The leadership often asserted by these countries is demonstrated, for instance, by the fact that they constituted four of the five members of the Colombo Conference of 1954 which took the initiative in calling the historical Asian-African Conference of Bandung in 1955.[4] The fifth Colombo member, Pakistan, though undoubtedly a very important representative of Asia, is not dealt with in this thesis, because it has – at least in the eyes of many Asians – allied itself with the Western powers by joining the SEATO pact. This policy decision has naturally so greatly influenced the foreign policy of Pakistan that it has set her apart from the above-mentioned four countries in many an issue. The latter consideration holds equally true for the other Asian members of the SEATO, Thailand and the Philippines.[5]

A further consideration for the selection of the four states – especially of India and Indonesia – is the fact that their control of resources and of people mark them among the most important

[2] *Cf.* Fifield, *The Diplomacy of South East Asia 1945–1958* (1958); Panikkar, *Asia and Western Dominance* (1953); Bowles, *Ambassador's report* (1954); Lasker, *New Forces in Asia* (1950); Van Mook, *The Stakes of Democracy in SE Asia* (1950); Mills, *The New World of South East Asia* (1949); Brodie, *South East Asia in the World To-day* (1950). The degree of unity has been considered more directly in: Thompson & Adloff, "Asian Unity: Force or Façade," 16 *Far Eastern Survey* 97–99 (1947); Venkatasubbiah, "Prospects of an Asian Union," 5 *India Q.* 99–112 (1949).

[3] Schwarzenberger, *Power Politics* 124 (2d ed. 1951); Hatta, "Indonesia between the Power Blocs, 36 *For. Aff.* 480–490; Fenwick, "Legal Aspects of Neutralism," 51 *A.J.I.L.* 71–74 (1957). Fifield, *op. cit. supra* at 523.

[4] The great significance attached to this conference is demonstrated by the equally great number of books and articles which have appeared in all parts of the world. A few examples may follow:

Kahin, *The Asian-African Conference* (1956); Romulo, *The Meaning of Bandung* (1956); Richard Wright, *The Colour Curtain – A Report on the Bandung Conference* (1956); Appadorai, *The Bandung Conference* (1956); Chaudri, "The Asian-African Conference," 8 *Pakistan Horizon* 1955; Chou En-lai, "The Asian-African Conference at Bandung," 7 *United Asia* (1955); "La Conférence de Bandoeng," 8 *Chronique de politique étrangère* 387–399 (1955); Abendroth, "Die völkerrechtliche Bedeutung der Bandung Konferenz," 6 *Archiv des Völkerrechts* 55–61 (1956).

[5] Fifield, *op. cit. supra* note 2, at 102; MacMahon Ball, "A Political Re-examination of SEATO," 12 *Int. Org.* 1–16 (1958); Boutros Ghali, "Le Pacte du Sud-Est Asiatique," 6 *Jahrb. f. Int. Recht* 167–177 (1955).

countries in the area. In this respect it can, of course, also be contended that Communist China, Japan and the Philippines are of at least equal importance and deserve to be included too. Here, however, some other factors eliminate them as possible examples to be used in the context of this work. Communist China, regardless of her actual or potential power, has still so few official contacts with the other states of the world that a review of her international law practices has to be postponed till the time that she will be able and willing to join the world community in a more intimate way. Her exclusion from the United Nations and other international conferences (e.g. the Geneva Conference on the Law of the Sea) has not provided us with the views of this country on important and current issues of international law.

Japan – and, for that matter, most of the states of West Asia also – although a very powerful member of the Asian world, cannot be called "newly established." Moreover, there is to-day the unspoken but clearly observable fact that Japan and the Philippines are apparently not regarded as fully representative of Asian views. This is not the place to examine the reasons for this fact. It is sufficient to state here that this opinion prevailing in Asia prevents these two countries from playing the important parts of which they are potentially capable on account of their advanced position in many fields.

If, therefore, the above considerations are made the criteria for the selection of "some newly established Asian states," which are dealt with here, it is clear that states of West Asia (including Israel which occupies a unique position in Asia), Pakistan, Thailand, Cambodia, Laos, North and South Vietnam, North and South Korea, Nationalist and Communist China, Japan, the Philippines and Malaya will in general not come into the picture. Only when they are involved in matters of international law which deal directly with one of the four countries, will they be drawn into the picture.

Having thus qualified the "newly established Asian states" we should now give some consideration to the term "development." This term implies a gradual change of the principles and prescriptions of international law into new ones which will more closely represent the contemporary views on justice and the expectations of the greatest possible part of the world community. Thus they will become more adequate to cope with the problems of our time.[6]

[6] See Hudson, "The International Law of the Future," 38 *A.J.I.L.* 278–281 (1944); Jenks, *The Common Law of Mankind* 62–64 (1958).

This concerns the important question mentioned earlier whether present world conditions have indeed changed so much that traditional international law has become inadequate to deal with the great international problems. It is the contention here – without minimizing the great merits of present international law – that the world has indeed experienced such far-reaching changes that it has at times become increasingly difficult to find in traditional international law clear answers to the great problems of our time.[7] To support this contention, a closer examination of these changes is the logical initial consideration.

WORLD CHANGES AND THEIR RAMIFICATIONS

1. Bipolarization

It is generally contended that the greatest change, and therefore problem, of our time has been brought about by the introduction of atomic and nuclear energy. However, from the viewpoint of international affairs, it seems more accurate to preface this fact by the other principal phenomenon of our time: the bipolarization of the world community. Even before atomic science reached its present development, the concentration of the world into two power blocs had already deeply influenced the global scene. It may even be contended that without the existence of two rival powers, which fear and distrust each other, the harnessing of atomic and nuclear energy would not pose such an ominous problem to mankind.

The bipolarization of the world can be seen as the result of a long and gradual process. During the last four or five centuries the number of states in the world has gone up and down, but it is easy to see how, in general, this number has dropped in the course of time. The well-recorded history of Europe and America illustrates with sufficient clarity how the unification of such countries as

[7] *Cf.* Kunz, "The Changing Law of Nations," 51 *A.J.I.L.* 77–83 (1957); Jessup, *Transnational Law* (1956); McDougal, "International Law, Power and Policy – A Contemporary Conception," 82 *Hague Recueil* 137–258 (1953); Morgenthau, "World Politics in the Mid-twentieth Century," 10 *Review of Politics* 154–173 (1948); H. A. Smith, *The Crisis in the Law of Nations* (1947); Grayson Kirk a.o., *The Changing Environment of International Relations* (1956); Samore, "The New International Law of Alejandro Alvarez" 52 *A.J.I.L.* 41–55 (1958); Fenwick, "International Law – What is its Function To-day?" 121 *World Affairs* 8 (1958); Yoshitaka Horinouchi, "Cold War Diplomacy Makes International Law and World Court Obsolete," 7 *Gaisei* (For. Aff.Q.) i – xi (1957); Vasudev Pillai, "International Law in a Changing World," 2/3 *Justitia* (Osmania Univ. Law College) 116–133 (1956).

Germany, Italy, France, The Netherlands, and the U.S.A. has been achieved by the incorporation of several separate states into one new unit, in which process the component units either gave up voluntarily or were forced to abandon their separate independent status.[8] This diminishing trend can equally be observed with respect to the select group of powerful states which determined the main course of history.[9] The policy by which peace was preserved, the so-called balance of power theory, was realized by shifting coalitions of these big powers. With a greater number of powerful states, more power combinations and greater flexibility in handling political issues were possible.[10] In the 18th century, the number of leading nations was at least six. Since then, international politics have been dominated by what was popularly called the Big Six, Big Five, Big Four, and Big Three.[11] For the first time in history, however, the entire world has come under the spheres of influence of only two nation-states, the U.S.A. and the U.S.S.R. It is obvious that the emergence of just two dominant powers leaves little room for another power combination and must necessarily lead to two huge rival blocs.[12]

This bipolar struggle has reduced the roles of other participants in the world power process (and here we mean particularly the nation-states) to that of more or less important allies, but allies without any decisive, independent power. The recent example of the Suez Canal crisis showed with painful clarity the secondary role now played by such erstwhile big powers as Britain and France. Without the express or tacit consent of the U.S. or the U.S.S.R. their military operations were doomed to failure. It is even less hard to conceive of the insignificant power positions of nation states of lesser stature than Britain and France.[13] The same trend holds true,

[8] Schwarzenberger, *op. cit. supra* note 3, at 104; Germany, for instance, comprised towards the end of the Thirty Years War about 900 sovereign states. This number decreased to 355 in 1648, 200 in 1803, 36 in 1815. Morgenthau, *supra* note 7, at 157.

[9] Schwarzenberger, *op. cit. supra* note 3, at 39.

[10] *Id.* at 178–185; Morgenthau, *supra* note 7, at 158; Kaplan, "Balance of Power-Bipolarity and Other Modes of International Systems," 51 *Am. Pol. Sci. Rev.* 684–695 (1957).

[11] For the shifting and changing pattern of the power struggle, see Schwarzenberger, *op. cit. supra* note 3, at 113–117.

[12] *Id.* at 121, 123. Schwarzenberger, at the time of writing his book (1951) regarded "The British Commonwealth" as a world power.

[13] Not long ago Senator William F. Knowland, Senate Republican Leader, suggested that Norway should pull out of the NATO, in return for a withdrawal of Soviet Russia from Hungary, and disarmament negotiations in London in 1947 included an inspection plan for the whole of the Arctic circle. The opinions of Norway and neutral Sweden were not mentioned at all. See James Reston in the *N.Y. Times*, June 13, 1957.

and without doubt even more so, in the communist orbit.[14] In other words, one feature of the bipolarization is *its total character*. The two big powers continually exert their influence on the other nation states in order to keep them in or bring them into their orbit, leaving little opportunity for the third state to ignore the existing power struggle. For ideological, political, economic or other reasons several states have already committed themselves.

The relevance of the process of bipolarization to the Asian states with which we are dealing lies in the fact that they have made it their policy to refuse a commitment to either bloc, an attitude which gave new life to the controversial question of neutralism.[15] As yet they have been surprisingly successful in maintaining their uncommitted position. Neither the fact that this policy of non-commitment exists actually only by the "courtesy" of the big powers, nor the accusation that this policy is applied by playing one big power against the other, can minimize the significance of that achievement.

The most important side issue developed by the bipolar struggle is at present the production of atomic and nuclear weapons, a small number of which is capable of wiping out human habitation over large sections of this earth.[16] These non-conventional, non-traditional weapons have created problems of great magnitude, which conventional, traditional international law is as yet unable to solve.[17] This is, of course, not a very new phenomenon. Traditional international law has not even been able to solve completely the problems raised by so-called conventional weapons, but the disagreements about these weapons did not threaten such disaster for the world. The magnitude of the problems raised by the new lethal weapons lies in the fact that the consequences of a failure to reach a complete agreement are so much more serious and may directly concern the survival of mankind.

It is interesting to note in this context the attitude towards these

[14] The example of Hungary is still fresh in our memory. It also seems erroneous to consider Poland as an illustration of communist states independent from the U.S.S.R. orbit. There is little reason to believe that they would be able to resist Soviet pressure if that is directed towards them in all its strength. Communist China, although apparently enjoying a great degree of independence, is clearly committed to the Communist bloc.

[15] *Supra* note 3.

[16] According to Lord Attlee and the military expert Lidell Hart a small number of hydrogen bombs (not more than five to ten) should make the British islands uninhabitable. See "*Nieuwe Rotterdamsche Courant*" – hereinafter cited as N.R.C. – April 20, 1955.

[17] Mathon, "De Nieuwe Wapens," 9 *Internationale Spectator* 63–73 (1955); U.S. Govt. Publication, *The Effect of Nuclear Weapons* (1957).

new weapons. Right after the creation of the first atom bomb, President Truman intended to keep the secret of the atom bomb as long as possible in order to secure the dominant position of the U.S.A. The shock, literally and figuratively, of the bombs dropped on Hiroshima and Nagasaki stirred the world to such a degree that it raised strong protests everywhere and aroused strong reactions in favour of outlawing such destructive devices.[18] Others proposed the internationalization of the bomb. To this end an international organization was proposed which would insure that the new invention should be used only for peaceful purposes.[19] Gradually, the world recovered from the first shock, acquainted itself further with the nature and potentials of the bomb, and again took heart.

Thus, when the two power blocs failed to agree on the banishment or regulation of the bomb, the atomic race was renewed; and the bomb reassumed its role of chief threat and deterrent.[20] Britain, particularly, having mastered the production of the hydrogen bomb, issued a government policy statement proclaiming her official adherence to the so-called "policy of deterrence." This would make Britain's main defence solely dependent on the deterrent effect of the hydrogen bomb, a policy which means in effect the return to the old Roman principle of "Si vis pacem para bellum."[21] This also brings up the argument that, with the possession of the hydrogen bomb, the U.K. (and now also France) has broken the exclusiveness of the U.S. and U.S.S.R. as leaders in the bipolar struggle and has now changed the bipolarization of this world into a three-power struggle. This thought is openly admitted and espoused by

[18] *Cf.* Kissinger, *Nuclear Weapons and Foreign Policy* 372 (1957), .

[19] Oppenheimer, "International Control of Atomic Energy," 26 *For. Aff.* 239–252 (1948); Gullion, "The Attempt to Secure International Control of the Atom," 25 *Am. For. Service J.* 7–9, 30–40 (1948); Whitman, "Developing Atomic Energy for Mankind's Benefit", 3 *U.N. Rev.* 42–44 (1957); Bachhoefer & Stein, "Atoms for Peace – The New Atomic Energy Agency," 55 *Mich. L. R.* 747–798 (1957); Tammes, "De Internationale Organisatie voor Atoomenergie," 11 *Internationale Spectator* 155–183 (1957).

[20] At the end of June 1957 Harold Stassen, speaking for the US Government, assured the NATO powers that the Western plans for disarmament will not involve the abandonment of a deterrent to global war through nuclear arms defence. Drew Middleton in *N.Y. Times*, July 2, 1957.

[21] On April 4, 1957, the British Government issued a White Paper on "Defence: Outline of Future Policy." The *N.Y.Times* of April 5, 1957, carried an excerpt of it, point 17 of which states: "Since peace so largely depends upon the deterrent power of nuclear retaliation...."

See also the three articles of the London correspondent of the *Nieuwe Rotterdamsche Courant* written in 1955, with predictions on the British attitude with regard to the hydrogen bomb. N.R.C., April 20, 21, 22, 1955.

See also Gaitskell: "Disengagement: Why? How? 36 *For. Aff.* 539–556 (1958); John Slessor: *The Great Deterrent* (1958).

the British.[22] It seems rather improbable, however, that the mere possession of the hydrogen bomb should raise the status of a state to the level of a leading power. A logical extension of such a contention would make big powers not only of Germany, France and Italy, but also of smaller states whenever they are capable of producing such weapons. Certainly the value of Britain as an ally has increased considerably, but the stature of a big power is dependent on more than the possession of hydrogen bombs. Britain's control of people and resources is as yet very limited.[23] It is, therefore, safe to say that the bipolarization of the world is still a fact.

What is the significance of these developments for Asia? Besides the experience of Hiroshima and Nagasaki the danger of these weapons has more recently become very real to them again as a result of the effects of radioactive fall-out after test bombs were detonated in the Pacific area. The Bikini tests of 1954, with their deplorable effects on Japanese fishermen and fishing industries, aroused violent protests from various Asian nations against the holding of such tests in waters so close to their territories.[24] No solution, however, can as yet be expected although world-wide pressure is being exerted to arrive at some restraint in the hydrogen bomb race.[25] The possessors of this lethal weapon have not yet been able to agree on the terms of such a settlement.[26] Meanwhile, the many protests raised against the dangers of radioactive fall-out have resulted in an intensive research for a "clean" bomb, i.e. a

[22] The editorial in the *N.R.C.* of May 16, 1957 mentioned the jubilant comments of the *Daily Express* and *Daily Mail* which stated that England "after one of the greatest events in the history of the world," has "regained its independence" and is now again a "big power," and no longer a "nuclear satellite of the U.S." Obviously, these statements should not be taken too seriously, but they are, nevertheless, characteristic of the aspirations of the British.

The *N.Y. Times* of May 1, 1957 ("Britain's nuclear bomb") says that "In some ways the British hydrogen tests will restore that country to the status of a first-rate power".

[23] Knorr, "Nuclear Weapons" – "Haves" and "Have-nots," 36 *For. Aff.* 167–178 (1957); *Cf.* Schwarzenberger, *op. cit. supra* note 3 at 121 for description of World Powers and Middle Powers.

[24] Oda, "The Hydrogen Bomb Tests and International Law," 53 *Die Friedenswarte* 126–135 (1956); further *infra* note 29.

[25] Pressure for a ban on or limitation of the bomb tests have come from such personalities or institutions as the Pope, *N.Y. Times*, May 4, 1957, Dr. Albert Schweitzer, *id.*, April 24, 1957, Adenauer, *id.*, Jan. 12, 1957 (although he later agreed to the equipment of the West German Armed Forces with atomic weapons, *id.*, April 15, 1957), Stevenson, *id.*, Oct. 17, 1956, the Bundestag (German Lower House), *id.* May 11, 1957, the Yugoslavian Parliament, *id.*, June 19, 1957; from Asia: e.g. from Nehru and Bandaranaike, *id.* May 18, 1957, Romulo, *id.* Nov. 12, 1956, and the Asian Socialist Conference, *id.* Nov. 9, 1956.

[26] The Three-Powers Conference on Nuclear Disarmament in Geneva has as yet not come to very concrete results.

hydrogen fusion explosion producing a minimum of radioactive residue.[27] The enormous destructive powers of these devices, however, have strongly caught the imagination of the world and the reassurances of clean bombs are unable to offset the fears, least of all in Asia. Moreover, the nuclear experts are among the first to perpetuate the general confusion by publicly disagreeing with each other on the possibility of such clean bombs. The newspapers have lately been full of controversial articles by leading scientists and other men of world renown, all of which indicate the global nature of concern over this problem.[28] It is easy to imagine the difficult task of the international lawyer who, although a layman in this field, is nevertheless obliged to appraise these technical data in order to arrive at an opinion on the legal aspects.[29]

2. Progress and Interdependence

In recent times, great scientific and technological progress has been made in many fields. It is an unfortunate fact, however, that the introduction of atomic and nuclear energy was made in the form of a devastating blast. Since then, world opinion has been focused on its destructive character rather than on its other potentialities. Public information furnished by mass media has done its share in blowing up the more sensational side of the new invention. No less sensational, however, though less spectacular, are the peaceful uses to which this new source of energy can be put. Its appearance, in fact, could not have been more timely. Experts have predicted

[27] Teller & Latter: *Our Nuclear Future* (1958) ; *N.Y. Times*, July 4 and July 6, 1957.

[28] A great number of scientists have felt obliged to express themselves on this issue. To give an impression of the seriousness of the debate, some names may be given here. Against the continuation of the bomb tests were: Dr. Linus Pauling, Nobel Prize biochemist of the California Institute of Technology, who claimed to have the endorsement of 2200 other scientists, *N.Y. Times*, June 12, 1957; the Executive Committee of the Federation of American Scientists, *id.* June 13, 1957; Professor Joliot-Curie in Paris, Nobel Prize Winner, *N.R.C.*, April 24, 1957; four prominent geneticists: Dr. James Crow (University of Wisconsin), A. H. Sturtevant (California Institute of Technology), Hermann J. Muller (Indiana University) and H. Bentley Glass (Johns Hopkins University), *N.Y. Times*, June 5, 1957; a group of scientists working directly or indirectly for the A.E.C., *id.* May 30, 1957; Professor Stanley Livingston of the Massachusetts Institute of Technology, and Dr. Charles Price of the University of Pennsylvania, *id.* May 13, 1957; 18 German physicists among whom were four Nobel Prize winners, *id.* April 13, 1957.

The list of scientists in favour of the bomb tests is not less impressive: Dr. Edward Teller, Head of the University of California Radiation Center, Nobel Prize winner, *id.* Nov. 6, 1956; Dr. Willard F. Libby, scientist-member of the A.E.C., *id.* April 26 and June 6, 1957; Dr. Frank H. Shelton, Technical Director of the Armed Forces Special Weapons Program, *id.* May 1, 1957.

for some time that with regard to world resources mankind will be facing a critical period of great shortages in the second half of the 20th century.[30] Although the world seems to have sufficient potentials for feeding and clothing of all mankind,[31] only an efficient exploitation and distribution of the resources throughout the globe will avoid a crisis. At present, the overall picture is not too encouraging. The fast growing world population and the corresponding decrease of available resources do not ensure to all people of the world a reasonable amount of all the necessities of life. Add to this the fact that millions of people, once living on a subsistence level, are now clamouring for better living conditions, and the picture of the critical situation is complete. These underdeveloped masses now demand an equal role in the shaping and sharing of values, and the inability to satisfy their demands may lead to more global tensions. It is for this reason that the fast development of science and technology are most welcome. Particularly the introduction of atomic and nuclear energy as a new power source gives new hope to the world. Already it is rendering great services to the industrial and communications field as a substitute for the conventional sources of power, such as coal, oil, gas and waterpower. Its usefulness, moreover, has spread to other fields. It has brought about great improvements in agricultural and medical practices and in other fields too its potential is unlimited.[32]

The above facts on world demands and world production illustrate with sufficient clarity another of the main characteristics of our time: the interdependence of the world. Agriculturally, industrially, economically and politically, it is undeniable that the peoples of the world have become more dependent on each other. The problems of world magnitude are today increasingly discussed on a global level. The great progress of international organizations is just one such example. The trend is clearly for a more intensive contact in

[29] The difference of opinion and of approach will become clearly evident when one compares the articles of McDougal & Schlei, "The Hydrogen Bomb Tests in Perspective – Lawful Measures for Security," 64 *Yale L. J.* 648–710 (1955), with Margolis, "The Hydrogen Bomb Experiments and International Law," 64 *Yale L.J.* 629–647 (1955). See also *supra* note 24.

[30] Professor D. H. Webster: *De Toekomst Onzer Samenleving* (The future of our society) (1952); Professor Archibald V. Hill of London, Nobel Prize winner, quoted in *Haagse Post* (The Hague) April 14, 1956.

[31] *N.Y. Times*, May 21, 1956 on the "speculative projection" of the resources of the world, drafted by faculty members of the California Institute of Technology.

[32] For abundant literature on the political, economic, social and scientific aspects of atomic energy, see *An International Bibliography on Atomic Energy*, U.N. Doc. No. AEC/INF/10/Rev.1 (1951).

the future. But with the increasing interaction, we are bound to have more international tension. It is to be hoped that the international law of the future will be able to keep pace with the progress of the world and provide it with prescriptions that will offer reasonable solutions of the mounting number of disputes. Paradoxically, it should always be remembered that the interdependence is largely a material one. Ideologically, there is another trend in the world towards more self-determination, more "sovereignty," as a result of strong local and regional sentiment.[33]

The new Asian states, for instance, are torn between these two thoughts. On the one hand, being economically underdeveloped they know that they can only benefit from closer contact with other countries. On the other hand, like most new states, their hard-fought struggle for independence gives the newly acquired sovereignty a halo of national sanctity and all state activities start from this point.

3. New Expansionism

One of the characteristics of the progress of our time is that it has succeeded in bridging the previously large gap between scientific knowledge and its application. Scientific progress in one field of learning cannot fail to affect ultimately other sciences. It is, however, remarkable how fast international law becomes involved in the technological advancement. Traditional prescriptions concerning the air space, the occupation of Antarctica and the jurisdiction over the continental shelf, territorial waters and the contiguous zone, all need reconsideration and revision in the light of new expansive developments.

The exploration of space presents a perfect example of how world prescriptions become obsolete and inadequate as a result of progress. The utilization of such fast, highflying and long range objects as missiles or rockets makes the principle of state sovereignty over space "directly above its territory" inadequate and infeasible. Even were one to retain this theory, difficulties with regard to celestial bodies would arise. A projection of the territory of a state into space would divide space into irregularly shaped cones according to the territory of the countries. The revolution of the earth on its own axis, its simultaneous rotation around the sun and the motions of other celestial bodies cause a constantly changing content of the

[33] *Infra* at 134 (Kashmir) and 168 (Indonesia and the Law of the Sea).

respective space cones. The concept of a space cone of sovereignty thus becomes meaningless and unworkable.[34] The extension of man's reach far beyond the atmosphere brings such an infinite space into consideration that a traditional claim of national sovereignty, for instance, also becomes rather meaningless in this context.[35]

It is understandable that the above evolutions took international law by surprise and that it has as yet only reached the phase of preliminary examination of the facts. Therefore, the result of these examinations must necessarily have a speculative character. One must, however, face the changes and try to adapt the traditional body of law accordingly, for "while it is healthy that the evolution of the law should follow rather than anticipate that of life, there are circumstances in which the possibility of developing the law on sound principles depends primarily on an initiative being taken in the matter before *de facto* situations have crystallized too far."[36] True to its name and nature, the law of outer space now actually tends to soar into the highest realms of legal speculations, a tendency which also needs some caution.[37]

The growing importance of Antarctica further illustrates the impact of modern technology. Only twelve years ago this vast territory was regarded as so inaccessible and insignificant as not to make it really necessary to try to settle the long pending questions of jurisdiction. In spite of the long assumed presence of huge mineral resources and the value of this area for strategic and meteorological purposes, one renowned polar expert stated, as recently as 1947, that the "imperial partition of the (Antarctic) continent is a fantastic conception. The installation of meteorological observatories is the sole permanent habitation that can be contemplated."[38] No sooner, however, were answers found to the technical obstacles to life in the polar areas than the significance of Antarctica increased considerably. Consequently disputes on territorial jurisdiction immediately assumed more serious propor-

[34] Jenks, "International Law and Activities in Space," 5 *I.C.L.Q.* 99–114, at 104 (1956); see also Jessup & Taubenfeld, *Control for Outer Space and the Antarctic Analogy* 205–206 (1959).

[35] See Bin Cheng, "International Law and High Altitude Flights," 6 *I.C.L.Q.* 487–505, at 493 (1957).

[36] *Id.* at 101.

[37] See McDougal and Lipson, "Prospects for a Law of Outer Space," 52 *A.J.I.L.* 407 (1958).

[38] Rudmose Brown, "Political Claims in the Antarctic," 1 *World Aff.* 393–401 (1947).

tions and received more attention as well. Argentina, Chile, Britain, France, Norway and the U.S. reasserted their – often conflicting – claims.[39]

The two above-mentioned subjects (space activities and Antarctica) represent relatively new and unexplored problems of international law. This is not the case with such questions as the internal and territorial waters, the high seas, the sea-bed and sub-soil which have for a long time engaged the attention of writers on the law of the sea. Here again the growing demand for new resources coupled with the invention of new technical skills were the stimulating factors for territorial expansion.[40] The proclamations of the U.S. with respect to the fish conservation zones and the natural resources of the sub-soil and sea-bed of the continental shelf of 1945[41] found many eager supporters. The formulation of claims by other states, however, was not always identical to that of the U.S. and there appears to be some disagreement among these states as to whether the claims of sovereignty over sea-bed and sub-soil of the continental shelf could be extended to the high seas above it. Some Asian states, anxious to reserve to themselves the few available resources, have quickly made claims to their continental shelves.[42]

SPECIFIC CHANGES

Thus far, we have dealt with general trends of a global character which may affect and determine the development of international law. The active, though not the passive, role of the newly established Asian states in these events has been minor. Lacking most of the necessary base values[43] and institutions, their individual participa-

[39] Jessup, "Sovereignty in Antarctica," 41 *A.J.I.L.* 117–119 (1947). Hayton, "The 'American' Antarctica," 50 *A.J.I.L.* 583–610 (1956); Toma, "Soviet Attitude towards the Acquisition of Territorial Sovereignty in the Antarctica," 50 *A.J.I.L.* 611–626 (1956); Sullivan, "Antarctica in a Two-Power World," 36 *For. Aff.* 154–166 (1957). Hayton, "The Antarctic Settlement of 1959," 54 *A.J.I.L.* 349–371 (1960).

[40] Visser 't Hooft, *Les Nations Unies et la Conservation des Ressources de la Mer* (1958); Borchard, "Resources of the Continental Shelf," 40 *A.J.I.L.* 53–70 (1951).

[41] 40 *A.J.I.L.* 45–47 (Suppl.) (1946).

[42] Kunz, "Continental Shelf and International Law," 50 *A.J.I.L.* 828 (1956).

McDougal and Burke, "Crisis in the Law of the Sea – Community Perspectives versus National Egoism," 67 *Yale L.J.* 539–589 (1958).

[43] The term "values" indicates general value categories, such as power, wealth, enlightenment, well-being, respect, skill, solidarity and rectitude. Each of them can be used as a means (base value) or an end (scope value), see Laswell and McDougal, "Legal Education and Public Policy: Professional Training in the Public Interest," 52 *Yale L.J.* 217 (1943); Lasswell & Kaplan, *Power and Society* (1950).

tion was necessarily quite restricted. Combining their respective small powers, however, they have succeeded – as will be seen below – in achieving a position which enables them to participate more fully and significantly in the world power process.

The recent emergence of so many Asian states as new participants in the world arena had two principal ramifications which will be discussed below. First, it has changed the number and composition of the participants. Secondly, it has already influenced the traditional prescriptions applicable in the world power process.

1. Change of Composition in the World Arena

In considering this particular point, it is perhaps possible to simplify the entire process and its consequences into three main phases: the emergence of Asian states and their admission into the world arena; the realization by these states of their numerical power in the decision making process, especially in international organizations; and, as a logical consequence thereof, their support of and reliance on these international organizations, particularly the United Nations.

Active Asian participation in the decision making process is a recent phenomenon. Most of the present Asian states did not come into being until recently and the older ones (except for Japan) were often not powerful enough to be respected. For instance, between the beginning of the 20th century and the creation of the League of Nations in 1919, the diplomatic conferences which were of significance to the development of international law were the First and Second Peace Conferences at The Hague in 1899 and 1907, and the London Naval Conference of 1908–1909. The First Peace Conference was attended by twenty-six countries, which number increased to forty-four for the Second Peace Conference, representing twenty European, nineteen American and five Asian nations. The Asian states were China, Japan, Persia, Siam and Turkey.[44] The Naval Conference at London of 1908–1909, which was an extension of the Peace Conference, dealt with the restricted subject of the maritime law of war and neutrality. Consequently, only the leading naval powers were represented, and of these only one was an Asian state, namely, Japan.[45]

[44] 2 Scott, *The Hague Peace Conferences* 529 (1909).
[45] 1 François, *Handboek van het Volkenrecht* (Manual of the Law of Nations), 619 (1949).

The list of members of the League of Nations did not indicate an increase of Asian states worth speaking of. Of the forty-five original members, Asia was represented by China, Japan, Siam, Persia, India (which was still part of the British Empire), and Hejaz (which, however, never participated as a member, not having ratified the Treaty of Versailles). Turkey and Iraq were subsequently admitted in 1932, and Afghanistan in 1934.[46] The League of Nations also had an African nation among its original members (Liberia) while later on Ethiopia (in 1923) and Egypt (1937) were admitted to membership.[47] The sixty-four nations which were at one time members of the League of Nations (seventeen of which withdrew afterwards or were expelled) consisted of twenty-eight European states, twenty-two American, eight Asian, four African, and Australia and New Zealand.[48]

The real influx of Asian participants into the world arena came after World War II. These years saw the creation of several newly independent Asian states that were successively admitted to the U.N. where they caused a further shift in its composition.

At the end of 1945 the U.N. was composed of fifty-one member states, i.e., fourteen European, twenty-two American, nine Asian, four African, and Australia and New Zealand. During the next five years[49] nine new members were admitted (Afghanistan, Burma, Iceland, Indonesia, Israel, Pakistan, Sweden, Thailand, Yemen), of which seven were Asian. During the following five years the U.N. experienced the full impact of the cold war. Both the U.S. and the U.S.S.R. blocked the admittance of members which might strengthen the voting power of the other bloc. This deadlock was not broken until December 14, 1955, when a so-called "package-deal" gave sixteen new states the so coveted status of U.N. member, i.e. Albania, Austria, Bulgaria, Cambodia, Ceylon, Finland, Hungary, Italy, Ireland, Jordan, Laos, Libya, Nepal, Portugal, Rumania and Spain. Subsequently, seven more states were admitted (Morocco, Sudan and Tunesia on November 12, 1956; Japan on December 18, 1956; Ghana on March 8, 1957, Malaya on September 17, 1957 and Guinea on December 12, 1958), bringing the membership (June 1960)

[46] *Id.* at 345.

[47] Goodrich and Hambro, *The Charter of the U.N.* 560 (1949).

[48] *Id.* at 567.

For a comparison with the U.N. membership Australia and New Zealand are separated from the British Empire membership of the League of Nations.

[49] See *U.N. Textbook* 26 (Leiden, 3rd ed. 1957).

to eighty-two nations,[50] of which twenty-six are European, twenty-two American, twenty-two Asian, ten African, Australia, New Zealand.[51]

The admittance to the U.N. meant to many of these new Asian states the culmination of a victorious struggle. Like other new states, their main objective during the first years of existence was to be recognized and accepted as full-fledged members of the world community. Such recognition was in their eyes not complete without membership in this world body. The high prestige of this international organization was in part due to the fact that in the past many erstwhile dependent states, (e.g. the former protectorates and Indonesia) owed their independence to some extent to the intervention, good offices or other services by the League of Nations and the U.N.

Not until they participated in the organs of the U.N. and voted in the General Assembly and other organs, where every state was entitled to one regular vote, did this Asian group realize fully how important their group was numerically. The Asian-African Conference at Bandung in 1955 also contributed to the more concerted activities of these nations, especially in the U.N. The Afro-Asian group is meeting regularly under a rotating chairmanship to exchange views on various issues.[52] Although it would be an overstatement to say that a solid Afro-Asian bloc exists,[53] the group formation is undeniable, and it is apparent that in certain cases, such as that regarding trusteeship territories, it is virtually impossible to get a two-thirds majority vote without the support of the Afro-Asian group.[54]

[50] Two members (Egypt and Syria) merged into one state (United Arab Republic).

[51] It is admittedly rather unscientific and even misleading to divide the countries of the world along such geographical lines. The cultural background of the U.S. and Canada make it possible to consider them closer to Western Europe than to their South American neighbours. It can equally be held that the inclusion of South Africa among the African states is incorrect. However, there cannot be any serious objections to an examination of the geographical distribution of the nation-states, a principle which has even found a place in the charter of the U.N. (art. 101, para. 3, with respect to the staff of the Secretariat as well as Art. 23, para. 1 as regards the election of non-permanent members to the Security Council).

[52] In the case of Algeria, for instance, the Asian-African bloc in the U.N. has several times supported the side of Algeria (*N.Y. Times*, October 3, 1956: "Genocide in Algeria charged to France," and *id.* June 18, 1957, "Asian-Arab Bloc at U.N. Urges Inquiry into Algeria Massacre." See also Maung-Maung, *Burma in the Family of Nations* 140 (1956). Recently, the Asian-African states again acted to bring the South African situation before the Security Council after the shooting of tens of negroes by the South African police during demonstrations, *N.R.C.* March 25, 1960 p. 1 col. 1.

[53] The SEATO Pact and the voting results in the Hungary case before the U.N., for instance, show clearly that there is no such thing as a general Asian-African stand.

[54] It is, of course, also true that the Latin American group and the Communist bloc, although not so numerous, play an equally decisive role.

It is interesting to note the reactions of some member states to these developments in the voting pattern of the U.N. The newly established Asian states, having benefited by the actions of the U.N. and now realizing their strong voting power, are among the most ardent supporters of this organization. Some European states, however, realizing their declining voting power, have become increasingly concerned with this trend and their enthusiasm for the organization, the creation of which was mainly their responsibility, has cooled considerably. Of course, it would be a great injustice to these states to say that their discontent was solely the result of such a technical point as the voting pattern. Their disappointment is indeed based on more substantial matters, but the concern for their numerical weakness has been very clear. It is, therefore, not surprising that the suggestion of "weighted" voting has come principally from this group.

If we consider the list of present non-members, most of which have expressed their desire to be admitted to the U.N.,[55] as well as those new countries which are about to become member states, [56] it will become even clearer that the trend is definitely towards a non-western, non-European, non-Christian majority. This sounds rather ominous but it is certainly unwise to close one's eyes to the indications of a changing world pattern. This then leads us to the next question: How and where will the growing power of the Asian states be reflected?

2. Impact of Changes on World Prescriptions[57]

The entry of the new Asian states into the world arena did not represent the first time that they came into contact with prescriptions governing the interactions of world participants. Even as colonies they did participate, although only to a limited degree. India, for instance, became a member of the League of Nations while still being part of the British Empire. Treaties between the Asian colonies, e.g. on extradition, were common. But it is often

[55] Communist China, the Mongolian People's Republic, North and South Korea and North and South Vietnam; in Europe: Germany.

[56] In September and October 1960 (just before this manuscript went to press) 17 new states were admitted to the U.N. of which 16 were African and the other was Cyprus. This brought the total U.N. membership to 99 states, i.e. 27 European (Cyprus included), 26 African, 22 Asian, 22 American, and Australia and New Zealand.

[57] For a more detailed discussion of such terms as prescription, arena and participant, see McDougal & Lasswell, "The Identification and Appraisal of Diverse Systems of Public Order," 53 *A.J.I.L.* 8–9 (1959).

forgotten that before the arrival of the Europeans in Asia at the end of the 15th century, the area was already occupied by several kingdoms and other states which formed an arena of interaction not much different in principle from the present one. What is more, the European powers which entered the Asian scene recognized most of the existing principalities and were aware of their jurisdiction. They treated them as sovereign states.[58] The subsequent disappearance of Asian states or their demotion to a colonial status cannot take away the fact that we are dealing here with an area to which international contact is not foreign at all. In this respect Asia differs from Africa. At the time of the first sea-voyages to Asia, Africa did not consist of well-organized states, though it had known some important states in its past. This enabled the European powers to establish their spheres of influence over the African continent without too much opposition from the autochthonous population and in the light of these circumstances it was understandable that the European powers could regulate their future colonial policies with respect to Africa at the Berlin Conference of 1884–1885 on African matters over the heads of all the African peoples. Such a "scramble for Africa" was not possible in the case of Asia which was already occupied by relatively well-established states. This fact should always be taken into account when dealing with the so-called "newly established Asian states."

Asians are fully aware of their great history, although it was a long time ago that Asia counted in the world. They seem to have a different sense of time from Europeans. This is reflected in their interpretation of some international issues. When after World War II the Western Europeans returned to Asia and claimed the territories as their rightful possessions, they did it on the basis of their sovereignty over the area before the illegal conquest by the Japanese. The fact that they had ruled the area for three or even more centuries was, in their opinion, sufficient title to the territories. To many Asians, however, the European domination was just another illegal occupation. Because of their different sense of time, as well as their lack of familiarity with modern international law, the duration of the foreign domination had no bearing whatever on the illegality of the European rule. The Asian interpretation of the principle of sovereignty seems to differ on this point from the European one.[59]

[58] See Chapter II *infra*.
[59] See further Chapter III *infra*.

This somewhat elaborate introduction leads us to the core of this section, i.e. the impact of the increased participation of Asian states on the interpretation of traditional prescriptions of international law. Little has as yet been written on this subject and the following analysis and predictions therefore have a personal and speculative character.

As has already been said, the new Asian states are on the whole well aware of the existence of traditional world prescriptions for the interactions of participants in the world arena. This does not imply, however, that they always applied or used them. Although the post war years have proved that these new nations have, in general, paid due attention to the so-called established rules of international law, numerous also are the moments in which their practices aroused the anger of other states which charged them with violation of the "well established" rules of international law.[60]

Looking for the reasons for such violations, one can detect at least two of them, namely, misunderstanding and inexperience, or, resentment and disagreement, with regard to those so-called established rules of international law.

The practice of law is an old universal profession existing in some way or other in the highest and lowest developed communities. Generally, however, the legal rules applied deal with the organization of the particular community only. The study and practice of prescriptions dealing with inter-communal activities have never been equally well developed. This complaint, which is heard in Western countries as well, obtains even more so in the Asian nations. Although it is a general phenomenon that Asian intellectuals have always been attracted to the legal profession, their objective usually is to enter politics or to practise municipal law, not international law. Moreover, the limited participation of a colony in the world arena did not give much opportunity for the practice of international law. Consequently, the unexpectedly fast achievement of independence as a result of World War II caught these young countries without the services of many capable international lawyers.[61] It was, therefore, inevitable that in their interaction with other participants,

[60] For instance, in cases of sovereignty, recognition, renunciation of treaties, expropriation.

[61] Maung Maung tells how during the Japanese occupation in World War II, "independent" Burma's Foreign Office remained idle most of the time. The international law library of this department consisted principally of an old edition of Oppenheim's International Law. Maung Maung, *Burma in the Family of Nations* 99 (1956).

they often deviated from what was to the others, a clear rule of international law.

The other reason, resentment towards traditional international law, may have been caused by various factors. It has been a general feature of these new countries that they have only achieved their independence after years of long struggle, spearheaded by a strong nationalistic movement. Active nationalism, which necessarily emphasized in the first place the welfare of the national state, could not possibly give much attention to the interest of the outside world. To achieve the all-important objective of political independence much was allowed and little forbidden. The achievement of independence did not mean the end of nationalism. Its spirit still dominates these new countries, giving preference in international issues to the national interest, and scarcely encouraging limitation on national sovereignty. For this reason the principle of sovereignty has again assumed greater proportions.[62]

Nationalism, however, has more objectives than the political independence of the country only. It also involves the revival of the indigenous culture and traditions, and a rejection of cultural elements which are considered foreign. In this respect it would not be surprising if some resentment would be expressed towards the present world prescriptions which are steeped in Christian, Western European traditions.

Such a trend weakening the development of international law is not new. Modern international law came into being as the product of frequent interactions among the nations of Western Europe in the 16th century.[63] In spite of serious disagreements, they basically shared a common cultural background as a result of the impact of Greek and Roman civilization and, above all, of the Christian religion. The role of the Church in international politics of that time contributed significantly to the formation of a relatively closely connected society of European nations. The Reformation, however, marked the decline of the Church as a political power, and from that time on the trend has been towards a secularization of the law of nations which increasingly gnawed at the moral foundations of the system.

The emergence today of so many new states, which lack the common bond of the West-European, Christian tradition, may well

[62] See Chapter III *infra*.

[63] Brierly, *The Law of Nations* 1 (1949); Nussbaum, *A Concise History of the Law of Nations* 1 (1950).

accelerate this centrifugal trend in international law. It is true that the growing interdependence of the world may have a favourable influence on the development of world prescriptions, but this interdependence being principally of material rather than of ideological nature, will certainly not lead to the strengthening of the Christian principles of international law. This weakening development, which is becoming more obvious in our time, has rightly been analysed as

> the expansion of the system from being the law of the small family of nations among which it arose into one that is world-wide and now claims the allegiance of nations which had no part in building it up, and which either have never known, or no longer accept, the fundamental beliefs and sentiments on which it was originally founded. Some of these nations at least are inclined to look on international law as an alien system which the western nations, whose moral or intellectual leadership they no longer recognize, are trying to impose upon them, and in effect they have begun to claim the right to select from among its rules only those which suit their interests or which arise out of agreements to which they have themselves been parties.[64]

Strangely enough, this resentment towards the Christian background of traditional international law did not prevent some objectors from advocating a similar role for their own religions. As a result of the nationalistic movements with their concomitant revival of indigenous traditions, the religions in Asia gained new strength and aspirations. Islam, Hinduism and Buddhism all experienced a period of cultural boom. Legal scholars, also in the field of international law, studied the religious background of their systems and advocated the use of their religions as a source of law. Islam, particularly, with its wealth of legal sources, claimed the existence of an Islamic international law.[65] The bright side of this development is the strengthening of the moral foundations, a prerequisite for a strong legal system. The other side of the coin, however, is that such a trend might ultimately raise the same objections as were made in the case of the Christian religion.

THE SEARCH FOR A SOLUTION

Criticising a system is indeed an easier undertaking than finding the answers to its problems, and a mere analysis as the one given in

[64] Brierly, *op. cit. supra* note 63, at 44.

[65] *Cf.* Khadduri, *War and Peace in the Law of Islam* (1955); Hamidullah, *The Muslim Conduct of State* (1945); Gibb, *Modern Trends in Islam* 85–105 (1947).

the preceding pages would not be very fruitful if not accompanied by a more positive contribution. Fortunately, many international lawyers have already done the initial work and have devoted themselves to the observation of the impact of present world conditions on international law. What is more, they have extended this task to making speculations as to the prescriptions which are to regulate future interactions in the increasingly dynamic world. Authors like Jessup, Kelsen, Kunz, McDougal, Schwarzenberger and others are doing pioneer work in studying the conditions and trends in the world community. Their approaches, of course, are not the same, nor are their expectations. Some of them view the future with pessimism, the others see more hope.

A discussion of the above-mentioned problems in the light of the conditions in Asia draws attention to three main points:

(a) due consideration should be given to the changing conditions affecting this part of the world.

(b) the present inadequacies of international law should be closely examined.

(c) the legal principles prevailing in this arena should be taken into account.

(a) The impact of the changing conditions has already been discussed above and it led, among other things, to the contentions that the increase of new states of non-Western nature might demand a reconsideration of the established rules of international law.[66]

(b) Without minimizing the dominating part played by international law in world affairs, it is necessary to draw attention to some of its inadequacies. They are not of recent date but only because of the changing world conditions has their nature been clearly exposed now.

One of the weaknesses of contemporary theories of international law has been the overemphasis on technical rules and legal technicalities. The practice of abstracting general rules which are to decide future cases of a similar nature is a feature of the very advanced legal systems in Western countries. It is true that international law, perhaps more than municipal law, allows for broad interpretations, but one has only to refer to the highly technical doctrines of sovereignty and recognition to see how legalistically certain rules of international law have at times been applied, and thus have lost touch with the reality of changing conditions.

[66] *Supra* at 19.

In the less rationalistic systems of many Asian countries legal rules have a less rigid character and are open to much adjustment and compromise.[67] As has already been stated[68] the customary law in most Asian states is basically less technical than its western counterpart which is probably one of the reasons for the dislike of legal technicalities. These objections can perhaps best be described by the following quotation, although it has not been written with Asia in mind: "The law is still too often regarded as a body of doctrines or rules divorced from power and social processes. Studies are still organized in terms of technical doctrines of highest level ambiguities."[69]

To the Asians, the old controversy whether law and policy can and should be separated,[70] is no real problem. To them, the greater part of whom still live under their age-old customs and traditions, such a division is as yet entirely foreign. Life in Asia, as everywhere else, is a total process, in which law fulfills only one function, but a function which is not only inseparably connected to the political, economic, social and religious aspects of life, but which has also to be treated as such. It is not inconceivable that with progressive westernization or modernization, a separation of law and policy will inevitably be the result but at present such a technical system does not seem to be very popular.

In fact such a highly technical approach has also come under severe criticism even in Western countries. Objections have been voiced there against such a "normative ambiguity" which seeks to squeeze into one authoritative statement all the processes involved in decision making.[71] Such a statement purports to be at one and the same time the representation of what decision makers have decided in the past, how they will decide now and in the future, as well as how they ought to decide. These processes should indeed be considered separately in order to arrive, after a careful weighing of all relevant

[67] See Ter Haar, *Adat Law in Indonesia* 213–216 (1948); Supomo, "The Future of Adat Law in the Reconstruction of Indonesia," in Thayer, *Southeast Asia in the Coming World* 217–235 (1953); Maung Htin Aung, *Customary Law in Burma*, in Thayer, *op. cit. supra* 203–216.

[68] See also *supra* at 21.

[69] McDougal, "The Comparative Study of Law for Policy Purposes," 51 *Yale L.J.* 918 (1932).

[70] See McDougal, *supra* note 7, at 143, 156–157; but see Kelsen, *Legal Technique in International Law – A Textual Critique of the League Covenant*, Geneva Studies, vol. X, no. 6 (1939).

[71] Lasswell & McDougal, "Legal Education and Public Policy – Professional Training in the Public Interest," 52 *Yale L.J.* 203, 266 (1943).

data, at a prescription which is most adequate for the particular case.

(c) As far as legal principles are concerned, most of these countries have adopted a western type of legal system, in addition to the traditional native administration of justice. The higher courts belong to the former group, whereas the lower courts, especially the village courts, comprise the latter category. Since the great majority of the people still live in village communities, native administration of justice is still of great importance. It differs in many respects from its western counterpart. The main difference is perhaps that it aims at the *settlement* of the dispute rather than at a legal judgement. Here, too, the idea of compromise is prevelant.[72] Compromise is actually one of the main principles in traditional legal practice in Asia.

There is another factor involved in the legal practice in these regions, namely their moralistic approach to law. Morality still is a great driving power in Asia today. The important role played by customs, traditions and religion also testifies to this fact. The present political situation in the world, and in particular the threat of nuclear weapons, has strengthened this approach. There is a definite trend to bring to a greater degree moral considerations into the field of international politics and the statements of Asian leaders clearly demonstrate this. Progressive modernization may again eventually have a damping effect on these moral feelings and may lead them to draw a clear dividing line between international law and international morality, but as yet morality seems to be considered as a complement to international law in much the same way as Christian principles represented in earlier days the complement to international law in Europe.

Here, too, the answer seems to lie in modifying the rigidity of so-called established rules of international law, whenever it would be possible and desirable to modify them in order to give a more satisfactory solution. What is suggested here is that – as far as Asians are concerned – one should abandon the attitude which applies prescriptions as if they were absolute merely because they have served their purpose in other times and under different conditions. Instead, one should try to arrive at a solution which also gives due consideration to the actual processes by which decision makers arrive at authoritative prescriptions for concrete

[72] See also *supra* note 67.

instances of international disputes. Such a method should at least include the following questions:

(1) What are the facts, the events, the value changes between people, to which the decision maker must respond?
(2) What have been the decisions on comparable facts in the past and what facts appear to have influenced the decisions?
(3) Who are the probable decision makers and what variables are likely to influence their decisions.
(4) What ought to be the decision?

Such a method would be very acceptable to Asian nations for the simple reason that it shows striking similarities with their legal procedures. In fact, the settlement of legal disputes in village communities follows more or less the same stages of the above method.[73]

It is sometimes held that, in spite of these world changes and the alleged inadequacy of traditional international law, the participants in the world power process abide nevertheless to a very great extent by the established rules of international law. Those who hold this opinion can provide many examples in support of their contention. These are no doubt true, but they concern mostly non-Asian states. The attitudes of the Asian states are not yet well known. The relatively short time which has elapsed since they achieved independence has not yet enabled them to express their views more clearly. This situation is now changing and gradually Asian voices are becoming more audible.

This then is essentially the problem dealt with in this thesis. What has been the attitudes of these new Asian states towards a supposedly established international law of a world community to which they have now been admitted? What has been their state practices in a community whose structure and principles have apparently become less certain? Do they in general abide by the so-called established rules of international law? Or do they follow a path which deviates from established practice? And if so, is that different approach due to a general resentment towards an international law to the creation of which they have not been allowed to contribute in the past? Or is this resentment directed towards particular parts of present international law only, namely, to those parts which do not give attention to the specific circumstances of their particular case?

As has already been pointed out above, the influx of so many new members from outside the European orbit creates various problems.

[73] See e.g. Ter Haar, *Adat Law in Indonesia* 228–233 (1948).

If anything, it has made even more untenable the position of those who believe that there is a general philosophical, religious or cultural background which embraces all nations, and from which can be derived the general prescriptions which will apply to the whole world. Even today protagonists of such a theory continue to look for all-embracing principles. However noble and desirable such principles may be, they fail to prove that they really obtain today in a world the population of which shows such very contrasting elements as black, brown, white and yellow peoples, Buddhist, Christian, Hindu, Islam and other religions, Communist, Western and neutralist policies. To bring all these elements under the aegis of traditional international law which purports to have all answers for all problems, is to demand the impossible.[74]

One answer to this problem is obviously that nations sharing identical values form their own public order system within which their prescriptions can have full meaning, application and observance. The question here is, therefore, whether these Asian nations have not only similar experiences and interests but whether they indeed constitute a regional unit within which a public order system is developed or developing.[75]

It cannot be sufficiently emphasized, therefore, that the problem is not only one of a strictly legal nature. It has important anthropological, sociological and economic aspects as well. It is true that one cannot expect the international lawyer to find answers to these questions if they lie outside his field. However, the least one can expect of him is an awareness of such outside factors, for this may lead to a recognition by international law of the value of the study by other social scientists of the total world process, a study which

also requires the investigation by all the techniques of modern science of how predispositional factors affecting decisions such as character structure, class position, skills, attitudes, vary from nation state to nation state. Hence it would

[74] It is perhaps unnecessary to give many examples of authors who support the universal theory. Not, however, because they are difficult to find, but exactly because, until recently, it has been the almost universal opinion of all textbook writers that international law is essentially a universal system governing all nations in all their mutual relations. One recent book may be mentioned propagating a world public order acceptable for all nations: Clark and Sohn, *World Peace through World Law* (1958).

[75] For a detailed discussion on this matter, McDougal and Lasswell, "The Identification and Appraisal of Diverse Systems of Public Order," 53 *A.J.I.L.* 1–29 (1959). The need for further research, which they have stressed, is certainly necessary for the Asian countries. Indonesia, for instance, might be considered to fit into an Islamic system of public order. Such an inclusion might set her apart, however, from a non-Islamic regional system of Southeast Asia.

make possible a meaningful survey through time of how different decision makers, with varying dispositions, appropriately located in different nation states apply technical doctrines of varying degrees of equivalence to comparable problems to achieve identifiable effects on values.[76]

Since we are dealing here with the *development* of international law we will start with reviewing in Chapter II the historical facts of these Asian states before the achievement of independence. At the same time this account forms the basis for an examination of the changing nature of the legal relationship between the Asian and Western nations since their first contact. The pre-colonial time was apparently not considered of any value to the development of modern international law. Asian authors, however, stress the existence of an Asian international law in that same period.

The first part in the next era (the colonial period and the rise of the nationalist movement) was the heyday of the European Chartered Companies which came to the East primarily for trade benefits. The legal status of these Chartered Companies *vis-à-vis* their Asian opponents (princes, chiefs, tribes) is considered. The colonial empires which were subsequently established reduced these Asian entities to colonial dependencies. This situation only ended after World War II. The legal aspects of this period concern the nature of the colonial relationship between the motherland and the overseas territory. The main contention made here is that, although colonies did not constitute a separate subject of international law, their participation as separate units in international affairs has been unduly minimized and underestimated.

When World War II put an end to the colonial period of the four Asian states concerned, two important cases emerged. Firstly, there was the Japanese-created, independent state of Burma. Although it was generally held that the Japanese action in creating the state was illegal and thus void, it is contended here that – under certain conditions – such a war-time creation can be considered to be valid. The other case, which has some importance for international law, is that of Indonesia. It gives an opportunity to observe the changing legal nature of a revolting colony in the process of becoming an independent country. The relevance of Chapter II to the development of international law lies in the fact that it may give us

[76] McDougal, "The Comparative Study of Law for Policy Purposes," 61 *Yale L.J.* 945 (1952); Schwarzenberger, "The Interdisciplinary Treatment of International Law," in *Fundamental Problems of International Law* (J. Spiropoulos) 401–409 (1957).

some indications on the causes and motives of the actions of Asian states. Their suspicions, distrust, resentments and also their preferences may become clearer from a review of their first contacts with modern international law.

In Chapter III some contemporary international law practices of these Asian states are reviewed. Since it is impossible to examine all their practices within the limits of this thesis, three cases have been selected to serve as the subjects of discussion: The Burma-China boundary disputes, the Kashmir conflict and the case of Indonesia and the law of the sea. The justification for this choice is that it represents the leading cases in these countries on international law. A second consideration is that the first example demonstrates the important impact of historical facts for Asian countries; the second example concerns a problem which came up in the present time, whereas the last case reveals something of the attitude towards, and expectations of, the future. A brief discussion of "peaceful coexistence" is added because it is today regarded as the leading principle of Asian policy.

In Chapter IV a summary is given and an attempt is made to make some generalizations and speculations on future practices.

CHAPTER II

THE ORIGIN OF THE PROBLEM

The origin of the problem is wrapped in history. Some knowledge of that history is, therefore, necessary to an understanding of the present situation. Outside Asia, ignorance of the actual, historical development of this continent has often led to misconceptions and incorrect appraisals of the significance of what is taking place today.

In the Western world people have no difficulties in judging contemporary events in the light of their own history since the facts of this history are generally agreed upon. The history of European-Asian relations ever since the discovery of the sea-route to the Indies, however, is fraught with difficulties. Not only has this period received insufficient attention so as to present a complete picture of the contacts, but even basic assumptions of historiographers on this subject, have later proved biased and inaccurate.

It is understandable if, at this point, the international jurist would ask: "How much direct connection is there between these historical errors and modern international law?" The answer is: "Very much indeed. In fact it concerns the very basis of international law the development of which depends, among other things, on the data provided by related disciplines, not the least the study of international history."

With regard to the early contact between Europe and Asia, international jurists have drawn conclusions which were largely based on historical recordings of these relations and which have become the traditional views on the international status of former Asian states, principalities, tribes etc. However, on the basis of more recent research, historiographers have now adopted quite different theories; but, unfortunately, these have not yet attracted enough attention among international jurists. Thus, while new ideas appeared in the field of history, traditional international law proceeded on the basis of obsolete views.

For instance, a basic assumption of modern international law states that it was conceived in the state practice of European nations of the 16th and 17th centuries[1] and that Asian nations could not possibly have contributed to these rules since the conception of a Family of Nations ruled by international law was entirely foreign to them.[2] This view is today more and more contested, not in the least by Western historiographers. With regard to the history of Indonesia, for instance, Dutch scholars[3] have pointed out themselves the "colossal distortions"[4] brought about by former incorrect accounts of Asia after the arrival of the first Europeans.[5] The same mistake was often made in the case of British India.[6]

It is quite clear that if these distortions have found their way into present historic knowledge they must have affected those doctrines of modern international law concerned with these early contacts.[7]

What could be done about it today? In the first place more attention should be paid to this fundamental point: In making the Asian states the subject of a study (as is done in this work) it is essential not only to look at them from a Europe-centric point of view, but also to see them through Asian eyes. Only those who have made themselves sufficiently familiar with the Asian views (no matter how wrong they may seem at first sight) can hope to find a reasonable solution for these problems.

For a clarification of these Asian views a reappraisal of certain historical events is necessary. Their significance is borne out by

[1] Brierly, *The Law of Nations* 1 (1949). 1 Oppenheim, *International Law* 48 (8th ed. 1955).

[2] *Id.* at 72.

[3] These revolutionary theories are – as far as Indonesia is concerned – connected with the names of the late J. C. van Leur, Professor C. C. Berg (Leyden) and further Professor G. J. Resink (Djakarta). See also Van der Kroef: "On the Writing of Indonesian History," 31 *Pac. Aff.* 352–371 (1958).

[4] Van Leur, *Indonesian Trade and Society. Essays in Asian Social and Economic History*, 150 (1955).

[5] Van Leur has made himself one of the first outspoken critics of previous historical accounts when he stated that colonial historians who had at first developed an Indocentric approach later changed their attitudes and "with the arrival of ships from Western Europe, the point of view is turned a hundred and eighty degrees, and from then on the Indies are observed from the deck of the ship, the ramparts of the fortress, the high gallery of the trading house." Van Leur, *Indonesian Trade and Society. Essays in Asian Social and Economic History*, Bookreview by C. R. Boxer in 8 *Indonesië* (The Hague) 426 (1955).

[6] Boxer, *supra* note 5, at 428, note 3.

[7] Professor Resink of Djakarta, who makes it his speciality to study the legal aspects of the early contacts between Europeans and Indonesians stated that, as a result of these misconceptions there was in the West naturally no place for the international law history of Indonesia during the many centuries preceding the colonial time. Resink, "Onafhankelijke Vorsten, Rijken en Landen in Indonesië tussen 1850 en 1910 (Independent princes, principalities and countries in Indonesia between 1850 and 1910), 9 *Indonesië* (The Hague) 265–296 at 293 (1959).

recent happenings, for today there are few international issues involving Asian countries which do not take the observer far back into history. Such outstanding examples as the claims with respect to Tibet, Yunnan, Goa, Damao (with Dadra and Nagar Aveli), Kashmir and New Guinea demonstrate how these claims are firmly rooted in historical facts. A disregard for such facts (especially if combined with an unfamiliarity with the attitudes and reactions of the people) may create wrong or distorted impressions as has been proved sufficiently by the predictions with regard to the Asian-African Conference at Bandung in April 1955,[8] the first general elections in Indonesia in September 1955[9] and the second general elections of Burma in April 1956.[10]

With the above in mind, it is not difficult to speculate with regard to future practices that, lacking more recent experience in international relations as a result of their former colonial status, Asian

[8] Richard Wright in his *The Colour Curtain* 69 (1956) describes how some representatives of the most powerful newsagencies in the world at first looked at this, for Asia and Africa most significant event, with neither a sense of history nor an understanding of the attitudes of the peoples. He mentioned how some of these newspapermen had made a list of all the delegates going to Bandung and had checked them all according to their political leanings and had come to the conclusion that the West would emerge victorious from its clash with China's evil genius Chou En-lai.

[9] In the case of the Indonesian general elections the attitude of observers also led them astray. Besides ignoring the history of this country they were perhaps also deceived by their own wishful thinking and by an unwarranted reliance on personalities, parties and statistics. Such an attitude, already unsound in Western countries, was certainly wrong in the East.

"Political observers of long experience" (including some Indonesians) were rather disturbed by the election results since it had been "virtually axiomatic" that the liberal Masjumi (Moslem) party would gain a resounding victory in this most populous Moslem country of the world. Robert C. Bone Jr., "The Indonesian Elections," in "*News and Views on World Affairs*" (Canadian Institute of Int. Aff.). vol. XIX, No. 7, Oct. 24, 1955. Most of these observers did not expect the Communists to come out very well, thereby disregarding the fact that communism does not (yet) have the odium which it has in western countries. Moreover they also overlooked the ability of the Communists to impress the people with their election campaign.

The results startled these observers. The Masjumi Party won only 57 out of a total of 260 seats in the House of Representatives, sharing the lead with the Nationalist Party which, although expected to trail badly (*N.Y. Times*, Sept. 27, 1955), won the same amount of seats. Third came the more orthodox Moslem party, the Nahdatul Ulama, with 45 seats. But the greatest surprise was perhaps the Communist Party which defied the forecasts and became one of the "Big Four" in the House with 39 seats. *Id.* Sept. 27, 30 & Oct. 5, 1955; also *N.R.C.* Oct. 7, 1955.

[10] Apparently, the Indonesian example (note 9) did not shake the faith of some observers in their own method of assessing the political leanings of the population. Only half a year later they had another opportunity to report an identical event, namely the second general elections in Burma. Again they expected generally that the main opposition party (the NUF) would do badly against the government party (the AFPFL). Again the results showed how they blundered. Although the AFPFL indeed won easily, the NUF – which was even expected to lose some of its 12 seats – managed to win four times that number (48 seats). *N.Y. Times*, May 4, 1956.

nations will fall back on early historical experiences in support of the positions that they will take in various international matters. Knowledge of Asian history is essential for the future as well as the past.

The records of Asian history, however, – with the exception of modern times – are less abundant than those of the West. It is undoubtedly true that the best-recorded and most well-known history is that of the European world. One of the principal reasons for this is that the history of the modern world is to a great extent the history of the Western world, its cultural and political expansion, as a result of which the fate of many other parts of the world became permanently attached to that of the West. Western culture with its education, sciences and accompanying prolific literature spread its influence to places far beyond its geographical boundaries. It is for these reasons that many Asians and other non-Europeans, particularly the educated classes, have become familiar with Western culture. Among their leaders are men who have become thorougly acquainted with the Western way of life and thinking and have to a great extent made it their own.[11]

Conversely, the situation is unfortunately rather different. Relatively few westerners, even the educated ones, are familiar with Asian tradition, history and thinking. The thousands of Europeans who have worked and lived in Eastern dependencies were not very well acquainted with the people and country of their temporary settlement. To most of them life in these overseas territories was a temporary sojourn in a place where they lived and worked but where they did not intend to settle. Moreover, their lives were often confined to the European enclaves in which their daily activities were concentrated. They seldom spoke the native language well and their contacts with the indigenous population were limited. This is not to say that they were incapable of developing deep and sincere feelings for these territories and their populations, but these feelings often had a paternalistic tinge which was not appreciated by the objects of the sympathy. Western experts on Asia have not been blind to this in their analyses. This is how one of them has put it:

> Most of us, travellers and adventurers from the West, whether we come with a spiritual message or for material gain, look down into that mass from a remote point. When we are humanly interested we may come to know certain representatives of the higher classes somewhat more intimately; yet even of them we know only the face they turn towards our Western world and not the roots they have among the common people.

[11] Nehru and Sjahrir are perhaps the best known examples.

Continuing his self-criticism he said:

> And if some of us, missionaries or doctors or just queer fellows, bury ourselves in such a community to live there, we are either too much filled with a special purpose, or we bury ourselves too deeply, to be able to observe more than our direct environment.[12]

Although this last statement may perhaps be too severe – in as much as the works of many western scholars, civil servants and missionaries, although biased towards the West, have been of considerable value to Asian students – these reflections of a man who spent the greater part of his life in Asia, point to the wide spiritual abyss between the people of Asia and the European immigrants.

It is not the task of international law, however, to occupy itself with these problems and give a better account of the Asian peoples, their character, history and life. This chapter will, therefore, attempt only to throw some light on certain important conditions and events in the past, knowledge of which is thought to be desirable in order to understand the spirit of present-day Asia. Cast in political terms it means that we are concerned in this chapter with the establishment, development and termination of the Asian colonial regimes. It also means – seen from a different angle – the history of Asian nationalism, its origin, growth and achievements.

This all-important question of nationalism brings us to a central aspect of Asian life today. In the West it is generally felt that nationalism is a product of Western civilization and not older than the 18th century.[13] It is quite probable that Asian historians will reject this contention. The disagreement is grounded on differing interpretations of the concept of nationalism.[14] This debate, however, is of no great importance in our case. For, regardless of its exact meaning, the fact remains that nationalism – whatever its origin – has become the driving force in Asian thinking. It will, therefore, be useful to keep in mind that nationalism will necessarily affect the views of Asians on issues of international law.

[12] Van Mook, *The Stakes of Democracy in SE Asia* 27–28 (1950). See also Korn, "Oosterse Visie op Westers Bewind" (Eastern view on Western rule), 113 *Bijdragen tot de Taal-, Land- en Volkenkunde* 16–31 at 30–31 (1957).

[13] Kohn, *The Idea of Nationalism* 3 (1951).

[14] *Cf.* Prof. Korn ,emeritus professor of Indonesian adat law (= mainly customary law) at Leyden University, who contends (*supra* note 12 at 27) that Indonesian nationalism in fact existed for centuries. In its early form its main theme was the re-establishment of the old order before the arrival of the Dutch. In its recent form nationalism is said to concern the idea of an independent national state.

There is another point worthy of note now. Dealing with nationalism we have an opportunity to make some projections into the future, for Asian nationalism as the cause of political change continued to exist, even after having almost completely achieved its primary aim, i.e. the termination of the political domination of the Western powers. In spite of these achievements nationalism still reigns supreme today. The fact that there still are some remnants of colonial rule in this area is only partly responsible for the continued feelings of nationalism. It has now found other objectives connected with colonial and racial problems in other parts of the world.

It is proposed here to examine the origin of the problem under three headings: the pre-colonial time; the colonial period and the rise of the nationalist movement; the achievement of independence and the years after that. A historical account will only be given here to the extent that it can form the background for the issues of international law connected with each of the periods.

(a) The significance of the *pre-colonial* time for the study of international law lies in the question whether the political entities in pre-colonial Asia could be considered "states," and whether they were familiar with international law.

(b) *The colonial period and the rise of the nationalist movements* gave rise to the legal problems of

(1) the status of the Chartered Companies,
(2) the nature of their relations with the Asians,
(3) the colonial relationship.

(c) Finally, *the achievement of independence and the years after that* created other legal problems, particularly for the colonies of Burma and the Netherlands Indies.

THE PRE-COLONIAL TIME

Modern international law is essentially a creation of Western, Christian civilization. This contention automatically excludes from the realm of modern international law the pre-colonial period which lasted until the arrival of the Europeans in the beginning of the 16th century. It does not mean, however, that these areas in Asia were devoid of any system of rules and usages which were considered to be binding in their mutual relationships. These rules may well have been quite similar in nature to the body of rules existing in Europe, although they were created and developed separately from those in Europe.

However, by its very wording, the above description of the character of modern international law rules out the possibility that Asian countries in this period could have contributed in any way to the creation of modern international law. Underlying this contention is the idea that Asian nations of that time were unable to carry out their international contacts and obligations in a way similar to that of the Western world.[15]

What then was the political picture of Asia before the Europeans appeared? The vastness and diversity of the area makes it very difficult to give one combined historical account. Yet there are clearly general trends which enable us to treat the histories of some parts of this continent along broad lines.

Burma, Ceylon, India and Indonesia, the countries with which we are particularly concerned, existed as distinct societies long before the Europeans appeared on their shores. They had reached levels of civilization which compared favourably with the European countries of that time.[16] Their political development had gone through stages of tribal community, monarchy as well as republic, although they may have differed in many respects from the western types.[17]

However, the political map of that time did not follow the boundaries of what is today known as Burma, Ceylon, India and Indonesia. One of the main features then was the broken pattern of these areas. On the other hand, it should be immediately added here that, in spite of the broken political structure, the people of these areas saw their fate linked to greater units. It has always been a common feature in their history that repeatedly attempts were made by some of their leaders to unite the separate components to one greater entity.[18] This aspiration has seldom been achieved and then only for

[15] See the various articles of Prof. Sastri in the Indian Yearbook of International Affairs (*infra* note 17 & 18) and of Prof. Resink, *supra* note 7.

[16] This is again one of Van Leur's contentions which, though novel in the 1930's – has now become almost generally accepted. *Cf.* Boxer *supra* note 5, at 425, 427.

[17] See Sastri, International Law and Relations in Ancient India, 1 *I.Y.I.A.* 99 (1952); Vlekke, *Nusantara – A History of the East Indian Archipelago* 8 (1945); Maung Maung, *Burma in the Family of Nations* 3, 1956.

[18] Vlekke, *op. cit. supra* note 17, at 53–55 (the Empire of Mataram) and 30–31 (the Empire of Shrivijaya); Maung Maung, *op. cit. supra* note 17, at 13 (the Alaungpaya dynasty); Sastri, *supra* note 17, at 101; Sastri, "Inter-State Relations in Asia" (hereinafter cited as "Inter-State Rel.") 2 *I.Y.I.A.* 138 (1953); *cf.* Korn, *supra* note 12, at 27, on the frequent emergence of persons who claimed to be the awaited leader.

a short period. Indeed one of the main achievements of the European colonial powers was their ability to bring about in the end real unification, if only by force of arms.

Before the arrival of the Europeans, the area was covered by a great number of fully or semi-independent states, which dealt with each other either on a footing of equality or on that of suzerain and vassal. In many cases the latter relationship should not be taken too literally for the tribute of a so-called vassal often amounted to mere formality and was restricted to something like an annual token tribute to the suzerain, who did not interfere with other external or internal affairs of his vassal.[19]

The contacts of these areas with the world around them were of long standing. With respect to the countries in the West relations had already been established before the beginning of the Christian era and the adventures of the Persian Empire and of Alexander the Great further increased the acquaintanceship with the West.[20]

To the east there was the mighty Chinese Empire which, by virtue of its great power, could not possibly be ignored. China had an outlook on international relations in which it showed itself a worthy Eastern counterpart of the Greek and Roman Empires. To the great Chinese civilization all peoples outside its realm were barbarians and not to be treated as equals.[21] The other nations were expected to pay tribute to the Chinese Emperor and did so in a spirit of tacit acknowledgement of the dominating position of the Chinese Empire. Occasionally these tributes were forcefully imposed on stubborn princes, but in general they seem to have caused little trouble, mainly because the Asian states, rather than risk military reprisals from China, willingly paid the annual token tributes which represented in fact the only exercise of Chinese suzerainty.[22]

Situated along the communication lines which connected the East and the West, the four countries under consideration here were naturally included in the international contact of that time, especially through trade.

[19] Sastri, Inter-State Rel., *supra* note 18, at 138; Vlekke, *op. cit. supra* note 17, 49–50, 54–56.

[20] Sastri, Inter-State Rel. *supra* note 18, at 136.

[21] *Id.* at 143.

[22] However, that these token tributes were not completely without legal significance has become clear in more recent times during the Burma-Yunnan border question (see chapter III) and in the dispute between India and China with respect to the Tibet borderline. Sastri Inter-State Rel. *supra* note 18 at 141; Vlekke, *op. cit. supra* note 17, 49–50.

As early as the 3rd and 4th centuries Arabian and Chinese merchants frequented these countries. In the 10th century, trade with the West was carried out by the Chinese who took the products as far as Palembang on the island of Sumatra where the Arab merchants took over and carried them further West.[23]

Political expansion also threatened these areas, especially from the side of the Chinese. Kublai Khan is well-known for the military expeditions which he sent to punish the princes who were unwilling to recognize his overlordship. These events gave some insight into the powers and intercourse of the so-called "states" of those days. Burma felt Kublai Khan's strong hand in the second half of the 13th century[24] and a few years later he sent an expeditionary force to the East Indies where some states (like Singosari) had not only refused to pay tribute but had also maltreated Chinese envoys. A force of about 20.000 men landed on Java but was only partially successful in its military operations. Soon after, it withdrew from the island.[25]

The East Indies had also been constantly visited or invaded by foreign elements. India, especially had a great influence. Even prior to the 5th and 6th centuries states in South India expanded their trade relations to the Indies.[26] Cultural relations of this type had political ramifications as well for they were accompanied by an influx of Indians into the visited areas. Although their numbers were relatively small, their influence was great. Not only did they introduce their religions into the new fatherland. They also brought knowledge of new forms of state organization. In the East Indies the continuous influx of Indians from the Indian sub-continent from the beginning of the Christian era to the 8th century reflected itself, besides the religious change, in the establishment of several Hindu-Javanese and Sumatran kingdoms, some of which became very important.[27] An illustration of the strength of these states is furnished by the Hindu-Sumatran state of Shrivijaya which established itself as a great naval power. At one time it was said to control all commerce in this area as far as the Moluccas and the Philippines.[28]

[23] F. C. Cole, *The Peoples of Malaysia* 27 (1945).
[24] Maung Maung *op. cit. supra* note 17, at 11.
[25] Vlekke, *op. cit. supra* note 17, at 49.
[26] Cole, *op. cit. supra* note 23 at 17.
[27] Vlekke, *op. cit. supra* note 17, at 13, 14, 17; see also Krom, *Hindoe-Javaansche Geschiedenis* 415–428 (1931).
[28] 1 Stapel, *Geschiedenis van Ned. Indië* (History of the Neth. Indies) 278 (1938);

Having described briefly the nature and powers of these Asian states,[29] the question arises as to how these states and their relations compared with those of the western world. It is but natural that as a result of such continuous contact over a long period usages and rules were developed which governed their intercourse. Oppenheim analysed this process in antiquity in the following way:

> No nation could avoid coming into contact with other nations. War was waged and peace concluded. Treaties were agreed upon. Occasionally ambassadors were sent and received. International arbitration was resorted to. International trade sprang up. Political partisans whose cause was lost often fled their country and took refuge in another.... Such more or less frequent and constant contact of different nations with one another could not exist without giving rise to certain fairly consistent rules and usages to be observed with regard to external relations....[30]

But Oppenheim is on less solid ground when he states that the exclusiveness of modern international law is connected to the awareness of the conception of a Family of Nations. "It is a well-known fact," he says, "that the conception of a Family of Nations did not arise in the mental horizons of the ancient world."[31]

Western authors are certainly not blind to the existence of non-European rules of international law, but they are hard-pressed to explain what must then be their significance to modern international law. Oppenheim's suggestion that the concept of a Family of Nations was absent in the ancient world represents one such unconvincing attempt to minimize the significance of these ancient rules of conduct.[32]

Perhaps part of the difficulty must be attributed to the fact that not enough research has as yet been carried out into the political systems of ancient Asia. It is worth noting here that some Asian authors who have dealt with the same subject arrived at different conclusions.[33] In India especially, scholars are giving more and

Steiger, *A History of the Far East* 195–196 (1936); but *cf.* Berg, "De Sadeng Oorlog en de Mythe van Groot-Majapahit," (The Sadeng War and the Myth of Greater Majapahit) 5 *Indonesië* 412–413 (1952).

[29] For the significance of Buddhism and Islam in the Asian political arena, Vlekke, *op. cit. supra* note 17, at 17-71; Sastri, Inter-State Rel. *supra* note 18, at 144; Cole, *op. cit. supra* note 23, at 23.

[30] 1 Oppenheim, *International Law* sect. 37b. (8th ed. 1955).

[31] *Ibid.*

[32] It must be admitted, however, that it is not entirely clear whether Oppenheim includes in "the ancient world" other countries outside Europe. For, if he was dealing with ancient Europe only (and this may have been his intention in the quoted passage) then the criticism launched above (as well as that of Prof. Sastri) does not hold.

[33] See also the identical views of non-Asians in *supra* note 3–7.

more attention to this issue. As early as 1925 Viswanatha pointed out the similarity between rules and usages in Ancient India and those of Western institutions.[34]

Professor Sastri's study of early interstate relations in Asia led him to conclude not only that greater caution should be used in assessing the character of the ancient world, but also that

> Asia constituted a family of nations with established laws, conventions and practices of their own, long before the rise of the modern European law of nations and a strict regard to the facts of history may lead to a modification of Oppenheim's categorical denial of the concept of a community of nations among the ancient and medieval states outside Europe.[35]

Wherever the truth in this matter may lie,[36] the historical reality does not seem to be of decisive importance for our purposes here. Inasmuch as there was no direct contact between the Eastern and Western world it made little difference what misconceptions prevailed about the cultural and political maturity of either group. Thus while the fact that Asia may have had more awareness of a "family of nations" than is generally assumed might greatly interest historians, anthropologists and other scholars, it has little bearing on the role played by modern international law today. Yet it is worthwhile to keep the above points in mind, because they represent an Asian view different from the traditional one.

Recent research has forcefully exposed Western misconceptions of Eastern social and legal institutions.[37] While these misconceptions may have had no harmful effects during the bygone period when Asian states were unable to assert themselves, they are bound to cause greater conflict today. The newly emerged independent states in these areas are no longer passive objects of a theory but participate actively in international affairs as full-fledged subjects of international law.

[34] Viswanatha, *International Law in Ancient India* 5–12 (1925).

[35] Sastri, Inter-State Rel., *supra* note 18, at 145.

[36] A non-Indian author from Asia, on the other hand, states unequivocally that it was not until the 19th century that Asian states were admitted into the Family of Nations. He apparently accepted the traditional concept that the "Family of Nations" was a strictly European product to which outside nations have only been admitted after reaching an advanced stage of development. Maung Maung, *op. cit. supra* note 17, at 1.

[37] *Cf.* Supomo, "The Future of Adat-Law in the Reconstruction of Indonesia," in Thayer, *Southeast Asia in the Coming World* 220–226 (1953).

THE COLONIAL PERIOD AND THE RISE OF THE NATIONALIST MOVEMENT

1. The Establishment of the Colonial Empires

The end of the 15th century marked the beginning of a new era in East-West relations. Before this time there had been some contact and both sides were well aware of each other's existence. Yet it was not until the discovery of the searoute to the East that revolutionary changes took place in the history of both Asia and Europe.

Up to this time there had not been sufficient reasons for embarking upon such a hazardous undertaking as the search for these searoutes. Spices and other products from the East found their way to the Western markets along the trade routes of Persia, Egypt and the other regions of the Eastern Mediterranean. Towards the end of the 12th century, however, Islam had succeeded in establishing itself as the key power, controlling the lines of communication between Asia and Europe. European merchants, realizing how much safer and cheaper it would be to get the products directly from the sources became more and more interested in such an undertaking.

Perhaps the greatest single factor leading to the discovery of the East was the desire of the Portuguese and Spaniards to strike some mighty blows at Islam in the spirit of the Crusades, for

> ... to a devout and patriotic Iberian, Spaniard or Portuguese, the fight against Islam was a stern imperative, a combination alike of religious duty and patriotic necessity. Islam was the enemy and had to be fought everywhere. Much of Portuguese action in Asia will remain inexplicable unless this fact is constantly borne in mind.[38]

With full support from the Pope the Portuguese started work on the realization of their plans, i.e. the discovery of the searoute to the East around the south of Africa. When Vasco da Gama and the remainder of his ships and crew reached the southwest coast of the Indian sub-continent in 1498 and dropped anchor at Calicut, the discovery of the searoute was realized.

Western historians generally point to this fact as the beginning of a new era. Their Asian colleagues do not dispute this but the agreement ends right there, for the historiography of subsequent centuries shows the respective biases of the European and Asian points of view with which we will deal later. Suffice it to say here

[38] Panikkar, *Asia and Western Dominance* 28 (1953).

that whereas Europeans have generally described this period as one of glorious western expansion as a result of daring, energy, salesmanship, foresight, Christian devotion and duty, to the Asians it represents an unwelcome invasion of rude, ruthless, profit-seeking and evangelizing foreigners. It is a tragic, if perhaps understandable, fact that it has not been possible to reconcile these two views, and even in our time, which has seen the elimination of the main point of friction (i.e. Western colonial rule), the experience of a "three centuries' nightmare" still dominates Asian feelings.

The territorial gains made by the Portuguese were initially restricted to certain harbours and trading posts along the coast. Their first establishment was not in Calicut, where Vasco da Gama had landed, but further to the south in Cochin (circa 1502). This was followed by other conquests and establishments, e.g. Goa (1515), Malacca (1511), Colombo (1517), Canton (1517), Macao (1557).[39]

In the pursuit of their other objective, i.e. the defeat of Islam, the Portuguese attacked their enemy in his communication lines. Ormuz, at the Persian Gulf, was taken, as was the island of Socotra which controlled the Red Sea (1515). An attempt to capture Aden failed and battles with the Islam naval forces remained stalemated for a long period.[40]

Obviously, it was not possible for the Portuguese to prevent other European nations from coming to the East. The Spaniards approached Asia from the opposite side. Starting out from their bases in Central America, they sailed to Asia and arrived in the Philippines. Until the end of the 16th century the Portuguese and Spanish were able to keep these areas to themselves, without interference from other European rivals. The Dutch, English, French and other sailors then arrived on the spot and a ruthless struggle for maximum commercial gains and interests commenced.

In the course of the following centuries Western influence spread to other parts of Asia. For reasons of propinquity India was the first to be affected. From here Western influence spread east and southwards in the direction of China, Japan and the Indies. Commercial profits were still the primary objective and the Europeans were not too concerned with conquests as such. At times they even showed some reluctance to conquer territories in the face of the

[39] Barthold, *La Découverte de l'Asie* 111(1947); Latourette, *A Short History of the Far East* 61 (1946).

[40] Panikkar, *op. cit. supra* note 38, at 50–53; Latourette, *op. cit. supra* note 39, at 60.

strong resistance from the native populace. The few territorial acquisitions, which were made, were primarily designed to set up commercial centers and trading posts. This trade was initially carried out by private merchants, and not by their governments. Later on both joined hands and in the so-called Chartered Companies private as well as official interests were represented.

In the following years the Chartered Companies were to play a leading role in Asian history. Although in essence commercial enterprises, they had been granted extensive sovereign rights by their respective governments.[41] In their capacity of governmental representatives they made contacts with the native princes or chiefs and negotiated treaties. When these Chartered Companies were subsequently taken over by their governments the groundwork for the conversion of these territories into western colonies had already been laid.

These Western interests and objectives remained of a primarily commercial nature until the end of the 18th century. They could be achieved chiefly by peaceful means of negotiations and agreements, rather than by force and conquest of territory. However, fierce competition among themselves, with its resulting decrease of profits, soon made the Europeans aware that it would be more profitable to have one's own establishments in these areas rather than to depend for the products on the good will of the Eastern princes and chiefs. In order to assure a steady flow of products, it was necessary to gain more direct control over their production. This was one of the main reasons that forced them to a policy of more deliberate territorial expansion. Later on this trend was greatly accelerated by the industrial revolution. The colonies then gained added significance as potential export markets which induced the European powers to expand these dependencies.[42]

A review of this historical period inevitably raises the question of how much resistance was met in the process of empire building. It seems indeed incredible that the Asian states, with their wealth of human and material resources, were unable to eliminate or push back the small groups of Europeans arriving on their shores after months of rough sailing often in damaged ships. It may have been true, as is sometimes suggested, that their outfit was superior to that of their Asian opponents. Their superior guns certainly

[41] Lindley, *The Acquisition and Government of Backward Territories* 91–92 (1926).
[42] Van Mook, *The Stakes of Democracy in South East Asia* 42–49 (1950).

assured them a definite advantage in battle and the national solidarity of these small groups of Europeans functioning as well-organized units was in marked contrast to the rivalries between the native states in the Asian world. The Portuguese typified this superiority of organization as their commanders knew that new supplies of ships and troops from the home-country would be sent to their support at regular intervals.[43] It might have been equally true that the Europeans were smart strategists and could skilfully manipulate the local rivalries to their advantage by playing one party against another. Yet all these factors would have availed them little had the Asian princes made a determined effort to eliminate the foreign invaders. The decisive factor thus seems to have been a lack of sufficient determination to eliminate the westerners on the part of the Asian people as a whole. Several reasons for this passive acquiescence suggest themselves. Firstly, the profits of the Asian princes out of the trade with the West had previously to be shared with the merchants and middlemen who carried the products to Europe. With the arrival of the Europeans themselves in the East, the middlemen could be eliminated and the possibility of trade benefits was not unwelcome at all.

Secondly, the Asians no doubt miscalculated the intentions and underestimated the potential powers of the Western nations. For a considerable length of time they did not even seem to fear the invaders. This is borne out by the happenings during the first centuries of contact, although the historical records are controversial on this point. European historians tend to minimize the resistance put up by the Asian nations, whereas Asian historians emphasize their equality and even superiority in those days. For instance, as late as the middle of the 18th century the position of the Europeans in Asia was not significantly stronger than in 1515.[44] It was not until the 19th and 20th century, when the West had so greatly advanced technologically and materially, that their military preponderance became quite evident. During this same period the political structure in Asia had not gained in strength or stability. It was now too late to stem the progressing trend of European expansion and the way was paved for the establishment of the western colonial empires.

[43] Van Leur in bookreview of Stapel, *Geschiedenis van Ned. Indië*, in 79 *Tijdschrift Ind. T.L.V.* 591 (1939); Panikkar, *op. cit. supra* note 38, at 42.

[44] Panikkar *op. cit. supra* note 38, at 44–45, 93.

As noted earlier, the question whether Asia had a system of international law in the pre-colonial time is academic and irrelevant to modern international law. For even if they had a system of their own, it cannot possibly have influenced the development of modern international law, simply because there was no contact at the time between the pre-colonial Asian states and Europe, the place where modern international law came into being. The situation was quite different in the period now under consideration. One of the striking features of this era was the initial development of intercourse between the nations of the two worlds leading to the creation of a certain body of rules governing their mutual relations.

The official relations of this time were of a special type, since the native princes, chiefs or even communities dealt not with the European governments, but with their representatives, the Chartered Companies. The importance of this period for international law purposes lies in the study of the international status of the native parties, the Chartered Companies and their mutual relations.

We will start by considering the Chartered Companies. The first ships, which sailed to the East, were not sent by Chartered Companies, but by individual merchants. The highly competitive trade, however, soon forced them to adopt other methods of organization. Corporations were formed in which all the individual interests were merged. These corporations became powerful national monopolies when they were granted sovereign rights and powers by their governments for the areas oversea. These powers were embodied in a charter given by the metropolitan government. They contained an enumeration of the rights and duties of the Chartered Company and included besides a monopoly of trade and navigation, a great variety of privileges, such as the power to discover lands of "gentiles and infidels and take possession of them as the King's vassals," the right to "make laws for good and quiet government," to make contracts, agreements and alliances, to fit out men-of-war, to raise and maintain military forces, to erect fortresses, to declare war and make peace, to appoint governors and officers of justice, to coin money, further the monopoly of colonization and cultivation of the land and working of the mines.[45]

Although these sovereign powers were quite extensive, the Chartered Companies were not fully sovereign. They were always dependent upon and subordinate to the mother country. For this reason the

[45] Lindley, *op. cit. supra* note 41, at 92–99.

Chartered Companies were often called "dependent sovereigns."[46] The severability of their sovereignty is perhaps best illustrated by the fact that, while the British East India Company warred with its European rivals in the East, the respective mother countries in Europe were at peace with one another. On the other hand, no Chartered Company had territorial possessions of its own. It was always to the metropolitan state that these territories accrued. In this respect the authority of the French and Dutch Companies was even more closely linked to the metropolitan government than was that of the British Company.[47] The Dutch Charter, for instance, made the Company an agent of the government.[48] The relationship between these two types of sovereignty came up for review in the *Palmas* case (1928) where the arbitrator found that

> ... The acts of the (Dutch) East India Company, in view of occupying or colonizing the regions at issue in the present affair, must in international law be entirely assimilated to acts of the Netherlands state itself.... Art. V of the Treaty of Munster... show that the East and West India Companies were entitled to create situations recognized by international law.... The conclusions of conventions, even of a political nature, was by art. 35 of the charter of 1602 within the powers of the Company.

The first European sailors did not come to Asia complete strangers. The East had always had some attraction to Europe and by way of the commercial contacts with Mediterranean countries more information about those distant countries filtered through.[49] One thing, therefore, seems clear: the Western sea-farers did not expect to arrive in a "dark" world bereft of organized states and inhabited by wild tribes, as they did with regard to Africa.[50] That they knew better is testified to by their ships' papers and other documents from their governments. For instance, merchants on board the Dutch ships carried with their letters patent such documents as an open letter in the nature of a passport which served as a request to foreign kings for protection. They also carried "friendship letters" containing a request to enter into commercial relations, written in Latin and sometimes in Arabic or Portuguese. The historical accounts of this period by Western scholars supply sub-

[46] *Id.* at 98.
[47] See for differences with the German and Portuguese East India Company, Lindley, *supra* note 41, at 103.
[48] *Id.* at 99.
[49] *Supra* at 40.
[50] Even this assumption with regard to Africa has now been questioned. *Cf.* Prof. Herbert Passin: "What is Africa?" in *World Assembly of Youth Forum* 3 (Spring 1959); Herbert Passin, "The Ancient Jar of Dahomey," 13 *Encounter* 37–38 (Sept. 1959).

stantial evidence of the existence of many political entities which were, at that time, considered as full-fledged states, even by the Western nations which had to deal with them. While many of them may not have met the rigid concept of a modern state, the same could equally be said of some of their European contemporaries. Asian historians are obviously convinced of this fact.[51]

In the light of these facts, it seems rather strange that modern textbooks of international law have adopted a different view. Little attention and space is devoted to these times, apparently because these facts have for the greater part only historical value. Yet this does not entirely justify the cursory treatment of this particular period. What is primarily open to criticism is not so much the amount of space given to these facts, but to the contents of the description. The terms used to indicate the Asian political entities, whether they were states, chiefs or tribes, do not give enough attention to the historical facts.

The terms used vary from "primitive society" or "savages" on the one hand, to "native states" on the other, and refuse to accord the status of equal to any of these eastern entities, a status which – it is submitted here – was undoubtedly acknowledged by the European India-farers, either explicitly or implicitly.

In between the two extremes of "primitives" and "native states" there is a whole range of other terms, such as tribal communities,[52] native communities,[53] backward societies,[54] non-civilized nation,[55] semi-civilized nation,[56] and non-Christian nation.[57]

If indeed there were clearcut criteria which set these Asian political societies apart from their more highly regarded Western counterparts of those days then the division may be harsh, but yet not unjustified. It is at this point, however, that the whole system breaks down. The real criteria are seldom mentioned, but only implied. What then could have been the real criteria? The answer can be derived from a closer examination of the above terms, for it is obvious from the very terminology used that the distinction is based on the concept of either civilization or Christianity, terms which were usually equated, but sometimes distinguished. Both

[51] Panikkar, *op. cit. supra* note 38, at 36.
[52] H. A. Smith, *Great Britain and the Law of Nations* 30 (1932).
[53] Schwarzenberger, *International Law*, vol. I, chapter IV (1957).
[54] Lindley, *op. cit. supra* note 41, at 11.
[55] Smith, *op. cit. supra* note 52, at 15.
[56] Lindley, *op. cit. supra* note 41, at 18.
[57] Oppenheim, *op. cit. supra* note 30, at 48–49.

concepts refer back to the first beginnings of international law, for at that time international law was strictly a product and a creation of the Christian, Western European world.[58]

Since the community of European nations was clearly delineated, it was easy to determine which communities did or did not fall in the pale of (European) international law. This factual division was indeed a well-working instrument, but the development of international law into a universal system made certain revisions necessary. No longer is "European" or "Christian" a condition for admission into to the Family of Nations. However, such a change of ideological concepts is seldom able to keep pace with political developments which explains the fact that, for example, the term "civilized nation" is still frequently implied or even used. Present definitions of international law still employ this term.[59]

Since international law does not provide us with a satisfactory definition of the elusive adjective "civilized" a look at the related disciplines may help. Schwarzenberger,[60] in dealing with this subject, suggests that good services can be rendered by the sociology of international law. In this respect, he says, one must look at civilization in its relation to nature as well as to man. In relation to nature civilization means intelligent exploitation. On the other hand, in relation to man exploitation is proof of *un*civilized behaviour. Seen in this light, one can readily understand that he urges the international lawyer to use this term cautiously.

One may perhaps go further and query, whether more recent studies of Asian and other so-called backward peoples have not confirmed the proposition that the term "uncivilized" has often been used too loosely and therefore superficially. Certainly, if intelligent exploitation is one feature of civilization, as Schwarzenberger suggested, it would be inaccurate to label some Asian nations "uncivilized" because they never showed an urge to explore nature more extensively than they seemed to need at the time. It is also significant in applying the term "intelligent exploitation," whether the word "intelligent" or the word "exploitation" is emphasized.

[58] Schwarzenberger, "The Standard of Civilization in International Law," 8 *Current Legal Problems* 219 (1955).
[59] Brierly, *The Law of Nations* at 1 (1949); Oppenheim, *op. cit. supra* note 30 at 4 (7th ed); 1 Hyde, *International Law* 1, note 1 (1951).
[60] Schwarzenberger, *op. cit. supra* note 58 at 218.

With regard to the concept of civilization in the relation of man to man, it is said that the more civilized a human association is, the less it has to rely on the exploitation of man by man, or of one group by another, and the more it is based on the principles of agreement and voluntary cooperation.[61] The nature of an eastern rural community has rarely been so well described.

This is not to say that the Asian states, which consist mainly of rural communities, should always have been considered as civilized nations. It only goes to show how fallacious the use of such terms in international law can be if not based on more solid grounds.

The above arguments are derived from the related field of the sociology of international law. There are, however, other contentions which are more directly related to international law itself. Prof. Smith[62] states that, after the expansion of European international law into a world wide system, the decisive test for statehood had shifted from Christian or European to that of a certain minimum of order and stability. He illustrates this contention with some examples from the middle of the 19th century and thereafter, a period which was to see the stabilization of the western world. Consequently, stability became a practical test for statehood. However, this test only arose in more recent times and it certainly did not apply in the first part of the colonial period when intercourse between the East and West was in its infancy. In order to determine what may have been the decisive test at that time, it may be useful to recall a ruling which is most clearly expressed in the *Palmas* case:[63]

> It is admitted that international law underwent profound modifications between the end of the Middle Ages and the end of the 19th century as regard the right of discovery and the acquisition of uninhabited regions or regions inhabited by savages or semi-civilized peoples. Both parties are also agreed that a *juridical fact must be appreciated in the light of the law contemporary with it.*[64]

In the same case the arbitrator stated that the continued existence of a right, in contradistinction to its creation, is *not* to be judged by the law contemporary with it, but that it should follow the conditions required by the evolution of law.[65] This important principle does not apply here, however, since we are not dealing with a right now, but

[61] *Ibid.*
[62] Smith, *op. cit. supra* note 52, at 30.
[63] U.N., 2 *Reports of International Arbitral Awards* 845 (1949).
[64] Author's italics.
[65] *Supra* note 63.

with the concept of a state at the time of the appearance of the Europeans in the East.

In order to determine whether Asian countries were regarded as states at that time, it would not be correct to apply a test which was developed in later times and which may, subsequently, set up conditions with regard to stability of government, settled frontiers, self-government and attitude towards international obligations.[66] Rather we should look at the structure and practices of these countries during the period concerned. Historical accounts seem to indicate that the Asian scene was dominated by a number of political societies which had such a high degree of internal organization and external relations, that they were – *in fact* – considered states and treated accordingly by their contemporary world.[67] The power to make laws, to conclude treaties, to exchange envoys, to maintain an army, to coin money and other prerogatives of a sovereign were all represented in the political machinery of these countries.[68] The first European sailors and later the representatives of their governments had no alternative but to treat these Asian states on a footing of equality.

Nor can it be said that these states were disorganized, unstable and unable to defend themselves. Although European historians minimize the strength of these Asian states a recent Asian account of the period gives ample proof of their powers.[69] It describes that at the end of the 15th century India was organized in states of considerable power and internal stability. The military (especially naval) power of the Portuguese was met on at least equal terms. Few military conquests succeeded in the first two hundred years and for about one hundred years a naval rivalry existed between the King (Zamorin) of Calicut and the Portuguese.[70]

It is not easy to determine what the legal conditions of statehood were at the time,[71] but it would be inaccurate to deny the existence

[66] Smith, *op. cit. supra* note 52, at 30.

[67] Resink, "Onafhankelijke Vorsten, Rijken en Landen in Indonesië tussen 1850 en 1910" (Independent Kings, Kingdoms and Countries in Indonesia between 1850 and 1910), 9 *Indonesië* 265–296 at 290 (1956).

[68] Vlekke, *op. cit. supra* note 17 at 49, 88, 90, 101.

[69] Panikkar, *op. cit. supra* note 38, at 36.

[70] Van Leur, in bookreview, 79 *Tijdschrift Ind. T.L.V. supra* note 46, 589–595 at 591 (1939), on the Asian equality in guns and commercial policies; Panikkar, *op. cit. supra* note 38, at 36–52.

[71] Alders, *Internationale Rechtspraak tussen Indonesische Rijken en de V.O.C. tot 1700* (International Administration of Justice between Indonesian Kingdoms and the V.O.C. till 1700) 7 (1955). According to Alders at the time the modern concept of states was not known anywhere else either.

of a factual equality between European and Asian states which seemed to have been quite sufficient to serve as the basis for official intercourse.

In modern international law the typical subject of international law is the sovereign, independent state, and the chief means of acquiring such status is recognition by other members of the international society. If we adhere to the view that during the colonial expansion in Asia no states, and, therefore, no subjects of international law, were in existence there, then no international law applied in the relations with these political societies.

Lindley pointed out that the prevailing opinion was that, although these areas were not without sovereignty, they were yet not regarded as full-fledged members of the international society. As suggested above, however, one could take the opposite stand and maintain that these Asian states were in fact recognized as sovereign, independent states and indeed dealt with on a footing of equality.

It is interesting to note that those who have taken the view that backward peoples were not to be regarded as possessing any rights within international law, were mainly modern authors. The farther one goes back to earlier authors the more willingness one encounters to give due consideration to the international rights of these "backward" countries. The contemporaries of the European discoverers of the searoute were, with certain exceptions, of the opinion that the native population had equal rights of sovereignty over the territory. This, it is contended here, is another indication that, if one looks at the facts in the framework of its time, international personality cannot be denied to the native states of that period.

The question of *territorium nullius* and occupation or conquest is also related to this matter. After making a survey of the opinions of the leading authors, Lindley comes to the conclusion that there can be no question of *territorium nullius* in the area inhabited by a political society, but that a tract inhabited only by isolated individuals could be regarded as such.[72] State practice seemed to have followed this attitude and territorial claims were based on cession or conquest rather than on occupation of *territorium nullius*. One may arrive at the same conclusion, by contending, that there was indeed

[72] Lindley, *op. cit. supra* note 41, at 23.
See also: Van Kan, "De Rechtstitels der Compagnie" (The Legal Titles of the Dutch East Indies Company) in 5 *Mededelingen der Ned. Akademie van Wetenschappen* 377–441 at 386 (1942).

no place for *territorium nullius*, but not so much because native states possessing some sovereign rights actually existed but because their status as sovereign independent states was neither doubted nor contested. One logical corollary of this theory is that the Asian nations at all times possessed the right of re-conquest, something explicitly denied to the aboriginal population in the Eastern Greenland case.[73]

Summarizing the Western theories on East-West relations in this period, it should first be noted that they represented in large parts an *ex post facto* rationalization of and justification for the establishment of a colonial empire. It is particularly unfortunate that these theories often made use of non-legal terms like "civilization" which were inadequately defined. Recent ethnographic research has exposed the unscientific and haphazard character of these terms. The introduction of other theories deriving their justification from the Christian religion was not very helpful either.

The inevitable result of such theories based as they were on a combination of unjustified legal, anthropological, social and moral considerations was a lack of coherence and consistency, which immediately becomes evident whenever their practical application is tested. The inconsistency can perhaps best be clarified as follows: When the Europeans arrived in the East, they were compelled to acknowledge the fact that the Asian states were so strong that they had to be accepted as equals.[74] On the other hand, the Europeans were unwilling to accord them the treatment reserved for what they regarded as more advanced, civilized and Christions nations.[75] A compromise resulted; where the native states were not strong enough to resist the Western invasion, they were soon subjugated and lost their independent status.[76] Where the Westerners ran into strong

[73] P.C.I.J., ser. A/B no. 53, at 47 (1933).

[74] See Van Leur, *supra* note 43, at 591.

[75] Speaking about the American Indian, Justice Story remarked on the ambiguity of the Western attitudes in their contacts with each other as well as with the native peoples:

"The Eurpeans nations ... claimed an absolute dominion over the whole territories afterwards occupied by them, not in virtue of any conquest of, or cession by, the Indian Natives, but as a right acquired by discovery ... The title of the Indians was not treated as a right of propriety and dominion, but as a mere right of occupancy. As infidels, heathen, and savages, they were not allowed to possess the prerogatives belonging to absolute, sovereign and independent nations. The territory over which they wandered, and which they used for their temporary and fugitive purposes, was in respect to Christians, deemed as if it were inhabited only by brute animals ..." Lindley, *op. cit. supra* note 41, at 29.

[76] See Korn, "Oosterse Visie op Westers Bewind" (Eastern View on Western Rule) 113 *Bijdragen tot de Taal-, Land- en Volkenkunde* 18-20 (1957).

resistance, however, as they did in many places in Asia, they were forced to adopt a temporary policy of equality.

Is there then no justification for the acts of the contemporary Westerners? Reviewing these facts, it seems apparent that there was really no need for such *ex post facto* justifications as outlined above. For if the situation is viewed in the light of the standards of that period it becomes clear that aggression or territorial expansion, however condemnable morally, was not prohibited by the international law of that time. Herein lies a real justification for the Western expansion, not however in the vague, ambiguous and confusing concepts of "civilized" or "Christian" states.[77]

2. *The Growth of the Nationalist Movement*

Whilst a broad outline sufficed in the presentation of the history of the early period, recent and better recorded times are not so easily dealt with. To attempt concision is to court the dangers. But since an extensive historical account is out of the question it will be attempted to give a brief but fair review which will prepare a better understanding for the legal matters to follow. The emphasis will be on the development of nationalism as the principal cause of the great political and constitutional changes in this part of the world.[78]

The founding of Western empires in Asia by European nations

[77] Lindley, *op. cit. supra* note 41, at 47.

[78] The brief and factual nature of this historical account makes specific references to sources often desirable. For a more detailed discussion reference may be made to the following books which have been consulted throughout this chapter:

Burma:
Hall, *A History of SE Asia* (1955).
Maung Maung, *Burma in the Family of Nations* (1956).
Panikkar, *Asia and Western Dominance* (1953).
Human Relations Area Files, *Handbook on Burma* (1956).
Ceylon:
Codrington, *A Short History of Ceylon* (1947).
Perera, *Additional Chapters to H. W. Codrington's A Short History of Ceylon* (1952).
India:
Majumdar and others, *An Advanced History of India* (1950).
Griffiths, *Modern India* (1957).
Panikkar, *Asia and Western Dominance* (1953).
Moreland & Chatterjee, *A Short History of India* (1937).
Indonesia:
Yamin, *Proklamasi dan Konstitusi Republik Indonesia* (1951).
Hall, *A History of SE Asia* (1955).
Vlekke, *Nusantara, a History of the East Indian Archipelago* (1944).
Kahin, *Nationalism and Revolution in Indonesia* (1952).
Human Relations Area Files, *Handbook on Indonesia* (1952).

was not accomplished everywhere at the same rate.[79] So far it has generally been said that by the end of the 19th century, the whole of South East Asia, save Siam, had come under European control.[80] More recent research has discovered the gross errors of this assumption. Only in the 20th century were the Western colonies really subjected.

From the end of the 19th century on, the political history of these areas was dominated by the efforts of the European governments to find a fitting place for the overseas territories in the constitutional structure of their empires. This meant in some cases that the colony was brought under the direct supervision of governmental organs of the mother country,[81] while in others under the control of a colonial government set up in these overseas areas. In either system many of the former sovereign native kingdoms or princedoms were allowed to carry on, though no longer as independent states, but as a portion of the colonial territory.

The further development of these colonial territories within their respective empires has little actual relevance to international law proper. The very diminution of their status to mere extensions of the mother countries, brought them into the realm of the municipal law of their European motherlands. This realm falls outside our scope. We shall, therefore, proceed to the second part of this section which will deal with the rise and development of nationalism.

It is this nationalism which ultimately led the colonies back on the road to independence, thus completing the historical cycle which these Asian countries went through in the course of about four centuries. They each completed this cycle in their own way, depending on the internal conditions of the territory concerned. Such was the isolation in the developments that there was in general little mutual contact between the nationalist leaders of very similar movements in the various Asian nations, let alone coordination and cooperation.[82] There is little justification for sweeping generaliza-

[79] Resink describes how for Indonesia complete Dutch domination was only established in the last forty or fifty years. Resink, "Veronachtzaamde Uitspraken" (Neglected Decisions), 8 *Indonesië* 1–25 at 1 and 19 (1955).

[80] Hall, *op. cit. supra* note 78, at 615. With respect to India, Panikkar. *op. cit. supra* note 78, gives as the exact date 1848.

[81] It is realized here that such terms as mother country, motherland, parent state have a certain emotional appeal, but the use of these terms is only adopted because of their universal application. Moreover, it is difficult to find less emotionally charged terms in current speech.

[82] Hall, *op. cit. supra* note 78, at 619.

tions with regard to the methods applied and the paths followed by each of the nationalist movements. Some generalizations, however, are possible in discussing the feelings of these nationalists and their reactions to foreign events, especially those happenings which became the stimuli for their movements.

On the road back to independence at least three milestones can be noted all of which marked major events in the development of Asian nationalism.

They are:

(a) The Russo-Japanese War of 1904–1905;
(b) World War I of 1914–1918;
(c) World War II of 1939–1945.

(a) The Russo-Japanese War of 1904–1905

It is difficult to assess in retrospect the patriotic feelings of the Asian peoples at the turn of the century. Historical material of this period does not expand very much on this subject. Perhaps one can make the following generalization.

Due to natural resentment at the European conquest in Asia, which resulted in the loss of power of the princes and chiefs, patriotic feelings never died in the upper layers of Asian society. It was a somewhat different matter with the masses, who were seemingly concerned only with their daily lives, their occupations and chores. This apathy led many to believe that they were largely indifferent to politics and cared little about the origin and legitimacy of their rulers.[83] That this appearance was false has been proved by recent history. For, otherwise, it would hardly have been possible for these "mute" masses to be aroused to such a degree as to be willing to leave their homes and families to take up arms for such vague and abstract notions as "freedom" or "independence." In order to receive such a response, these nationalist feelings must have been present, though perhaps dormant, for a long time. From the first there were intermittent riots and revolts to warn the unheeding Europeans of the existence of patriotism in Asia. Certain revolts were especially effective in firing the spirit of the nationalist movement in the whole of Asia, namely the Indian Mutiny of 1857, the Atjeh War till around 1904, the Boxer uprising in 1900, and the Russo-Japanese War of 1904–1905. Of these the Russo-Japanese War appealed most to the imagination of the people of Asia.

[83] Griffiths, *op. cit. supra* note 78, at 66; Kennedy, *The Ageless Indies* IX (1942).

The actual facts of this war were irrelevant so far as Asian nationalism was concerned. It was of no real concern to Asian nationalist feelings that the Japanese were not always victorious on land and that some of their victories were indecisive. What did matter to them was that an Asian nation with a relatively small army could gain major successes against a powerful, Western nation. The decisive defeat of the huge Russian Baltic fleet by a small but better Japanese fleet was of particular importance.

In the opinion of many Asians it meant "the explosion of the myth of Western superiority"[84] and "the victory of Asia over Europe."[85] It is obviously not the truth of these statements that is significant so much as their symptomatic aspect. The following quotation may further illustrate these points. For India (and similarly for other Asian countries) the impact of the Russo-Japanese War was described as follows:

> The main features of Indian response to these stimuli... were the growth of a feeling of national self-respect, a tendency to self-assertion, a claim that India should not be regarded as inferior to any other nation....[86]

The war gave impetus to the nationalist movement; it grew stronger, more self-confident, more aggressive. In face of the challenge, colonial governments gradually evolved a new policy of cooperation. Whilst the instinct of self-preservation inevitably led to retaliation and force of arms, foresight and a new understanding brought gradual response to the demands of the people and constitutional development culminating in independence. But the process was slow. One cannot write about the growth of the nationalist movement without emphasizing the role of education often provided by the colonial governments themselves. Education, at this time and later on, produced students who were to become the leaders of a movement which led their peoples to independence. At first in small groups, but later in greater numbers, Asian students visited Western institutions of learning. They wandered to Europe and America in order to discover and learn at the very wells of Western learning what had made the West so advanced.

There they studied the ideas and teachings of the Western thinkers. They were particularly attracted by the works of the liberal writers, and their stay abroad was often a time of training

[84] Perera, *op. cit. supra* note 78, at 224.
[85] Moreland, *op. cit. supra* note 78, at 429.
[86] *Ibid.*

for political activity and organization. On their return to their native countries, they soon were able to put their experiences into practice. An increased political activity in the colonies was the result. The first political parties came into being and they acted not only as a political instrument but also as a training ground for the upcoming politicians.

India, as was so often to be the case, led the way. As early as 1885 the Indian Congress Party had been established. Although secular in set-up, it could not keep the Moslim people under its wing and another party, the Muslim League, was founded in 1906.

In the other countries the first parties also came into existence in the years following the Russo-Japanese war. They too claimed to be the spokesmen of their peoples. The practice of politics was mainly confined to the intelligentsia and the middle classes,[87] and the full implications of the political struggle had not yet become clear to the common man. The time was now ripe for those personalities among the leaders who had the ability to understand the masses and speak the language that would awaken a response in their hearts.[88] This indeed was one of the greatest achievements, whatever their failures in other respects, of such dynamic personalities as Gandhi, Nehru, Sukarno, Aung San and others. Their continued activities brought them into frequent clashes with the colonial governments. The latter reacted severely with arrests, trials, convictions, imprisonments or banishments. But the nationalist leaders became heroes and provided the masses with a new focus of loyalty.

The colonial governments were not yet able to see the handwriting on the wall. The nationalist developments caught them unprepared and the resulting policies were thus equally unprepared and confused.[89] In the opinion of one author[90] there was even a setback during this period in the growth of liberal ideas in the mother-country as a result of the atmosphere of imperial pride and competition for markets and fields of investment. Although written with regard to India, this statement held equally true for the other areas concerned.

It should be noted at this point that the political arenas in the

[87] Panikkar, *op. cit. supra* note 78, at 265; Maung Maung *op. cit. supra* note 78, at 82–88; Perera, *op. cit. supra* note 78, at 222.
[88] Griffiths, *op. cit. supra* note 78, at 66–67.
[89] Lumby, *The Transfer of Power in India* 11 (1954).
[90] *Ibid.*

mother countries were never entirely devoid of great liberal thinkers and statesmen with foresight and imagination. It is indeed a golden page in the history of European colonial government that there was at no time a total absence of such men of courage, imagination and wisdom, who criticized the prevailing colonial policies and then also suggested a better method. To illustrate this point some quotations may be given here. Lord Hastings, Governor General of India in 1818 looked forward to "a time not very remote ... when England will on sound principles of policy wish to relinquish the domination which it has gradually and unintentionally assumed over this country and from which she cannot at present recede."[91] Lumby added to this: "even while (Lord Hastings) conducted a policy designed considerably to extend British rule."

In contemporary Holland a similar thought was expressed by the liberal statesman Van Hoogendorp:

> Yes, we shall one day loose the sovereignty over our colonies, but that day is still distant and when it comes it will bring us a profit equal to that of our present ownership. Our descendents, grown wise by the experience of what is happening before our eyes will no longer make war upon those overseas territories when they are prepared for independence, but will readily grant them their liberty and so enter into new relationships of friendship and commerce with them, which will fully outweight the advantages that we now enjoy.[92]

In the course of time more and more liberal voices were heard. They all had one thing in common which made them lose some of their value. To the impatient Asian leaders the allusion to a realization in the distant future only was far from satisfactory.[93] In later years other such theories emerged which were already more pronounced in their ideas. The British "sacred trust" idea,[94] the Dutch "ethical policy" and "New Course"[95] and the French "mission civilisatrice"[96] all testify to a new spirit. But actual progress was slow. Not content with what they regarded as a slow trend, the nationalists kept pressing for more reforms. It was in the context of this charged atmosphere that World War I broke out in 1914.

[91] *Ibid.*

[92] Van Mook, *The Stakes of Democracy in Southeast Asia* 7 (1950).

[93] These ever-returning ambitions of independence-hungry peoples are today once more underlined by the claims of African peoples who, though having had fewer opportunities than Asian nations to develop themselves administratively, still demand independence "immediately."

[94] Van Asbeck, "International Law and Colonial Administration," 39 *Trans. Grot. Soc.* 6 (1953).

[95] Hall, *op. cit. supra* note 78, at 633.

[96] *Id.* at 616.

(b) *World War I (1914–1918) and the inter-war period*

This war, although mainly fought on European soil, nevertheless became another milestone of nationalism in Asia. Although it has now generally become known as "World War I", the correctness of this name has sometimes been questioned. It was only because a great part of the world outside Europe was constitutionally linked to European states that they became involved in this war. So far as many Asians were concerned it was strictly an inter-European affair.[97]

Whatever the correct nomenclature of this war may be, there is no doubting its impact on Asian nationalism. Like the Russo-Japanese war this was a milestone in Asian political consciousness. The open split in Western solidarity on Asian soil (China) and the defeat of the Germans by the Japanese on the Kiauchiow Peninsula[98] undermined Western superiority in the eyes of the Asian peoples. At the same time their self-confidence was greatly increased by participation in the Allied war effort and the feeling that they had contributed something to the victory. Moreover, the contingents of Indian, Ceylonese and Burmese soldiers, which were rushed to the European battlefields, while small in numbers, underwent experiences which had a great influence on their compatriots at home. Fighting side by side with European soldiers, going through the same experiences, and seeing European conditions with their own eyes, these Asian soldiers came back to their countries with new ideas about human and colonial relationships.

President Wilson gave a great impetus to these feelings in 1917 with the doctrine of self-government included in his Fourteen Points.[99] It found an eager acceptance and enthusiastic support in the whole of Asia. Although the realization of this doctrine was not up to expectations, the very seed of the idea had found a lasting place in Asia's fertile, political soil, and its growth, though slow and difficult, could no longer be stopped. Add to these facts the in-

[97] *E.g.* Panikkar speaks consistently about the "european civil war" of 1914–1918, a term which seems technically incorrect in this case, since the concept of civil war in international law means a war between population groups within one and the same state. 2 Oppenheim, *International Law* 209 (7th ed. 1952).

[98] Panikkar, *op. cit. supra* note 78, at 260.

[99] Point 5 of Wilson's Fourteen Points reads:

A free, open-minded and absolutely impartial adjustment of all colonial claims based upon a strict observance of the principle that in determining all such questions of sovereignty the interests of the population concerned must have equal weight with the equitable claims of the government whose title is to be determined. Seymour, *Woodrow Wilson and the World War* 234 (1921).

fluence of the Russian Revolution and the attack of Communist theorists on imperialism, and it becomes clear that the cracks inflicted during World War I on the solidarity of Western colonial rule were more serious than appeared on the surface.

In considering these events one must keep in mind that Holland, and, therefore, her colonies, such as the Netherlands Indies, remained neutral, and though they did not completely escape the impact of the war, the effects in the Netherlands Indies were less pronounced than in the other countries.

Of these countries India was in many ways the most important, bearing the main brunt of the fight for constitutional reforms. In Burma (which at the time was a province of India) and Ceylon the nationalist leaders could often point to the Indian reforms and demand similar rights.

Later on, during the inter-war period the coincidence of unrest and reform continued. Unrest indeed was frequent and widespread. In Indonesia, for example, the Communists staged a serious but abortive revolt in 1926,[100] and Burma had its student strikes in 1920 and the Saya San Rebellion of 1930–32.[101] In this respect India too had the greatest share with the Punjab rebellion (1919) and the Jalliawalah Bagh (1919).[102] It was now that Gandhi rose to eminence. He succeeded in rallying the masses to his non-cooperative movement and civil disobedience campaign which brought about an intensive mass agitation. Simultaneously with these uprisings and perhaps as a result of them, constitutional reforms were introduced.

For India World War I meant the acceleration of the constitutional progress. Even during the war the Montagu-Chelmsford Reforms – better known as the system of dyarchy – were introduced, which among other things established for the larger provinces the principle of ministerial responsibility in certain transferred matters.[103] In quick succession other developments of similar political significance followed, namely the Simon Commission, Round Table Conferences in London, the Joint Select Committee of 1933 and finally the Government of India Act of 1935[104] which was the

[100] Hall, *op. cit. supra* note 78, at 638.
[101] Maung Maung, *op. cit. supra* note 78, at 83–84.
[102] Panikkar, *op. cit. supra* note 78, at 269; Griffiths, *op. cit. supra* note 78, at 76.
[103] Moreland, *op. cit. supra* note 78, at 461–462.
[104] Hall, *op. cit. supra* note 78, at 628; Griffiths, *op. cit. supra* note 78, at 76, Panikkar, *op. cit. supra* note 78, at 272.

furthest point reached before World War II on the road to self-government. It gave the provincial governments autonomy under ministries which were now responsible to elected legislatures.[105]

Burma, being a province of India, experienced identical political developments which finally led to the Burmese counterpart of the Government of India Act, namely, the Government of Burma Act of 1935.

As a separate colony, Ceylon had its own constitutional evolution and although this was temporarily suspended during World War II, Ceylon, encouraged by the progress of India, demanded similar rights which were granted in 1948.[106]

The Netherlands Indies, though the only non-belligerent of these four countries, nevertheless felt the impact of the war on its political scene. The nationalists kept making greater demands. The Netherlands Government in 1918 established the Volksraad (People's Council) as a first experiment in self-government.[107] Yet the nationalists were not very content with the composition of this body, for the European population comprised a majority of the total membership. Half of the members were to be elected by local and city councils, whereas the other half would be appointed by the Governor General. Its powers were very limited and mainly of an advisory character. In subsequent years the number of elected members, the number of Indonesian members, as well as the powers of the Volksraad gradually increased, but it never reached the level of a fully representative body.

All these facts tend to suggest how the nationalist movement was gaining momentum. Although the European colonial governments took early notice of the nationalist activities, they were understandably not inclined to concede easily or contribute willingly to the early elimination of their own regime. They resorted, therefore, to policies which – in the opinion of the Asian nationalist leaders – were in effect "delaying actions." The Europeans endeavoured to use their superior knowledge and experience to produce solutions which would accommodate the demands of their colonies without giving them exactly what they wanted.[108] They might well have succeeded in playing this game for quite some time, had it not been that another important historical fact interrupted abruptly

[105] Lumby, *op. cit. supra* note 89, at 17–19.
[106] Perera, *op. cit. supra* note 78, at 222.
[107] Vlekke, *op. cit. supra* note 78, at 346.
[108] Panikkar, *op. cit. supra* note 78, at 273.

this manoevre. When in August 1939 World War II broke out, this third milestone in nationalistic development caused, like the two preceding milestones, a great acceleration of political development, this time of such a forceful nature that it completely overthrew the colonial rule.

We will now consider the legal aspect of the period which constituted the heyday of the colonial empires. The legal significance of this period lies obviously in the nature of its colonial relationship. As in the foregoing sections, these legal aspects will only be considered in so far as they were concerned with the status of the interacting parties. In our example, we are dealing with the European mother-country on the one side (Great Britain and the Netherlands) and the four colonies (India, including Burma, Ceylon and the Netherlands Indies) on the other. At the beginning of this period the colonies were no more than appendices of the metropolitan countries and thus included in their constitutional system.

The international law system of this inter-war period considered states as being "solely and exlusively" the subjects of international law.[109] Colonies, being just parts of a state, were not considered to be subjects of international law. In later years the concept became less rigid and more and more voices were raised favouring the recognition of other subjects of international law, like international organizations and individuals, a controversy which continues to occupy the minds of present-day writers. However, the predominant view was to make clear-cut distinctions between metropolitan countries and colonies, or in other words, between states and non-states which in turn led to the two distinct legal categories of subject of international law and non-subject of international law.

States, being subjects of international law, are bearers of rights and duties under international law. They entertain mutual relations falling within the domain of that law. Colonies, on the other hand, are not bearers of rights and duties under international law and cannot have relations governed by international law. Their legal relations are governed by the municipal law of the mother country and by a colonial constitution, the latter of which often incorporates it into the motherland.

As this viewpoint was generally accepted in the pre-World War I period no practical difficulties evolved. Nevertheless, some voices were raised quite early challenging the correctness of such a sharp

[109] 1 Oppenheim, *International Law* at 17 (3rd ed. 1920).

two-fold distinction.[110] They pointed to the fact that actual practice showed more nuances than is allowed and accounted for by the accepted dichotomy.[111]

Van Asbeck, for instance, writing in 1916 demonstrated how rough the division was by examining contemporary examples which clearly did not fit into this dichotomy. He cited as an example, the English colonies with international status (Australia and Canada), other colonies with just a beginning of international contact (Netherlands Indies), the states of the German Empire before World War I (e.g. Prussia and Bavaria) which did conclude treaties and receive envoys, the "provinces" of Canada, which like the States of the North-American Union had a full-size administration, and furthermore "native states" which had their own administration, judiciary and police.[112]

The main argument of this deviating opinion was that the creative power of international practice had given rise to the existence of autonomous entities which, however, had not yet been absorbed by contemporary theory. This is not to say that their existence was completely ignored by contemporary international law but it only gave an explanation of their position under international law which seemed far from satisfactory. Oppenheim, for instance, dealt with them and called them "not-full sovereign states which are in some way or other international persons and subjects of international law." This seems to say that colonies have sovereign powers (though not full) yet he considers them anomalies, exceptions to the main rules.[113] At first sight these entities seemed indeed to have no lasting existence and to be destined to disappear slowly but gradually. Indeed, if one considers the internal (constitutional) relations of these not-full sovereign states and their metropolitan countries, it is noticeable that there is a certain tendency to absorb them into the mother country, after which they lose their own identity and continue to exist as part of a new all-embracing unit. However, if one were to look at the international side, as opposed to the internal side, one

[110] This period should be clearly distinguished from the era of the establishment of the colonial empires (*supra* at 61). As has been pointed out there, the Asian countries, in spite of Western claims, were still independent. In the period now under discussion by "colony" is meant a completely subjected territory.

[111] Van Eysinga as quoted in Fievez de Malines Van Ginkel, *Overzicht van de Internationaal Rechtelijke Betrekkingen van Nederlandsch Indie* 1850–1922 (Review of the International Relations of the Netherlands Indies) 4 (1924).

[112] Van Asbeck, *Onderzoek naar de Juridische Wereldbouw* 3 (1916).

[113] 1 Oppenheim, *International Law* 115 (7th ed. 1952).

would see that the international relations of these not-full sovereign states were continually expanding, a fact which seems to refute the idea of anomaly. Such was the increasing degree of foreign contact by some of these units that Van Asbeck categorized them at one point as "states which more and more approach the status of ordinary international states."[114] What is more, it was the deliberate intention of the mothercountries to make their colonies more active participants in matters of government. Policy statements of that time, like the Speech from the Throne by the Dutch Queen in in 1901,[115] and the famous announcement of Mr. Montagu in 1917[116] point to a future of greater participation, certainly also in international affairs. The question whether these promises were fulfilled is irrelevant at this point.

There is a further inconsistency in the traditional distinction between only two groups, viz. subjects and non-subjects of international law. Such a view will hardly consider the existence of colonies whereas the status of colonial protectorates is regarded as having sufficient merit to be dealt with more extensively, although, as will be shown below, such protectorates are in fact identical to the colonies.[117] If, therefore, colonial protectorates are considered subjects of international law then colonies should equally fall in that category.

It seems, therefore, that the rough but sharp division between states and non-states did not give full credit to the existence of various intermediate forms. This is particularly regrettable since this matter is not only of an academic nature, as was the case with the foregoing legal sections with regard to the ancient Asian states. On the contrary, the colonies and other dependencies are not yet historical facts. They may now have disappeared by and large from the Asian scene, but, for example, in Africa colonies are still very much alive. Furthermore, the exceptional attention given by the UN Charter to non-selfgoverning territories, especially trust-territories, has given life to this matter and has even brought it on a higher international level.

After having attempted to expose the international aspects of colonies, we will now proceed with trying to determine the nature of a colony, before we establish its status under international law.

[114] Van Asbeck, *op. cit. supra* note 112, at 6, 244.
[115] *Id.* at 7.
[116] Panikkar, *op. cit. supra* note 78, at 268.
[117] *Infra* at 64–65.

Rather than giving a vague definition of a colony as such, it may be better to quote here a description of the mutual relationship between a metropolitan country and its colony. Dr. Moresco, in an article on colonial relationship, starts with saying: "Les métropoles et les colonies ... sont des collectivités de droit public qui habitent des territoires non contigus, font partie d'un seul et même État, mais se trouvent sous des régimes gouvernementaux différents et inégaux, la métropole exerçant l'autorité suprême dans l'empire entier. Leur caractère spécial tient donc à trois elements: la distance, la spécialité de régime et la subordination."[118]

For our four countries, as opposed to other types of dependencies such as the American colonies, it has the following implication, namely, that we are dealing here with peoples of different races and cultures. This is indeed the implication of the word "distance," for it comprises "distance mentale" as well as "distance physique."

The relationship of a colony to the metropolitan country can have various characteristics. It may have become an ordinary part of the metropolitan territory; Algiers, for instance, was at the time a "prolongement de la métropole."[119] It may also have become a loose appendix to that territory (e.g. Puerto Rico and the Philippines at the beginning of the 20th century). A more advanced stage has been reached by certain colonies, which together with the metropolitan territories have been coordinated into a unit of higher political status, e.g. the Netherlands Indies, along with the metropolitan territory of the Netherlands, Surinam and Curaçao, were grouped into the Kingdom of the Netherlands.[120]

Ceylon, India and Burma[121] too, could be categorized as colonies which have been brought into a greater and higher unit, namely the British Empire-Commonwealth.[122]

A fourth example of a colony, although perhaps not such an obvious one, is the colonial protectorate. The word "protectorate" does not signify a distinct concept. Van Asbeck, for instance, urged caution whenever dealing with so-called protectorates. He pointed out that at least three concepts of protectorates existed at the time, namely,

[118] Moresco, "Les Rapports de Droit Public Entre la Métropole et les Colonies, Dominions et Autres Territoires d'Outre-Mer," 55 *Hague Recueil* 511 (1936).

[119] *Id.* at 515.

[120] Van Asbeck, *op. cit. supra* note 112, at 7.

[121] Keith, *The Governments of the British Empire* 20–25 (1935).

[122] *Id.* at 19–20.

(a) the colonial protectorate, i.e. the constitutional relationship between a state and a territory not yet possessing any real state-life, e.g. the colonial protectorate of the Berlin Congo Act of 1885.

(b) a constitutional relationship between one state and another state, the latter of which has entirely lost its separate international life, as well as the authority to deal at its own discretion with its domestic affairs, e.g., the self-governing native states in the Netherlands Indies.

(c) the international protectorate, i.e. the relationship of a state which, although it has lost its international status, is still master of its own internal affairs.[123] The difference with the "colonial" protectorate is, firstly, the qualification "international," but there is, in addition, a more substantial distinction. Both kinds of protectorates are based on a treaty in which the protective relationship is laid down. In this document the conduct of foreign affairs is reserved for the protecting state, leaving to the protected party only powers with regard to internal affairs.[124] In the case of the colonial protectorate, however, the treaty was not more than a façade to cover up the intentions of the protector. There was no real intention on his part to make mutual benefit the purpose of such a merger. The intended purpose was rather annexation and complete subjection of the protectorate to the protector, a relationship which is reflected in the insignificant powers left to the colonial protectorate itself.[125] On the basis of these and other similar evidence, Van Asbeck came to the conclusion that a colonial protectorate is in effect not more than a colony, though in a disguised form.[126]

After the above review of the internal, constitutional, relationship between colonies and their metropolitan countries, we will now examine the second and external relationship, i.e. the extent to

[123] Van Asbeck, *op. cit. supra* note 112, at 4.

[124] *Id.* at 200.

[125] *Id.* at 9–12.

[126] In a more recent lecture Van Asbeck dealt with another aspect of these two kinds of protectorates. The international protectorates were established in native states with a relatively high level of state organization and cultural sophistication, whereas the colonial protectorates, especially in Africa and Oceania, were regarded as not yet having reached this level. Van Asbeck, *Samenhang van Internationaal en Koloniaal Recht* (Relationship between International and Colonial Law) (1931).

which colonies, in spite of their not-full sovereign status, participate in international affairs. For this purpose the following scheme of not-full sovereign states will be adopted with respect to their international relations:

(1) states which only maintain foreign relations with one country,[127] e.g. the international protectorates of San Marino, Andorra, Monaco.
(2) Parts of a state which maintain foreign relations,[128] e.g.
  (a) members of confederations,
  (b) members of federations and of real unions.
(3) Parts of a state which more and more approach the level of an ordinary international state[129], i.e.
  (a) seceding parts of a state, e.g. the former Turkish provinces, like Serbia and Egypt.
  (b) colonies.

Of these types it is obviously group 3b with which we are particularly concerned here. The very heading "Parts of a state which more and more approach the level of an international state" describes by itself the development of colonies. It also demonstrates that there was a more significant international aspect to these territories than would in general appear from its definition. The question is: How significant? A survey of their foreign relations, which will follow below, will show several instances of direct, as well as indirect, participation.

One of the most important and frequently quoted examples of colonial participation in foreign affairs is the membership of colonies in such administrative unions as the Universal Postal Union and the Universal Telegraph Union. In these unions the colonies-members had their independent representation and a separate vote. On the other hand, it would go too far to conclude from this membership that these colonies were regarded as sovereign states.[130]

The next important example was created when the League of Nations was established after World War I. India again demonstrated its advanced status by becoming the only one of the four colonies which became an original member. It shared this honour with another example of not-full sovereign states, namely the British

[127] Van Asbeck, *op. cit. supra* note 112, at 191.
[128] *Id.* at 216.
[129] *Id.* at 240.
[130] See Van Panhuys, "The International Aspects of the Reconstruction of the Kingdom of the Netherlands in 1954," 5 *Neth. I.L.R.* 4–5, 9 (1958).

dominions which, however, were constitutionally more advanced. Membership of a colony in the League of Nations, does not *ipso facto* give the colony a status equal to that enjoyed by full-sovereign members of that Organization.[131] Although an original member of the League of Nations, India's position was inseparably connected to that of the British Empire. Moreover, from the political point of view the Indian delegates appointed by a government which did not directly represent the Indian people, could not really be the Indian representation, and indeed complaints were heard in India about the "paper equality" which it enjoyed on the international level.[132] A more significant recognition of India's international status appeared to be its inclusion into the group of eight members of "chief industrial importance" in the Governing Body of the International Labour Organization.

Still another example of participation in such matters governed by international law is concerned with the conclusion of treaties. A colony, not being a sovereign state, cannot, in general, be an independent party to a treaty. However, some of the few exceptional cases have already been mentioned above, namely the participation of colonies and protectorates in administrative unions. In other cases colonies did become parties to a treaty, but were represented by their respective mothercountries.[133]

Another example in the case of India as well as the Netherlands Indies refers to the beginning of this century. The Governor General of India was then given the power to maintain political relations with "second-rate" neighbouring states like Afghanistan, Tibet, Siam, Persia, Bhutan and Nepal. He could conclude treaties with them, and, under certain conditions, he was even entitled to declare war or conclude peace.[134] Similarly, the Governor General of the Netherlands Indies could under the 1836 constitution conclude provisional treaties in case of urgency, which treaties had to be communicated as soon as possible to the Government of the Netherlands which had to ratify them.[135] These examples, however, do not strengthen the views of those who attach more significance to the

[131] See for the distinction between sovereign state, full membership of non-sovereign states to international organizations, and party to a convention, Van Panhuys *id.* at 4–5.

[132] Lanka Sundaram, *India and the ILO* in Zimmern, 1 *India analysed*, 68 (1933); Van Panhuys, *supra* note 130, at 4.

[133] Fievez, *op. cit. supra* note 111, at xi.

[134] Van Asbeck, *op. cit. supra* note 112, at 256.

[135] *Id.* at 295.

international status of a colony. This is because the underlying reason for this particular treaty power was not the recognition of the international nature of a colony, but rather the fact that the means of communication at the time were so poor, that some treaty power had to be left to the overseas territory. With the introduction of modern means of communication such emergency treaty powers became superfluous and were consequently withdrawn.

The Netherlands Indies Government had some other special powers. For instance, the Governor General could conclude provisional agreements with governments of other European powers in the East with respect to matters of legal aid.[136] He also had some powers with respect to foreign consuls, and in some matters of extradition as well. In the latter case it is worth noting that his powers were in fact not always based on a constitutional provision, but rather on an established practice.[137] Several instances are reported of such extradition-without-treaty cases.[138] In general, extraditions had to be carried out on the basis of treaties concluded by the metropolitan country on behalf of its colony. The colonial officials were in such cases directed by organs in the motherland.[139]

These examples of participation in foreign matters which belong essentially to the foreign affairs of a sovereign state prove that a colony although not having a fully independent status, is not entirely excluded from foreign relations. Actually, this is seldom contested, but it is often tried to fit the different foreign relations of dependent, semi-dependent and independent states forcefully into the rigid, traditional dichotomy of "state" and "non-state" and thus of "international law" and "municipal law." In so doing, one has overlooked the fact that states as well as non-states (such as colonies, protectorates and dominions) have arrived at their present status only after a slow and gradual process which had to pass through various stages of political maturity. By having regard only for the opposing ends of this development (i.e. states and non-states), one overlooked the many existing intermediate stages in the development of political entities from one end to the other.[140] It is evident that of the many intermediate stages the dominions were closest to the status of full sovereign state. The colonies on the other hand,

[136] Fievez, *op. cit. supra* note 111 at xi.
[137] *Ibid.*
[138] Fievez, *op. cit. supra* note 111, case 282, 283.
[139] Van Asbeck, *op. cit. supra* note 112, at 267.
[140] See *id.* at 307.

in spite of their participation in certain parts of international affairs, were not so advanced.

The position of the British colonies and dominions at that time has been reviewed by Keith who expressed the contemporary views (1935) by accepting the well-known dichotomy when he stated that

> whatever the autonomy of the dominions in international affairs, for international purposes the Imperial Government was solely responsible.

Though we are not dealing here with dominions, but with colonies, this statement is worth quoting, because of India's special status which lay between a colony and a dominion, so that a denial of the status of subject of international law to a dominion would automatically exclude India. Even the fact of the membership of the League of Nations enjoyed by the dominions and India did not make any difference in Keith's opinion, although he had to admit that it made the maintenance of a dichotomy very difficult.

> The Covenant, however, makes no definite attempt to give its members fully self-governing status of units of international law; it contemplates the admission of any fully self-governing colony which can give effective guarantees of its sincere intention to observe its international obligations; it assumes thus that a territory can be a colony, therefore not an independent state, be fully self-governing, and possess international obligations which prima facie cannot attach at all to a colony as such, seeing that an international obligation normally and properly must be incumbent on an international person and not on a dependency. No light is thus thrown on the real position of the dominions and India in international law beyond the sphere covered by the Covenant of the League of Nations.[141]

The above lines apply to the dominions and India in the 1930's. As far as the ordinary colonies were concerned, Keith was unhesitating in stating that "the conduct of all relations with foreign states, which are intended to be capable of recognition under, and enforcement by the sanctions of international law, rests entirely with the Crown..." and many relations of a "business character" entered into by the governments of dominions and colonies are not regarded as treaty relations.[142]

To summarize: it seems that Keith's ideas with respect to the international status of colonies reflect the prevalent attitude of the period here discussed, whereas Van Asbeck, though not claiming the status of full subject of international law for less advanced political entities, was expounding a doctrine which emphasized the more complex reality.

[141] Keith, *op. cit. supra* note 121, at 87.
[142] *Id.* at 107.

The factual existence of some intermediate position between the two extremes of "state" and "non-state," of "subject" and of "object" of international law, is undeniable, and often conceded. Yet, when it comes to drawing the consequences from this fact, traditional international law hesitates and rather retreats into its accustomed dichotomy of sovereign and non-sovereign state. If we now once more return to the earlier quoted opinion of Oppenheim that colonies should be regarded as "not full-sovereign states which are in some way or other international persons and subjects of international law,"[143] the emphasis should now more and more be laid on the last part of his statement.

The increasing contact of these entities would in the long run have demanded a fairer appreciation of their status, either as a subject or perhaps as a more distinct intermediate status between subject and object of international law. For if it is true what was said of the status of individuals, namely that "if the present subjects of international law (i.e. states) choose to transform the status of the individual from that of an object to that of a subject of international law, they are free to do so,"[144] then these states are equally capable of bestowing the status of subject of international law on colonies which had come even closer to that level than individuals.

The evolution of these political entities was disrupted, however, by the outbreak of World War II. This will be dealt with in the following section.[145]

WORLD WAR II AND THE END OF THE COLONIAL ERA

Asia did not get seriously involved in World War II until the surprise attack on Pearl Harbor by the Japanese forces on December 7, 1941. This aggressive act did not leave much choice to the U.S., Great Britain and the Netherlands but to declare war on Japan. The overseas territories of Britain and the Netherlands in Asia had no say in this matter and thus became automatically involved. Yet they were neither militarily, nor mentally, prepared for such an undertaking.

[143] *Supra* at 62 where it was also contended that Oppenheim's view on the anomalous position of a colony was incorrect.

[144] Schwarzenberger, "The Protection of Human Rights in British State Practice," 1 *Current Legal Problems* 153 (1948).

[145] *Cf.* for a new and unique development in the relationship between the Netherlands and her former colonies of Surinam and the Antilles, Van Panhuys, *supra* note 130, at 20–31.

Militarily, the defence of the colonies had never been entrusted to the inhabitants themselves. The training and recruiting of native forces had never been introduced on a nation-wide scale. Such a policy did not agree with the attitude of the colonial government of the time. The territorial armies consisted mainly of selected native troops under the command of European officers, although in more recent times many natives were admitted to the officers corps, especially in the Indian Army.

The mental unpreparedness of the peoples, as demonstrated during the war, did not result so much from a lack of "hardness," or from inexperience with modern warfare, as from a lack of awareness of what was at stake in this world conflict. To them slogans like "the defence of democracy" or "the struggle against totalitarianism" were empty words and could not arouse any genuine enthusiasm. The European governments could hardly expect their colonial subjects to rally to the defence of democracy, if that meant, in effect, the continuation of the *status quo*, which was not particularly popular among the colonial peoples. It is therefore, in retrospect, hard to believe that the colonial governments did, after all, expect the support of their colonial subjects in the fight against the Japanese. They again overlooked the fact, which should have been clear to them after the Russo-Japanese and the First World War, that the challenge of European superiority by an Asian power generally receives the moral, if not actual, support of the other Asian peoples.

Furthermore, whereas the Japanese victories during the Russo-Japanese War were known to the peoples only from hearsay, during World War II they could see with their own eyes the sweeping Japanese victories at the beginning of the war, and what is more, also the demoralization of the Western forces. It did irreparable harm to Western prestige.[146]

The apathetic attitude of the people towards the defence of their homelands thwarted the task of the colonial armed forces as much as it facilitated the Japanese military operations. Thanks also to their preponderance in materiel as well as personnel, the Japanese were assured of great successes. Immediately after the Pearl Harbor attack, they embarked on military operations from their home and mainland bases. Even before this date Thailand and (Vichy) French Indo China had already been forced to conclude treaties of

[146] Hall, *A History of SE Asia* 683 (1955).

"friendship" and in the latter country the Japanese were given several concessions which paved the way for the stationing of military forces in these areas. After such a privilege a military occupation seemed to be the next logical step. It indeed happened without meeting much actual resistance.

At the same time the Japanese Army and Navy invaded the Philippines, Malaya and Burma. Their superior forces struck with great force and speed, and the Allied defences, in spite of sometimes heroic resistance, crumbled faster than was thought possible. The occupation of these territories was soon a fact. Singapore, said to be an invincible bastion, fell too. Before this happened, landings were already made in the Netherlands Indies Archipelago. One island after the other fell into the hands of the invader without much resistance and, after the surrender of Java on March 9, 1942, organized resistance ceased in the whole of the Dutch colony. After only five months of war Japan had already gone a long way towards the realization of its military plans. Yet it did not get much further. Apparently the extensiveness of the territory to be occupied and controlled, coupled with the amazingly quick recovery of the U.S. forces, prevented Japan from making further advances. Thus the following years saw the Japanese contained in the areas they had already occupied.

At this point we have to separate the joint account of the events in the four colonies. For, whereas Burma and Indonesia, with the exception of some frontier areas, were occupied, Ceylon and India were spared such an experience. Consequently, the latter countries were able to continue their constitutional progress during war time. This was speeded up after the war under the pressure of nationalistic activities. In India the political situation seemed to lead to a quick solution, but it was aggravated when the Moslem population pressed for the creation of a separate Moslem state. The final solution came on August 15, 1947, when the British Government transferred power to two separate, independent states: India and Pakistan.

Ceylon, again following in the wake of India, made similar claims proving the impact and significance of political precedence in colonial history.[147] Ceylon did not have to wait very long. On February 4, 1948, it became an independent state.

As far as the occupied territories (Burma and Indonesia) were concerned, it became necessary for their inhabitants to decide upon

[147] Perera, *Additional Chapters to H. W. Codrington's a Short History of Ceylon* 242 (1952).

their future attitude towards the Japanese occupant. As was stated before, the Japanese invaders were, in general, not officially supported by the nationalist movements. Yet they could count in the beginning on the sympathy of the peoples, and in certain cases they were actually aided by some rebellious groups, like the student nationalists in Burma. The reason behind this attitude is rather obvious. Japan was an Asian nation which had defeated the Western forces and might thus also liberate them from European domination. This was exactly what the Japanese propaganda promised. However, the peoples soon began to realize the emptiness of Japanese slogans like "Asia for the Asians" and "Greater Asian Co-Prosperity Sphere." Besides, the Japanese occupation forces, particularly the feared Kempeitai (Military Police), did not always behave like friendly liberators. Their cruelties and terrorism caused, at first, the loss of popular sympathy and, later on, even armed resistance.

For the sake of their countries some nationalist leaders decided to collaborate with the new masters. In so doing they hoped to be able to keep an eye on their country. Another section of the nationalists, however, decided to carry out an underground resistance. In the case of Indonesia the decision to split up into these two factions was even made by mutual agreement among the nationalist leaders. It is further worth mentioning that in most cases the underground resistance was carried out or led by Communists, who in later days claimed for themselves the honour – and not entirely without justification – of having constituted the main forces which resisted the Japanese invaders.[148]

Both nationalist groups, whether above or underground, had one common experience. They were more actively involved in matters of government than ever before. Because of the absence or internment of European officials, native officials had to take over all branches of the administration. The underground movement, on the other hand, created an opportunity for military training which – as the leaders foresaw – could become of major importance for the years to come. These facts not only gave rise to greater political experience, but they also created more self-confidence as well as nationalist fervour,[149] especially when it became clear that Japan was going to lose the war.

[148] Hall, *op. cit. supra* note 146, at 687–690; Maung Maung, *Burma in the Family of Nations* 91 (1956).

[149] Maung Maung, *op. cit. supra* note 148, at 97.

The turn of the tide became apparent for the first time by the middle of 1942. The Allied forces had gained considerably in strength and Japan became more and more aware of their formidable striking power. Worried by these trends, the Japanese decided to make an all-out effort to ensure themselves of the support of the peoples of the occupied areas in case of Allied invasions. To this end they were even prepared to fulfill the most important wishes of these peoples which were obviously concerned with independence. Burma was the first to become an independent state on August 1, 1943. The Philippines followed on October 15, 1943. It needs no further explanation that the independence conferred upon these states was of a rather nominal character. Actual control and ultimate decision remained in the hands of the Japanese, especially in military and foreign affairs.[150]

In Indonesia the military situation seemed at first less critical for the Japanese and therefore no such far-reaching changes were contemplated in the beginning; instead, promises were made for independence at some date in the near future. In spite of all these efforts Japan remained on the losing side and the outcome of the war became more and more a matter of time only. The details of the military developments are well-known and it is unnecessary to dwell upon them any longer. Suffice it only to conclude by saying that Japan surrendered on August 10, 1945, after the droppings of the atom bombs on Hiroshima and Nagasaki made it clear that further fighting would be senseless.

The political evolution in the occupied territories had strengthened the nationalistic aspirations of the peoples and, although the independence which they enjoyed under the Japanese was not very great, the very toying with this concept greatly stirred their minds and emotions. As one Asian author put it: "Independence was empty, (the people) knew, but it gave them more selfrespect."[151]

There were other factors which added to the growth of nationalism. The Atlantic Charter, for instance, proclaimed in 1941 by the U.S. and the U.K. met with a great response in Asia. The idea, that one should "respect the right of all peoples to choose the form of government under which they will live" had the same effect of raising hopes as that other document of the same nature, namely, President Wilson's Fourteen Points after World War I.[152]

[150] *Id.* at 96.
[151] *Id.* at 97.
[152] *Supra* note 99.

Thus, the end of World War II saw political conditions in Asia which demonstrate the repetition of historical events. The similarity with the period after the Russo-Japanese war and World War I was striking. The above-mentioned developments after the second World War again accelerated the nationalist movement, this time to such a degree that it could no longer be suppressed. The goal and demand of the Asian peoples became "independence and freedom immediately."

It is characteristic of British statesmanship in recent times that it was able to make a correct appraisal of the depth of nationalist feelings, before deciding on a future policy. The British were able to sense how desperate the Asian peoples were to achieve independence, and that they were willing to achieve this goal at all cost, regardless of the fact whether they understood the real implications of such independence or not. Few countries have been, and are, willing to part with their colonies. Fewer still know to part at the right time. Britain was able to make that difficult but great gesture. As it stands today, it seems that Britain is going to reap the fruits of its sensible policy of that period.

India and Pakistan were the first to become sovereign, independent states after World War II. Ceylon and Burma followed soon after them. Unfortunately, the Dutch-Indonesian relations failed to follow the example set in India. The demands and claims made by one party were unacceptable to the other. Four years of intermittent bloody fighting and tiring negotiations passed before finally a solution was reached. On December 27, 1949, Indonesia also reached the stage of independent state.[153] The colonial period in Asia had virtually come to an end. With this fact all four former colonies had passed into a new era of their history. They were now to continue their existence as sovereign, independent states in the Family of Nations.

1. *The Status of Burma during and after the Japanese Occupation*

We shall now turn to the question of Burma's legal status during this period.

The regular achievement of independence by India and Ceylon

[153] Since the legal aspects of the Dutch-Indonesian conflict, which will be dealt with later on, are closely related to the historical facts of that period, a more extensive historical account of that time will be postponed till we are treating the legal part of this question (see *infra* at 93).

presented no legal difficulties. It is the cases of Burma and Indonesia which gave rise to a number of problems. These were inseparably linked to the time of military occupation which both countries went through, and which will, therefore, be reviewed first.

Military occupation, and more specifically belligerent occupation, is generally defined as the occupation of part or all of the territory of a country which continues to wage war against the occupying power.[154] What stands out in this definition is the emphasis on the factual situation, for indeed the whole concept of belligerent occupation starts from the presumption that the enemy power has succeeded to gain actual control of the occupied territory. The Hague Regulations on the Laws and Customs of War on Land of 1907 clearly stressed in art. 42 that factual nature by stating that "territory is considered occupied when it is actually placed under the authority of the hostile army." Having achieved the essential condition of actual control, occupant states tend to neglect or ignore other conditions which are attached to the status of occupying power. It will be attempted now to look into the behaviour of Japan in occupied Burma. Due consideration will be given to the legal construction as well as to the underlying principles of belligerent occupation because they have both been made the bases of the claims by the returning colonial government at the end of World War II.

Seen in their historical context the rules of international law with regard to military occupation grew out of a mainly European war experience and, consequently, bear the marks of their European origin. They were not made to include a situation such as that which arose in the Asian colonies during World War II. The possibility that a colonial territory outside Europe would become occupied by an enemy power whereas the motherland remained free (like respectively Burma and the U.K.), or of the colony being occupied by a different power than the motherland (for example, Indonesia and the Netherlands) were never conceived of by contemporary doctrine, perhaps chiefly because such an event seemed to be highly improbable at the time.[155] One could of course

[154] Von Glahn, *The Occupation of Enemy Territory* 27 (1958); Briggs, *The Law of Nations* 1024 (1952).

[155] There is another significant facet to the colonial relationship which, however, is only partly relevant to the present discussion. After the occupation of West-Europe, countries like Holland and Belgium were said to remain as international entities since the legitimate government still administered vast colonial territories. Ph. M. Brown, "Sovereignty in exile," 35 *A.J.I.L.* 666–668 at 667 (1941). Such an opinion implies,

try to find the solution of such an unforseseen event by deducing it from the existing rules of military occupation by way of well-known methods of legal interpretation.

One such interpretation would in the case of Burma probably rationalize in the following manner:[156] "Burma, which was a British colony during World War II, came under Japanese occupation. The British government of Burma was temporarily driven out, but the war was carried on from outside the actual territory. The Japanese did not become the sovereign authority as a result of their military success. They only became the occupant which gave them no more power than that of a military authority under the laws of war.[157] In this capacity they were not allowed under international law to make thorough constitutional changes, especially not those which were intended to be permanent, such as the creation of an independent state in territory held under occupation. Therefore the granting of independence to Burma was an illegal act and thus void."

The merits of this theory, at least with regard to Burma, have not received much discussion, mainly because the Japanese-sponsored Burmese state did not survive the defeat of its protector. Hence, when afterwards Great Britain appeared to be willing to grant Burma independence along more traditional lines, a further discussion of the above-mentioned issue (i.e. whether an occupying power was allowed to grant independence) was side-tracked. Yet it may be worthwhile to consider this topic for a moment, since, in the first place, it still has some significance for existing dependent territories. But, more importantly, it may expose some contrasting attitudes of the colonial governments and the nationalist movements.

Contemporary international law is said to contain some clear-cut rules on military occupation and it may perhaps be best to make them the starting point of this discussion in order to decide afterwards whether they are applicable in the case of Burma or not.

however, that if the colonies are also occupied (as in the case of Indonesia, with the exception of a very small part) they cease to exist as an international entity.

156 These are the arguments expressed explicitly or implicitly by the returning government. Therefore, they are also the arguments with which the Asian nations are acquainted. It is for this reason that these arguments, though often facticious, are made the starting point of this discussion.

157 According to McNair: "The most important principle of law incident to belligerent occupation... is that occupation does not displace or transform sovereignty. The occupant is entitled to exercise military authority over the territory occupied, but he does not acquire sovereignty unless and until it is ceded to him by treaty of peace." McNair, "Municipal Effects of Belligerent Occupation," 56 *L.Q.R.* 34 (1941).

In former times occupation by itself was said to be sufficient to establish the sovereignty of the occupant over the territory. In effect occupation was then equal to conquest or annexation and the occupant derived all sovereign power from his military achievement.[158] This theory is now generally regarded as being no longer valid.[159] Today customary as well as convential international law makes a distinction between occupation and conquest. In the case of occupation no sovereignty is transferred to the occuping power, whereas conquest does signify such a transfer of sovereignty including, of course, the power to grant independence. This technical point must be qualified, however, as a result of recent war experiences. Feilchenfeld writes:

> Ever since 1914 it has been definitely held that a phase of mere occupation persists as long as the allies of the conquered state continue to fight, particularly where the conflict is still supported by a government in exile and at least some troops of the conquered state.[160]

This was indeed the case with Burma, the northern part of which was never really occupied, and from here as well as from beyond the Indian frontier Allied forces kept harrassing the Japanese till they were finally able to reconquer the whole country.[161]

The reasoning against the validity of the Japanese act of creating an independent state in such occupied territory[162] rested on the following points:

(a) Burma, even during occupation, was a British colony and therefore part of the mothercountry.
(b) Sovereignty rested with the mothercountry and not with the occupant who had only a military authority.
(c) No permanent change of administration or laws, no grant of independence was therefore allowed.

[158] De Louter stated that, as late as the 19th century, occupied territory was considered as a conquest, 2 De Louter, *Het Stellig Volkenrecht* (Positive International Law) 261 (1910); 2 Oppenheim, *International Law* 435 (7th ed. 1952).

[159] The Japanese often, though not always, behaved as if they had conquered and annexed the Asian territories e.g. one of their first objectives was mostly the japanisation of the legal system. See Lyons,"The Courts of Singapore under the Japanese Occupation," 30 *B.Y.I.L.* 507–512 (1953); Zorab, *De Japanse Bezetting van Indonesië* (The Japanese Occupation of Indonesia) 143–149 (1954).

[160] Feilchenfeld, *The International Economic Law of Belligerent Occupation* 7–8 (1942).

[161] The fact that not the entire territory of Burma was under Japanese control and the continuation of the war from India also exclude the question of *debellatio*, or subjugation. Since there can, therefore, be no question of *debellatio* the authority of the Japanese can only be based on the laws of belligerent occupation (Van Essen, "Het Recht van de Bezetter in Duitsland" (The Law of the Occupant in Germany), 23 *Nederlands Juristenblad* 741–751 at 744 (1948); Oppenheim, *op. cit. supra* note 158, at 600.

[162] *Supra* at 77.

(d) Customary as well as conventional international law supported this thesis.

It will now be attempted to show that, regardless of their real merits, these contentions cannot be held fully applicable to colonial territories and other dependencies. To start with, one has to look for the basis of military occupation in international law.

The laws of war, of which the rules of military occupation are a part, are the outcome of a long and gradual development which took place mainly in the European society of nations.[163] This development gave rise to many usages which, through custom and treaty, were accepted as binding.[164] In our days an attempt has been made to codify these rules and lay them down in conventions, and military manuals, e.g. the Hague Conventions, the Geneva Conventions of 1949, the new U.S. Rules of Land Warfare, and the British Manual of Military Law.

The relevant rules for the present discussion on military occupation are mainly to be found in the fourth Hague Convention of 1907[165] on the Regulations respecting the Laws and Customs of War on Land, and more particularly Section III entitled "Military authority over the territory of the hostile state."[166]

They do not create new rules. On the contrary, they purport to be declaratory of existing international law; they do not claim to cover all possible claims.[167] There are a couple of factors, however, which

[163] There are few written documents on rules of warfare before the 19th century, but there always were customary rules. Only in the 19th and 20th century did such written documents come into being starting with the Declaration of Paris of 1856 on maritime laws in time of war. Lachs, *War Crimes – An Attempt to Define the Issues* 5 (1945).

[164] Oppenheim, *op. cit. supra* note 158, at 226, Von Glahn *op. cit. supra* note 154, at 3. Writers like Graber, *The Development of the Law of Belligerent Occupation* 1863–1914 (1949), and Mouton, *Oorlogsmisdrijven in het Internationale Recht* (War Crimes in International Law) (1947) trace back the present codified rules to the preceding documents on the laws of war. One thing which such studies expose is the different laws which prevailed not so long ago on certain points, e.g. arts. 26, 33, 59 and 60 of the Lieber Code (Lieber, *Instructions for the Government of Armies of the U.S. in the Field* (1898) appear to be contrary to respectively, arts. 45, 43 (as well as 45 and 52) of the Hague Regulations, art. 2 of the Convention of Geneve of 1929, and art. 23d of the Hague Regulations. Mouton, *op. cit. supra* note 164 at 67–69.

[165] Graber, in her treatise on belligerent occupation, mentioned other landmarks in the development of international law preceding the creation of the Hague Regulations, e.g. the Lieber Code, The Brussels Code of 1874, and the code of the Institute of International Law of 1880 (Oxford). This thesis limits itself to the Hague Regulations which, since they have not been formally revised, are still "the basic code to which international lawyers turn to determine what occupation law is..." Graber, *The Development of the Law of Belligerent Occupation* 1863–1914, 5–6 (1949).

The 4th Geneva Convention of 1949 relative to the Protection of Civilian Persons in Time of War, is excluded here because of its creation only after the Burmese occupation.

[166] Scott, *The Hague Conventions and Declarations of 1899 and 1907*, 122 (1918).

[167] "Until a more complete code of the laws of war is issued the High Contracting

should be taken into account. Firstly, the two World Wars have shown the inadequacy of the rules in modern warfare.[168] Professor Kunz, for instance, is of the opinion that an enormous task is awaiting the laws of war.[169] He comes to the conclusion that the laws of war, including the rules on *occupatio bellica*, are in a state of chaos and completely inadequate to face their task.[170] This is partly the result of its failure to deal with the changed conditions in the world in general, and in warfare in particular.[171]

Professor Kunz stated:

> This inadequacy of the laws of war in the great wars was further a consequence of the radical change of general conditions as compared with those prevailing in 1899 and 1907. These codifications presupposed the doctrines of democracy, capitalism, economic liberalism, the principle of the sanctity of private enterprise and economic activities by the strict distinction between armed forces and civilian population. The appearance of state socialism, even in democracies, and of totalitarian regimes, has changed those conditions basically.[172]

Parties think it right to declare that in cases not included in the Regulations adopted by them, populations and belligerents *remain* (italics added) under the protection and empire of the principles of international law, as they result from the usages established between civilized nations, from the laws of humanity, and the requirements of the public conscience..." (from the Preamble of the Hague Convention, Scott, *op. cit. supra* note 166, at 101). See also Lord Cave, "War Crimes and their Punishment," 8 *Trans. Grot. Soc.* XXI (1922).

[168] The inadequacy of the laws of war is, of course, not a new discovery. The development of the world community has at various times exposed such gaps. World War I proved that the problem of air warfare had not yet been fully understood. Lachs, *op. cit. supra* note 163, at 7. The totality of the modern wars affected the applicability of the traditional rules of war, e.g. in the matter of reprisals, indiscriminate mine-laying, general devastation. Lauterpacht, "The law of Nations and the Punishment of War Crimes, *21 B.Y.I.L.* 74–75 (1944). For problems raised by the dropping of the atom-bombs, see Stowell, "The Laws of War and the Atom Bomb," 39 *A.J.I.L.* 784–788 (1945).

Another fact which caused uncertainty with respect to the application of the traditional laws of war is the modern concept of international action for the collective enforcement of peace undertaken against an aggressor state. Opinions are divided whether the aggressor state should have the benefits of the laws of war (Lauterpacht, "The Limits of the Operation of the Law of War," *30 B.Y.I.L.* 206 (1953).

[169] Kunz, "The Chaotic Status of the Laws of War and the Urgent Necessity for Their Revision," 45 *A.J.I.L.* 38, 40, 52 (1951).

[170] To keep a sense of proportion it should be noted, however, that in spite of this chaotic status, the rules of occupation have still made the greatest progress of all rules of warfare. Oppenheim, *op. cit. supra* at 432. Mouton also points out that the Hague Regulations represent in general the existing laws of war. He admits their obsolescence, however, and stresses also the different attitudes of the big and small powers towards the obligation of the occupant, as a result of their contrasting vulnerability in time of war. Mouton, *op. cit. supra* note 164, at 139–140).

[171] Holland suggested as another reason that the drafters of the Hague Conventions refrained from being too specific in order not to add to the authority of the repulsive claims. Holland, *The Laws of War on Land*, 61 (1908).

Feilchenfeld stated that the drafters mistakenly expected that these rules would undergo a permanent progressive development and therefore failed to anticipate a deterioration of war practices. Feilchenfeld, *The International Economic Law of Belligerent Occupation* 14 (1942).

[172] Kunz, *supra* note 169, at 40.

It is suggested here that to these changing conditions may be added another characteristic of our time, namely, the release from colonial domination, and to the statement that

> ... the Hague Convention could, of course, not regulate methods of warfare unknown at this time...[173]

we may add the observation that it could not, and did not, intend to regulate situations unknown and inconceivable at the time. Therefore, it seems to be erroneous to apply automatically the somewhat obsolescent Hague Convention rules to our situation and say that the creation by Japan of an independent state in occupied territory was contrary to international law.[174] We must rather keep in mind the underlying reasons for these laws of war, and especially for the laws of belligerent occupation.[175]

As is very common in the present international society, rules of international law seem to be in conflict with each other. The origin of the problem lies, among other things, in the conflicting interests of the parties concerned which in turn give rise to equally conflicting theories on rules of international law. Actually these rules should be seen as the outcome of complementary theories. In the case of the laws of war the complementarity is illustrated by such competing concepts as military necessity against humanitarianism, and military interest against civilian interest.[176] With special reference to the question of military authority in occupied territory, one will find, for instance, on the one hand, the right of the occupant to demand obedience from the inhabitants,[177] and, on the other, hand the cor-

[173] *Id.* at 38.

[174] On the other hand, this gap does not imply a criticism of the Hague Convention itself. On the contrary; the Preamble of this document states that" ... the high contracting Parties clearly do not intend that unforeseen cases should, in the absence of a written undertaking, be left to the arbitrary judgment of military commanders." Scott, *supra* note 166, at 101. What is, therefore, objected to here, is only the too mechanical application of the given laws of war.

[175] See for an application of such a method of interpretation: McDougal & Schlei, "Hydrogen Bomb Tests in Perspective – Lawful Measures for Security," 64 *Yale L.J.* 658 (1951) and McDougal and Burke, "Crisis in the Law of the Sea – Community Perspectives versus National Egoism," 67 *Yale L.J.* 539–544 (1958).

[176] At present, war more and more becomes a total war with all its regrettable consequences, not the least the doing away with the distinction between military and civilian interests. In Asia the concern for the civilian population has been greatly aroused by the dropping of the atomic bomb on Japan in 1945 (Stowell, *supra* note 168, at 784–788) and the subsequent nuclear tests.

[177] The controversy about the validity of the traditional laws of war is clearly exposed with respect to this particular rule which has been generally accepted for a long time. As a result of experiences in World War II, however, opinions were expressed that a state is entitled to command its citizens to disobey orders which the occupant was

responding right of the population to be exempted from taking part in military actions against their own legitimate government. These rights of the occupant *vis-à-vis* the population are further elaborated by writers on international law, e.g. with respect to the taking of an oath, the rendering of services to the occupation army, the collection of taxes.[178] These rights and obligations spring from two main underlying principles of a competing and complementary nature, namely,

(1) The occupant is *entitled* on the basis of his successful military occupation to administer the territory in his military and other interests in order to pursue the purpose of war, i.e. the total defeat of his opponent.

(2) In doing so, however, he is *obliged* to give all possible consideration to the interests and the good of the population in the occupied territory.[179]

The division between these rights and obligations is generally explained in terms of sovereignty, that is, the sovereignty of the legitimate, ousted government, *vis-a-vis* the *de facto* authority of the occupying power. Neither the conventional, nor the customary laws of war give a conclusive answer to this problem. If we would consult a subsidiary source of international law, the writings of qualified publicists, we would find it generally stated that the occupant does not acquire the amount of sovereignty which the legitimate government possesses, but that it only exercises some of these sovereign powers by virtue of its military administration.[180]

entitled to give under international law. 2 François, *Handboek van het Volkenrecht* (Manual of International Law) 329–330 (1950).

[178] 2 Oppenheim, *op. cit. supra* note 158, at 438–456.

[179] Von Glahn, *op. cit. supra* note 154, at 34; Spaight, *War Rights on Land* 322 (1916). Such a process of balancing interests in terms of rights and obligations is obviously often coloured by national preferences. Germany has in the past often defended the position of the occupant, whereas Belgium and France tend to limit the powers of the occupant. Countries like Britain and the United States were inclined to take a middle position. Feilchenfeld, *supra* note 171, at 15. It is very obvious that in our time of bipolar struggle in which any aggressor is faced with a deadly counter attack and all states without exception are in danger of occupation, there is a great need of a fair balance of interests.

[180] Ph. M. Brown (*supra* note 155 at 667), discussing the problems of sovereignty, stated that "so long as people do not accept military conquest, as long as they can manifest in one way or another their inalterable will to regain their freedom, their sovereignty... still persists." This statement holds true for the British as the adversary of the Japanese in Burma. There is a significant corollary to an acceptance of Brown's theory, however, for it might well be used as a basis for Asian claims that their countries had only been occupied by the Western powers and never conquered or annexed since the Asian people never abandoned completely the idea of their own sovereignty, an idea which periodically came to the surface in the form of rebellions. Even the lapse of a few centuries did not affect the Asian views decisively. See also Von Glahn, *op. cit. supra* note 154, at 31.

In dealing with the laws of war one has, of course, to be aware of the continuous presence of the concept of "military necessity" which always upsets an attempted two-fold division of rights and duties. It seems, however, that in our case we are dealing with a subject where, for once, military necessity can be disregarded, for

> ... few, if any, of the measures likely to be undertaken by occupation authorities in enemy territory will reasonably contribute decisively to the end of the conflict, to the surrender of the enemy, or will be invested with supremely vital character... It must be remembered that practically all measures of importance undertaken by an occupant in hostile territory fall in a period of time when the military phase of active hostilities has passed from the occupied territory and when the occupant attempts to establish an orderly administration. Hence, there is an absence of nationally vital necessity and a lack of real necessity which enable a successful employment of the defense in question.[181]

Thus it becomes clear that the restrictions imposed by international law on the occupant are the result of a compromise between the competing interests of the inhabitants of the territory and of the occupant. Nothing suggests that this policy is imposed by any obligations of the occupant towards the legitimate, ousted government.

Nor does this doctrine mention anything which alludes to any duty to refrain from acts which may have a slackening influence on the allegiance of the people towards their legitimate government. For instance, it is generally contended that in carrying out its military administration

> the occupant is totally independent of the constitution and the laws of the territory, since occupation is an aim of warfare and the maintenance and safety of his forces and the purpose of war stand in the foreground of his interest and must be promoted under all circumstances and conditions ... But, ... as he is not the sovereign of the territory, he has no right to make changes in the laws, or in the administration, other than those which are temporarily necessitated by his interest in the maintenance and safety of his army and the realization of the purpose of war.[182]

If the occupant is therefore restrained from acting at will, it is clearly not because of his obligations towards the enemy, but because of the limitations imposed by international law for the

[181] Von Glahn, *op. cit. supra* note 154, at 226–227; see also Lauterpacht, "The Law of Nations and the Punishment of War Crimes" 21 *B.Y.I.L.* 75 (1944).

[182] 2 Oppenheim, *op. cit. supra* note 158, at 437. See also Van der Hoeven who discusses whether art. 43 of the 4th Hague Convention gives the occupant the power to give regulations other than those to ensure public order and safety. Van der Hoeven, "De Wetgevende Bevoegdheden van de Bezetter (The Legislative Powers of the Occupant), 16 *Nederlands Juristenblad* 233–235 (1941).

benefit of the *people* now coming under his military administration.[183] In other words, there is no obligation on the part of the occupant to perpetuate the authority of the exiled government. On the contrary, it could even be maintained that such a perpetuation conflicts with the very purpose of the war which it started, namely, the total submission of the legitimate government.

These conditions have not been treated very fully by contemporary writers. Part of the reason may have been that in the case of colonies traditional international law often made the mistake of applying automatically the European laws of war which equated the interests of the people with those of their government, in this case of their colonial government.

What then has caused the confusion, or more correctly, the equation of these two different interests, and why in fact are they different? In modern times an independent country possesses a legitimate government which is regarded as the guardian of the interests of the people. Established as a result of general elections, it not only guards but also expresses and formulates the wishes and interests of the people. Here then lies the apparent reason for the equation: Whether a government is firmly settled or ousted by the occupant, its legal and political status as the guardian and spokesman of its subjects remains unaffected. Like any other legitimate government, it is still entitled to claim allegiance and obedience from its subjects whom it had to leave behind in occupied territory.

It is precisely in this identification by the people of their interests with that of their government that the colonial example deviates from that of the independent country. It is also precisely here that we find a deviating opinion caused by the specific interests of the colonial people as opposed to the independent nations, a phenomenon to which e.g. Brierly has drawn our attention.[184] The population in these colonies differs in race, religion and other cultural features from that of the motherland. Their different interests have at one time been subordinated to those of the motherland. The government in the colony was as a rule not a government formed after general elections. If they were, as in Burma, then their repre-

[183] The relations during World War II between the German occupation forces and the population of the island of Guernsey in the Channel represent a good example of the actual interplay and balancing of their respective interests. See for a description of that situation Quincy Wright, "The Value of International Law in Occupied Territory," 51 *A.J.I.L.* 775–783 (1945).

[184] Brierly, *The Law of Nations* 44 (1949).

sentative character was still dubious, since a colonial administration always represents some sort of a drag on the formation of political parties and – more importantly – the final decision in important matters of government always lies with the mothercountry or its representative in the colony. In its top functions the colonial administration was not composed of mainly native officials. It did not represent the people as such. In spite of the fact that only a minor part of the population in the colonies was European, the overwhelmingly native majority had no direct say in the government of its country. Consequently, the people did not regard their colonial government as their spokesman or the guardian of their interests. What is more, there seems to have been a general feeling that, after all, this foreign government was not the legitimate government, although it had succeeded in usurping power for a couple of centuries. The very lapse of some centuries did not, in the eyes of the peoples, legalize the European conquest. Time seemed to play a different role in Asian thinking from that which it played in the Western world.[185]

Thus, when the Japanese forces started to roll southward, the native population showed little resistance since they did not feel a moral obligation to support the European ruler of their territory against his enemies. This is a point of some importance. For, if the Asian people had of their own will supported the colonial government, the above-mentioned considerations regarding non-allegiance to a non-representative foreign government might have been eliminated. In case of such a voluntary support the foreign colonial government would have proved that in spite of all the differences the people were willing to recognize it as its legitimate government and to uphold it in the face of a threat by another foreign power.[186] Indeed, some of the Asian peoples offered to support the motherland in return for a promise of independence.[187] This offer, however, was not accepted by any of the motherlands, and therefore they continued to be, at least in the eyes of many Asians, the illegitimate government of the territories concerned.

Nationalism gave new life to these feelings. War conditions in Asia were favourable for the further rise of nationalism and indeed we have seen the eruption of nation-wide responses to the appeal of

[185] See Chapter I *supra* at 18.
[186] *Cf.* the case of the Philippines and her support to the U.S.
[187] See Thakin Nu, *Burma under the Japanese* 7 (1957).

nationalist leaders. To hold that such a mass support was merely the result of negative anti-Western or anti-colonial sentiment is to minimize unduly the positive convictions of the people, however unformulated, that these nationalist leaders were in fact their legitimate spokesmen. That such a "political" consideration does enter into a legal debate in some way or other is demonstrated by professor Hyde who, in a discussion of the Indonesian revolt after World War II, makes the following statement:

> In a technical sense it is unimportant to stress a sinister historical background that differentiates the lofty aspirations of a downtrodden and tormented people from the ambitions of a few who get in the saddle and who foment a political situation that proves ultimately to be productive of revolution and perhaps even statehood.[188]

It seems that Professor Hyde, for once, has been guilty of a wrong appraisal of a situation which is perhaps more a political than a legal question. Once again: the nationalist leaders would never have been given the popular response if they did not stand for something that lived, however undefined, in the hearts of the people.[189]

The significance of this period lies in the fact that, for the first time after the European invasion into Asia in the 16th century, the legitimacy and domination of colonial government were seriously challenged. Before this time the power of Asian nations was so small that they could not make any effort to challenge the contemporary doctrines on the legitimacy of European rule. Consequently, the rules set by the European family of nations were accepted in most of the Western countries without the audible objection from the Asian peoples themselves.

With the outbreak of World War II and its subsequent developments finally came the opportunity for these colonies to express their different opinions. Because of the novelty and uniqueness of the situation, neither customary nor conventional international law had as yet a ready answer to the emerging problems. Even the writers did not seem to foresee the possibility of such a situation. Some of them had given some thoughts to the possibility of a native uprising, but they were mostly of a totally different nature.

Von Glahn, for instance, anticipated "native uprisings"[190] but he

[188] Hyde, "The Status of the Republic of Indonesia in International Law," 49 *Col. L.R.* 957 (1949).

[189] See also *supra* at 56.

[190] Von Glahn *op. cit. supra* note 154, at 50.

dealt mainly with occupation as practised in Europe. He did not, therefore, consider a native uprising in a colony. One could, of course, try to draw an anology from the European example with the occupation of a colony. Such an anology may show many identical features but in reality there is a world of difference between the two. Writing about the European resistance movements, Von Glahn mentions that these resistance forces have often succeeded in liberating considerable parts of their country "on behalf of the absent sovereign."[191] This statement perhaps holds to a certain extent even for some colonies. In Burma, for instance, some of the border tribes have been armed and trained by the British to harass the Japanese in guerilla warfare. It is conceivable that these tribes, who are now part of the population of Burma, did at that time fight for the return of the absent British Government. But the majority of the Burmese never did organize a resistance in order to promote the return of the British Government in exile. In fact, the characteristic element of an uprising such as that of the Burmese is that it was directed towards both occupying power as well as legitimate government and designed solely for the achievement of a national state.

Oppenheim came close to the core of the problem where, when dealing with the rights and duties of the occupant, he put in a footnote, which unfortunately he does not develop, that

> although the Hague Regulations cannot literally be applied in occupied enemy colonies populated by natives and having only a few white settlers – the latter must not be deported unless it is a military necessity to do so.[192]

All this goes to prove that the colonial revolt in time of military occupation has not yet been given serious consideration by the writers.[193] Probably because so far the traditional views on a colony as a mere appendix of the metropolitan country made a separate treatment of the colony, as such, unnecessary.

Meanwhile, however, the success of the popular uprisings under nationalist leadership during World War II gave rise to the emer-

[191] *Ibid.*

[192] 2 Oppenheim, *op. cit. supra* note 158, at 439, footnote 1.

[193] In a footnote Feilchenfeld gives an example which has much similarity with the Burmese case, i.e. "The following situation may also arise: A non-contiguous region, such as a colony, may be evacuated by a belligerent occupant and may then not be reoccupied by the old sovereign, his allies or third states. Unless the liberated colony engages in recognized secession, it would seem to return to the old sovereign." Feilchenfeld, *op. cit. supra* note 160 at 7, n. 4. The difference between the two examples was that the Japanese occupant did not (or did not intend to) evacuate the country, and the old sovereign did return. Moreover the Burmese act of secession found little recognition.

gence of a new element in the question of sovereign authority. In the ordinary European example of occupation, the sovereign powers were divided between the occupant by virtue of his military administration and the ousted government as the legitimate government. As is stated above, the tacit understanding is here that the government is indeed considered by its own subjects as the legitimate government, elected and obeyed by the people. This not being the case in the colonies, at least not in Burma, the nationalist leaders emerged as the *third factor* to be reckoned with, making it now a relationship between three parties: the occupant, the legitimate government, and the people represented by their leaders. This triangular relationship is admittedly not based on traditional rules of international law. It could not possibly be. Not, however, because it was in fact against the traditional rules of international law, but because there were no such rules relevant to this particular situation.

The new triangular relationship of authority was a factual one. Traditional international law still holds that the Japanese had no authority to create an independent state in occupied territory. This might have been true in occupied China, but to hold such an opinion in the colonial case is to close one's eyes deliberately to the hard facts. If international law is to be applied regardless of such factual realities, it may be claiming more authority than it deserves. In this case at least, it is hard to see what other alternative the Japanese had. As stated above, only gross ignorance of the movements present among the Asian peoples will lead a person to believe that the burning desire for independence was mainly caused and sponsored by the Japanese in order to injure the interests of the colonial governments. It has been one of the main purposes of the preceding brief historical review to prove that this desire existed long before the Japanese invasion.[194]

In the already mentioned duty of the occupant to refrain from creating an independent state is apparently also included the obligation to prevent the emergence of an independent state by popular uprising. The term "emergence" refers to a subtle distinc-

[194] This, of course, does not imply a denial of one of Japan's main war objectives, namely, the elimination of all Western influence in the occupied areas of Asia. See Jansma, *Het Bezettingsrecht in de Practijk van de Tweede Wereldoorlog* (The Laws of Occupation in the Practice of the Second World War) 19 (1953). But this objective was only true in its generality. In the realization of this objective, Japan was obliged to make several concessions one of which was the granting of independence to certain nations whose support she desperately needed in the struggle against the Western powers.

tion. Whether such an independence movement is instigated by the occupant as a means to injure the legitimate government, or whether it emerged spontaneously, is often difficult to establish without knowledge of the real facts. It is the contention here that the movement, though certainly aided and used by the Japanese, was nevertheless a spontaneous and popular one directed against the occupant as well as the colonial government. Its aim was exclusively the creation of a national state. Such an act of self-determination amounts in fact to a revolt against the legitimate government. However, once such a revolt is successful and the territory secedes from the mothercountry and establishes itself under an organized government, it can under certain conditions be considered to have a *de facto* government and the relevant rules of international law become applicable. Moreover, a subsequent number of recognitions raises the status of the new state.

Burma represented indeed an example of such a revolt, with the important difference that it took place indirectly and during the time that the mothercountry was engaged in a war and the colonial government temporarily ousted from the colony and thus unable to assert itself. Burma's status was indeed raised by the recognition of a fair number of states, although most of them belonged to the Axis powers. They were Japan, Germany, Italy, Thailand, Nanking-China, Manchukwo, Croatia, Slovakia, Bulgaria and the Vatican.[195]

Coming now to our final analysis we will restate and summarize the relevant facts in the form of two basic questions, namely:

(1) Does the inability of the legitimate government to assert itself during the occupation of its colony have any legal significance with respect to the creation of a new state in that colony?
(2) Was it one of the obligations under international law of the Japanese occupant to prevent such a popular uprising and the subsequent formation or proclamation of a new state?

With respect to the first point the legitimate government will obviously contend that it is the only authority for the introduction of changes in the constitutional system. No consideration will be given to any revolt. The very thought of it would appear to be a derogation from its sovereignty. Consequently, the colonial govern-

[195] Maung Maung, *op. cit. supra* note 148, at 97.

ments expected to return to a position of sole sovereign in their colonies at the end of the war.[196]

The opposing view, as already expounded above, is that a revolution, once it is successfully carried out and recognized, attains a measure of legality which gives it a certain status under international law. The temporary inability of the legitimate government to perform its sovereign task does not detract from the legal status achieved by the new state. To hold that a revolt during the incapacity of the legitimate government cannot achieve such a status does does not make much sense. For it belongs to the inherent characteristics of a revolt that it takes advantage of the weakest moments of its opponent to strike and gain effective control of the area. This is the essence of revolution and the objection to the use of an inopportune moment for the colonial government is identical to an attempt to lay down a legal rule banning all future revolts.

As far as the second question is concerned, it is generally held that the rights and obligations of the occupant consist of a compromise resulting from the purpose of war, on the one hand, and the interests of the population in occupied territory, on the other hand. It is further held that the creation of an independent state belongs to the series of actions from which the occupant has to refrain himself.[197]

Some remarks are perhaps appropriate before continuing along these lines. First of all, it is not correct to say or imply that it was the general Japanese policy to create independent states in Asian territories in order to injure the Western colonial powers. These policies are to be seen as part of the whole military strategy.[198] Only

[196] The position taken by the colonial governments is similar to the Roman principle of *jus postliminii* which restored ex-Roman persons or property to their original status as soon as they came again under the control of the Roman empire. See 2 François, *op. cit. supra* note 177, at 339; 2 Oppenheim, *op. cit. supra* note 158, 616–620; Feilchenfeld, *op. cit. supra* note 160, at 144.

[197] *Supra* at 77.

[198] This is not the place to dwell extensively upon the merits of the political and humanitarian ideals of the Japanese in "liberating" the indigenous people. The concept and application of the idea of a "Greater East Asian Co-prosperity Sphere" is well known. As so many other slogans, it contained a mixture of truly idealistic intentions and pure self-interest. This is not a new way of reasoning with regard to colonial dependencies, however. After World War I there was a similar case of the Cameroons. Marabail compared the merits of the French and the preceding German administrations of this territory and came to the conclusion that the French idea of a "mission sacrée" towards the native population of the Cameroons would make France a better administrator than the cruel and egotistic Germans. This is in his opinion the justification of France's role as the executioner of the "tâche civilisatrice," Marabail, *Étude sur les territoires du Cameroun occupés par les troupes françaises* 165–173 (1919). But *cf.* the German protest against the "Kolonialschuldlüge" (i.e. that German colonial administration before 1914 had

Burma and the Philippines were from the very beginning destined by the Japanese to become independent as soon as possible, in order to induce other Asian peoples to a better relationship with Japan, and not in the first place – as is so often thought – to injure the Western powers. Moreover, where military and strategic considerations did not make it directly advantageous to grant independence (e.g. in Indonesia) the Japanese were only too anxious to hold back such a grant of independence and keep the peoples under direct control. Sometimes even stern orders were given to prevent any independence movement. Again, these are facts proving a Japanese policy to grant independence in the first place for its own direct benefit.[199]

Secondly, even though an occupant may be willing to conform with the suggested rule of refraining from granting independence or making other constitutional changes, it is conceivable, particularly in such occupied colonial territories, that the nationalist demands for independence would become so strong, that the occupant would be faced with the alternative of either granting these wishes or else being forced to engage himself in another struggle, this time with an internal enemy, perhaps in a gruelling guerilla warfare which would certainly not be advantageous to his over-all military prospects. Such a situation seemed indeed to have existed in Burma soon after the invasion.[200]

Another consideration in support of the validity of independence achieved in time of occupation, lies in the time factor, in other words: How long should the occupant resist the popular pressure for an independent state? If the occupation were to last, for instance, ten years, is the occupant nevertheless obliged to uphold the constitutional *status quo* as he found it when he entered the colony?[201] Such a refusal to take notice of popular political claims would in effect amount to a static situation which is actually a step back if compared with the pre-war time when the population had at least

been far below standard) Von Freytagh-Loringhoven, *Das Mandatsrecht in den deutschen Kolonien*, i (1938).

[199] At one of the liaison conferences between the Japanese Cabinet and the General Staffs of Army and Navy, the future policies for occupied territories were considered. One of the decisions arrived at was that a pre-mature development of independence movements in the occupied areas had to be prevented. The autochthonous population had to be made fully aware of its dependency on the Imperial Japanese forces.

[200] Maung Maung, *op. cit. supra* note 148, at 95.

[201] François stated that the Hague rules started from the presumption that the occupation would be brief and that the military authority would always have complete control. François, *op. cit. supra* note 177, at 320.

the possibility of making some, though slow, constitutional progress. It can be neither the intention nor purpose of international law to set up rules which, while regulating the relations between sovereign states in time of war, at the same time fail to protect the interests of a people which is allegedly one of the major underlying policies of the laws of war.

In view of such considerations, particularly the popular pressure with the accompanying threat of a guerilla war, it does not seem unreasonable to say that the purposes of war, as well as the interests of the people would make the yielding by the Japanese to nationalist demands for independence, under certain conditions, a reasonable action. To hold in spite of all these considerations that it was a violation of international law is rather legalistic as well as unrealistic.[202]

Is this opinion compatible with present-day legal doctrine? For the subject of constitutional changes in military occupied territory we are again dependent on the writers of international law, but, unfortunately, they have not been able themselves to arrive at a fairly unanimous opinion, not even with regard to strictly European territories,[203] let alone colonies.

Without going so far as the German school, e.g. Heyland, who suggests that "the occupant has an original right of his own, granted to him in some manner by international law,"[204] it is again suggested here, that the so-called rule of international law demanding the occupant not to make constitutional changes is one of a broad nature and deserves to be scrutinized in the light of the facts of each particular case. This means that, although it might be valid for some European area which actually is a part of the mothercountry, geographically, ethnically and politically, it cannot possibly be fully applicable to a territory which was not only geographically and culturally different, but which in addition did not have the privilege of being a real part of the mothercountry in the sense that it could participate in the shaping and sharing of its policies. It is therefore reasonable to contend that the creation of the Burmese state by Japan was not contrary to international law and that it resulted in the creation of a legitimate state.

[202] This is not to say that Japan's attitude towards her other obligations as an occupant did not fall far short of a reasonable minimum. Japan was particularly guilty of violating arts. 46 and 50 of the Hague Regulations. Jansma, *supra* note 194 at 19, 122–125.

[203] Von Glahn, *op. cit. supra* note 154, at 36.

[204] Heyland, *Die Rechtsstellung der besetzten Rheinlande nach dem Versailler Friedensvertrag und dem Rheinlandabkommen* 8 (1923).

The happenings at the end of World War II obscured the legal status of this Burmese state. For, the defeat of the Japanese resulted in the simultaneous collapse of the Burmese state. The returning British government did not regard it as an actual independent state and thus restored the colonial status, but, after two full years of negotiations with the nationalist leaders, the British themselves agreed to grant Burma independence, this time along more traditional lines.

Thus Burma became again an independent state on January 4, 1948. As usual the U.K. cordially invited it to join the British Commonwealth of Nations. There were strong feelings in favour of such an association with the U.K., but the influence of some leaders and the impact of certain events caused a different result.[205] Burma finally chose not to become a member of the British Commonwealth of Nations, thus following a different course from that of its former sister-colonies India and Ceylon.

2. *Indonesia during and after the Japanese Occupation*

The developments in Indonesia[206] during this period were decisive for its future status. Though, in certain respects, these events were quite similar to those taking place in the other countries, there were also significant differences. In contradistinction to India and Ceylon, which remained free throughout the war, Indonesia shared Burma's fate of being occupied by the Japanese. Its further experiences, however, were quite unlike those of Burma, for it was never granted independence by Japan, although it came very close to that point. Furthermore, the former colonial government did not return immediately. As a result Indonesia experienced a second military occupation, this time by the British troops which liberated the country. Finally, independence was only achieved after a long and bitter struggle with the Dutch. In fact, Indonesia was the only colony of the group of four which fought against the returning government, a fact which gave rise to a number of questions on its legal status.

[205] Maung Maung, *op. cit. supra* note 148, at 112.

[206] For an account of the Indonesian question written in the English language, by American authors: Kahin, *Nationalism and Revolution in Indonesia* (1952); Wolf, *The Indonesian Story*; by an English author: Wehl, *The Birth of Indonesia* (1948); by Dutch authors: Vlekke, *Nusantara, A History of the East Indian Archipelago* (1945); Van Mook, *The Stakes of Democracy in Southeast Asia* (Book Two and Three) (1950); Gerbrandy, *Indonesia* (1950).

With respect to the policies for Asia the Japanese pre-war plans[207] made for Burma and the Philippines were unanimously accepted by her Foreign Office as well as by the members of the Imperial General Headquarters, the actual policy-making organ of Japan[208] composed of the General Staffs of Army and Navy. Both countries were to be granted independence as soon as possible in order to encourage other South East Asian peoples to cooperate with the Japanese. There was no complete agreement, however, on a policy for the Netherlands Indies.[209] The viewpoint of the Foreign Office in the latter case was to create there an independent federal state with the possible exclusion of some underdeveloped areas which would remain under direct Japanese supervision. Treaties with the new state would make sure that Japan would retain a strong diplomatic, military and economic position.[210] The General Staffs, however, opposed this plan. In their opinion, the best way to maintain control of the vital raw materials in the Netherlands Indies was to keep this area under direct supervision.[211] The war time strategy with respect to the Netherlands Indies indeed bore every mark of this controversy between the Japanese policy makers. Consequently, no very concrete plans were carried out in Indonesia during the occupation. However, when the luck of the Japanese was running out midway through the war, it became essential for them to be assured of Indonesian moral and material support. Consequently, the Indonesian demands for independence had to be considered more seriously and more concrete steps had to be taken in that direction.

In 1943 the Japanese Government and the General Staffs reviewed the general situation again.[212] They also discussed the problem of sovereignty in the occupied areas. It was decided to grant speedy independence to Burma and the Philippines which was realized respectively on August 1, 1943, and October 14, 1943.

[207] International Military Tribunal for the Far East (hereinafter cited as IMTFE), Exhibit Doc. No. 1335, *Establishment of East Asia. Maneuvers for the First Period of Total War*, 10–11, (1946–48).

[208] De Weerd, *The Japanese Occupation of the Netherlands Indies*, IMTFE, Pros. Doc. 2750. For a short description of the composition of the Japanese military and civilian High Command, see Zorab, *De Japanse Bezetting van Indonesie* (The Japanese Occupation of Indonesia) 3–10 (1954).

[209] Elsbree, *Japan's Role in Southeast Asian Nationalist Movements 1940–45*, 15–42 (1953).

[210] IMTFE, Exhibit Doc. No. 1333A, *Policy toward Neutral Powers and other Problems*, 1–2 (1946–48).

[211] IMTFE, Exhibit Doc. No. 1344, *Course of Events Leading up to Decisions on Political Control and Reversion of the East Indies in the Second World War*, 2–3 (1946–48).

[212] *Id.* at 1.

With respect to Indonesia no final agreement could yet be found. Finally, it was decided to annex this area to the territory of Japan, but to give the people at the same time more autonomy.[213] The decision to annex was not published at the time, nor was it ever carried out.

In 1944 the Japanese strategic position became very precarious and the new Cabinet of Prime Minister Koiso was, therefore, more inclined to introduce new policies in order to achieve an improvement of the over-all situation. It then showed a willingsness to consider a grant of independence to Indonesia[214] and on September 7, 1944, the Japanese Government made the first declaration which alluded to an independent Indonesian state "in the very near future."[215]

The end of 1944 and the beginning of 1945 saw the further retreat of the Japanese forces to their homeland bases. The defeats they suffered in the Philippines, Okinawa and other small islands in the neighbourhood cut off the Japanese forces in the more remote territories, like the Indonesian Archipelago, from the motherland. The forces left behind there, became even more dependent on the population and resources of these areas. Their precarious position did not remain unnoticed by the Indonesians who promptly demanded more political advancement. Under such pressure the Japanese had to yield. The authorities on Java then established an Investigating Committee for the Preparation of Independence in March 1945.[216]

In Japan a new Cabinet under Prime Minister Suzuki adopted a resolution on July 17, 1945, at the initiative of the Foreign Minister Togo. It stated that independence would be granted to the whole of Indonesia. It would be proclaimed by an Indonesian Independence Preparatory Committee consisting of delegates from all parts of the country. Because of the difficult communications with Japan it was later planned to send instead an Indonesian delegation to Field-marshall Terauti at Saigon, the highest regional representative of the Imperial Government. On August 11, 1945, Terauti received the delegation and assured them that the Japanese Government would

[213] *Ibid.*
[214] *Id.* at 2–3.
[215] Overdijkink, *Het Indonesische Probleem, De Feiten* (The Indonesian Problem, The Facts) 32 (1946); Kahin, *op. cit. supra* note 206, at 115.
[216] Aziz, *Japan's Colonialism and Indonesia*, 236–237 (1955); Overdijkink, *op. cit. supra* note 215, at 32–33.

transfer sovereignty to Indonesia on August 24, 1945.[217] However, on August 14, the Japanese Government decided to surrender unconditionally. This news was not published till a few days later, but on Java some members of the Indonesian Independence Committee, which was to meet for the first time on August 18, had become acquainted with the news. Fearing that the turn of events would endanger the grant of independence, they decided to act, and an independent Indonesian state was proclaimed by the Heads of the Committee (Sukarno and Hatta) on August 17, 1945.

Meanwhile the Allies had made preparations to take over the area. The liberation of the Indonesian Archipelago from the Japanese was assigned to the Allied forces of the South East Asia Command under Lord Louis Mountbatten.[218] One of the implied consequences was the return to power of the Netherlands Indies Government. But the Japanese themselves were either unable or unwilling – perhaps both – to go all out for the suppression of the newly proclaimed Indonesian state. Moreover, the Indonesians had taken their future in their own hands by organizing themselves politically as well as militarily. The fact that the first Allied (British) troops did not arrive till September 29, that is about six weeks after the Japanese surrender, gave the Indonesians enough time to go ahead with their plans. The British troops, which finally landed on Java, had set themselves a task of limited scope, namely firstly, accepting the surrender of the Japanese, disarming and putting them into internment camps and preparing them for repatriation; secondly, releasing Allied prisoners of war and internees; and finally, maintaining law and order until the Netherlands Indies administration was able to take over.[219]

In the performance of their task, the British ran into great difficulties in trying not to get involved in the political and military

[217] It is quite clear here that the intention to grant independence has little to do with the often repeated argument that the Japanese conferred independence only to injure the Western colonial powers (see *supra* at 91). Being on the losing side at this moment, the Japanese made an all-out effort to win the support of the colonial peoples and, according to one Indonesian opinion, no promise was too big for the Japanese to achieve this goal. Adam Malik, *Riwajat dan Perdjuangan sekitar Proklamasi Kemerdekaan Indonesia* (The Story and Struggle around the Indonesian Proclamation of Independence) 12 (1948). See also Aziz, *op. cit supra* note 216, at 250–252.

[218] For a more detailed account, *infra* at 100 and note 237.

[219] *Enquête Commissie Regeringsbeleid 1940–45*, (Report of the Investigation Committee into the (Netherlands) Government Administration during 1940–45) vol 8, 654–655 (1956). See also the views of the Dutch Parliamentary commission (Van Poll Commission) which investigated the factual situation in Indonesia in 1946. Van Poll, *Indonesië in het Parlement* at 23–24 (1946); Kahin, *op. cit. supra* note 206, at 141–142.

conflict which started between the Indonesians and the returning Netherlands Indies administration.[220] Gradually, more Dutch troops arrived on Java, the centre of revolution. They took over the areas occupied by their British predecessors. These areas were confined largely to the bigger cities and their surroundings. The greater parts of the islands of Java, Madura and Sumatra were under the factual control of the Republic of Indonesia, whereas in the other islands the Dutch troops and administration had not too much trouble in reestablishing the Netherlands Indies Administration.[221] After the British troops had completely withdrawn from Indonesian soil by the end of November 1946, fighting was carried on between the Indonesians and the Dutch, with intermittent periods of negotiations and cease-fire, until the final solution was reached in the transfer of sovereignty to the independent Republic of the United States of Indonesia on December 27, 1949.

This is not the place to examine the military and political achievements during this struggle for independence. Just a few major events should be mentioned which are necessary for a better understanding of the legal positions of the parties to the dispute, namely two agreements which have dominated the legal issue of the Indonesian case. They are the Linggadjati Agreement and the Renville Agreement, which were arrived at in the following sequence of events.

The first important results of the negotiations between the Dutch and Indonesians were achieved in November 1946 when both parties initialed the Linggadjati Agreement[222] which contained the Dutch recognition that the Government of the Republic of Indonesia was exercising *de facto* authority in the islands of Java, Madura and Sumatra. It further provided for the establishment by January 1, 1949, of a sovereign, democratic, federal United States of Indonesia (U.S.I.), composed of the Republic of Indonesia (that is the Republic controlling Java, Madura and Sumatra) and at least two other component states to be formed in Borneo and in the eastern islands. Finally the U.S.I. would be linked to the Netherlands in a Netherlands-Indonesian Union. The agreement was signed on March 25, 1947[223] but at that time relations had again deteriorated and on

[220] For the legal aspects of the second (= British) military occupation of the Netherlands Indies see *infra* at 100.

[221] Kahin, *op. cit. supra* note 206, at 145.

[222] For the English text of the Linggadjati Agreement, see Wolf, *op. cit. supra* note 206, at 175–178; *Dep. of State Bull.* XVIII, no. 454, 325–327 (1948).

[223] Foster Collins, "The United Nations and Indonesia," *Int. Conciliation*, March 1950, no. 459, 119–126; Kahin, *op. cit. supra* note 206, at 196–199; Wolf, *op. cit. supra*

July 21, 1947, the Dutch staged a "police-action" (or "military aggression" according to the Indonesians). The Security Council then entered upon the scene on the request of India and Australia.[224] The actions of the Security Council led, among other things, to a U.N. Good Offices Committee whose task it was to assist the parties in their search for a solution.[225] Indeed it succeeded in getting the parties to conclude the Renville Agreement on board the U.S.S. "Renville" on January 17, 1948, a document containing a truce agreement,[226] 12 principles[227] and eight additional principles.[228] The principles provided for the establishment of a sovereign, democratic, federal U.S.I. of which the Republic was to be a component state, and further for the transfer of Netherlands sovereignty to the U.S.I. at the end of a "stated interval." During the interim, Netherlands sovereignty was to be recognized and all states were to be granted fair representation in a central interim government. Plebiscites were to be held in various areas of Java, Madura and Sumatra to determine whether these areas desired to become a part of the Republic or of another state within the U.S.I. Following the delineation of states a constitutional convention based on proportional representation was to be held to frame the constitution of the U.S.I. Upon formation the U.S.I. was to be linked in equal partnership with the Kingdom of the Netherlands.[229] However, again difficulties arose in the implementation of this agreement and once again the Dutch felt that they were forced to launch a police-action (December 19, 1948). The Security Council once more intervened overrruling strong protests of the Dutch Government which contended, among other things, that the Charter of the U.N. dealt only with relations between sovereign states and that this conflict was a matter which fell essentially within the domestic jurisdiction of the Netherlands.[230] This then brings us di-

note 206, at 29–46; Smit, *Het Akkoord van Linggadjati* (The Linggadjati Agreement) (1959); Smit, *De Indonesische Questie* (The Indonesian Question) 90–135 (1952); Overdijkink, *Het Indonesische Probleem, De nieuwe Feiten* (The Indonesian Problem, The New Facts) 113–123 (1948).

[224] *U.N. Security Council,* Off. Rec. 2nd year, no. 67, 171st meeting, 31 July 1947, at 1615–1617 (1947).

[225] *U.N. Security Council,* (S/525) 26 August 1947, point II.

[226] *U.N. Security Council* (S/649) 10 February 1948 at 105–107.

[227] *Id.* at 111–112.

[228] *Id.* at 97.

[229] *Id.* at 20–25; Foster Collins, *supra* note 223, at 143–151; Kahin, *op. cit. supra* note 206, 224–229; Smit, *De Indonesische Questie* 150–160 (1952).

[230] Dr. Van Royen in a statement in the Security Council on 22 December 1948, Off. Rec., 3rd year, no. 132 at 4 (1948); Foster Collins, *op. cit. supra* note 223, at 118.

rectly to the question of the legal status of the Republic of Indonesia under international law. For this it is necessary to start at the Dutch capitulation to Japan in March 1942.

At the moment that the Dutch Government in Indonesia capitulated to the Japanese, the Netherlands Indies became Japanese occupied territory and thus shared the same experience as Burma. As was stated before,[231] Japan did not at first intend to transform Indonesia into an independent state. The farthest it went was to promise independence and allow the Indonesians to set up an Independence Preparatory Committee. Only at the very end of the war did Japan try to rush the creation of an independent state, but these efforts were overtaken by other events. This, of course, brings up the question whether such actions were valid under international law. In the preceding example of Burma such changes in the constitutional system have been discussed at length. We may, therefore, refer to that discussion in which it was attempted to prove that such an occupation policy in a colony is not necessarily always contrary to international law.[232]

Quite a different matter, however, was the intended annexation of Indonesia to the Japanese homeland.[233] In general, annexation of occupied territory is not allowed under international law.[234] Although the Japanese did not carry out their intention, it may be worthwhile to devote a few lines to the Indonesian case. Whether under the laws of belligerent occupation the Japanese had a right to annex occupied territories would have to be seen in the light of the underlying policies which – as was contended – struck a balance between the interest of the occupant and that of the inhabitants. In the case of Indonesia it seems to be a difficult task to

[231] *Supra* at 94.
[232] *Supra* at 92.
[233] *Supra* at 95.
[234] Annexation, like belligerent occupation and conquest, is another factual situation resulting from a war. In order to discourage wars traditional international law has been very hesitant to legalize the benefits which have been the outcome of war efforts. It has deliberately ignored the factual situation and has therefore become rather hypocritical at times. See Schwarzenberger, *Manual of International Law* 50 (1947); Fischer Williams, "Sovereignty, Seisin and the League," 7 *B.Y.I.L.* 41 (1926). In practice, annexations were carried out regardless of the apparent violation of international law. Though "premature" they were in time accepted as a valid title. See for examples, 1 Oppenheim, *International Law* § 239 (1955). For opponents of the above traditional theory, see the the German writers Von Liszt, *Das Völkerrecht* 150 (1925), Von Freytagh Loringhoven, *Völkerrechtliche Neubildungen im Kriege* 23 (1941). For the influence of the Covenant of the League of Nations, Hyde, "Conquest Today," 30 *A.J.I.L.* 472 (1936). For the influence of the U.N. Charter, see e.g. 1 Oppenheim, *International Law* § 241a. See also the case of Burma and the question of conquest, *supra* at 78.

prove either that such an annexation would in any way have been for the benefit of the people, or that military necessity forced the Japanese to such an act. There still remains one reason which could perhaps permit such an act, namely, that the peoples themselves requested an annexation with Japan. There is no evidence, however, that such a move was ever contemplated by the Indonesians. Therefore, since no valid justification can be found, an annexation must still be considered to be contrary to international law.

The proclamation of the Republic by the Indonesian leaders at the end of World War II gave rise to a new political entity, which claimed to be an independent state. It created a triangular relationship between the legitimate Dutch Government, the British occupying forces and the newly created Indonesian state which was similar to that described above in the Burmese situation[235] though with significant nuances. First of all, the Republic of Indonesia was neither established by the Japanese occupant (as Burma was) nor by the subsequent British occupation forces. Instead, it was proclaimed by the Indonesians themselves.[236] Secondly, the British occupation forces, unlike the Japanese in Burma, held the territory on behalf of the legitimate Dutch government.[237] In fact, Admiral Mountbatten, the Supreme Commander of these Allied occupation forces, acted, in the beginning, in that spirit. He even ordered the Japanese Commander in the Southeast Asian territory, Marshall Terauti, to annul the proclamation of the Republic of Indonesia, an order which, of course, did not achieve much, although the Japanese Commander on Java subsequently issued a statement in which he denied that the Indonesian government had taken over power on Java and stated that the Japanese would transfer their powers to the Allied forces.[238]

Subsequent facts have greatly blurred the legal relationship between the parties concerned[239] and the Indonesian leaders suc-

[235] Supra at 88.

[236] Japanese connivance was not so general as is sometimes contended. Zorab mentions how the opinions of the top military officials in Java were divided. Zorab, *op. cit. supra* note 208, at 120.

[237] For a Dutch view on the reasons behind the transfer of the Netherlands Indies from the South West Pacific Area Command of General MacArthur to the South East Asia Command of Admiral Mountbatten, see Enquête Commissie Regeringsbeleid 1940–45, *op. cit. supra* note 219, 484–523 (1956). See also 2 Helfrich, *Mémoires* 198–201 (1950). For a contrasting British view justifying their actions, see Wehl, *op. cit. supra* note 206, at 31–49.

[238] Overdijkink, *op. cit. supra* note 215, at 46 (1946).

[239] The Van Poll Committee attributed the cause of the uncertain situation to the fact that, although the Allies recognized Dutch sovereignty over the Netherlands Indies,

ceeded in getting effective control over extensive parts of Java and Sumatra. As a result the British troops which initially only recognized the legitimate Dutch Government were later forced to ask the Indonesian government for their support in the maintenance of law and order, and made the Indonesians responsible for the government of the territories under their control.[240] With this request the British Commanding Officer, General Christison, practically recognized the *de facto* authority of the Indonesian Government, an act which was greatly resented by the Dutch government.[241] The resulting situation defies any rigid theory on the division of over-all sovereignty. This is but natural. Facts often occur regardless of existing legal claims and when afterwards the new situation must be construed again in terms of sovereignty, the legal construction arrived at often fails to clarify the picture. The Dutch Government maintained, however, that the establishment of the Indonesian Republic was just a revolutionary movement against its legitimate authority.[242] There is no doubt that the proclamation of an independent state in a colony amounts, in effect, to a revolt against the sovereign and thus places the label of "insurgents" on the movement. The matter thus becomes, as it were, a race between both contenders to assert themselves. If the sovereign would be able to crush the uprising, no further problem would arise from the status of the insurgents. However, if the latter would be able to consolidate their position and set up a political entity with all the necessary attributes of statehood such as territory, people, government and independence, and even be recognized by some states, then inevitably the question would arise whether the new unit should be considered a state under international law or not.

Before proceeding with the merits of the Indonesian case, it may be worthwhile to consider another point. Apart from the considerations of effective statehood, there was another and interesting argument which was put forward by the Indonesians.[243] They

this sovereignty did, in fact, not rest with the Netherlands or Netherlands Indies Government, but with the British occupying power. Van Poll, *op. cit. supra* note 219, at 24.

[240] Enquête Commissie, *op. cit. supra* note 219, at 655–657.

[241] *Supra* note 219.

[242] See for a Dutch view, Van Kleffens in the Security Council, *U.N. Security Council*, Off. Rec. 2nd year, no. 67, at 1619, 1645 (1947). For an Indonesian view, see the discussion of the status of the Republic of Indonesia, in Sastroamidjojo and Delson, "The Status of the Republic of Indonesia in International Law," 49 *Col. L. R.* 344–361 (1949).

[243] Still another, but weaker, Indonesian argument is the one put forward by Maramis

contended that the creation of the new Indonesian state was justified because of the abandonment of sovereignty over this area by the Dutch colonial government and subsequent seizure of power and establishment of a new government by the autochthonous inhabitants of the colony.[244] The contention is here, apparently, that the Dutch, by giving only a feeble display of military resistance against the Japanese, followed by their unconditional surrender, have in effect abandoned the territory and thus caused terrible hardship on the Indonesian people who were left to the whims and terrorism of the Japanese. By failing to defend the country and its population adequately, the Dutch have forfeited their sovereign rights over the territory, so the Indonesians say.[245]

If the Indonesians could establish that the Dutch government intended to, and indeed did abandon the territory, they would have some sound points in favour of their contention. However, the facts do not seem to support their view sufficiently. It is true that the military resistance of the Dutch forces was on the whole inadequate. It is equally true that the subsequent occupation caused considerable hardship on the people. Nevertheless, it cannot be denied that there was not the slightest intention on the part of the Dutch to abandon the Netherlands Indies. They even carried out a continued resistance in certain parts of Indonesia, like in New Guinea, which island was never entirely occupied. In Australia too, Dutch forces prepared themselves for an eventual invasion of Indonesia, thus proving that the Dutch Government had every intention to return to the islands as soon as possible. In fact the whole argument for their return to power after World War II was based on the fact that they had never abandoned the area but were compelled by force of arms to move out temporarily.[246] The feebleness of military resistance

in his pamphlet "*No more Legal Power of the Netherlands in Indonesia,*" 5–11 (1946). Maramis deduces the independence of Indonesia from the fact that the Governor-General governed in the name of the Queen whose authority, it is alleged here, had become unconstitutional when the seat of the Dutch government was removed to London contrary to the provisions of the Dutch Constitution. From this violation Maramis draws the conclusion, without further elucidation, that Indonesia constituted an independent state as of the moment of the removal of the seat of the Dutch government from the Netherlands. Afterwards, however, this Dutch action has found its justification in the theory of "state emergency law." See e.g. Kranenburg, *Nederlandsch staatsrecht* (Netherlands Constitutional Law) 448–450 (1947).

[244] See written statement by Dr. Roem, Chairman of the Indonesian delegation, in Sastroamidjojo and Delson *supra* note 242, at 348, note 14. This argument, if true and valid, would then equally hold for some other colonies in Asia.

[245] Kahin in Holland, *Asian Nationalism in the West* 70 (1953).

[246] P. M. Brown states that sovereignty remains with the legitimate government so long as the people in occupied territory "can manifest in one way or another their

does not seem to be a sufficient argument to establish the fact of abandonment. Judging from the outcome of the fighting in Asia, the Dutch did not do worse than the British in Malaya and Burma, or the French in Indo-China.

Therefore, we will return to the first argument which – it is suggested here – offers more chances for making a good case. If insurgents succeed in establishing an organized government in their territory, a factual situation is created which cannot be ignored and is often recognized *de facto*. Then the question to be answered is: What is the relationship between the new *de facto* government and the legitimate sovereign? In other words: What is the status of the new political body in international law? It is said that the very existence of such a political body does not entitle it yet to one of the rights of a full-sovereign state, namely, the right of intercourse[247] and it is thus unable "to live the normal life of a State of international law until some of them (= members of the Family of Nations) acquiesce and permit it to do so."[248]

After a revolution the problems involved in matters of recognition are mostly the result of the competing claims of the two political entities, both of which pretend to be the principal authority in the territory. If formal authority as well as effective control are indeed still in the hands of the legitimate government there are no problems whatsoever. However, the insurgents may succeed in completely controlling part of the territory of the state. Then, although not yet having formal authority under international law, it must be admitted that they in fact control the area. Reversely, the legitimate government might still possess formal authority, but in fact it has lost the effective control over that territory. In the battle of arguments the legitimate government will now, of course, defend its position, firstly, by emphasizing its formal authority, and, secondly, it will try to prove that the insurgents do not possess enough authority and organization to be considered a state able to fulfill international as well as national obligations. The insurgents, on the other hand, go all out to prove that their government is sufficiently

inalterable will to regain their freedom." P. M. Brown, "Sovereignty in Exile," 35 *A.J.I.L.* 667 (1941). Such a contention applied fully to the Dutch people in Indonesia, but it obviously did not apply to the Indonesians who did not regard the Dutch government as the legitimate government in the strictest sense of the word.

[247] Briggs, *The Law of Nations* 65–66 (1952).

[248] Hyde "The Status of the Republic of Indonesia in International Law," 49 *Col. L. R.* 956 (1949).

effective, and that there are reasons why they should even be regarded as a government with formal authority in the territory under their control. Indeed, the legal controversy between Indonesia and the Netherlands took place exactly on these grounds.

In dealing with recognition one will inevitably run into the conflicting doctrines of the declaratory and constitutive nature of recognition.[249] Sastroamidjojo and Delson deal extensively with this question and they expound the familiar view that "the existence of a State is independent of its recognition by other States and that such a recognition, when forthcoming, is merely declaratory of the already established fact of statehood." Reference is then further made to the Tinoco arbitration case.[250] after which they proceeded to prove that the other, constitutive, view is not very useful, at least not in their case.[251] In the case of Indonesia the question of recognition received a more substantial, legal basis after the Linggadjati Agreement, although it still came nowhere near a solution.

In the terms of Article 1 of the Linggadjati Agreement "the Netherlands Government recognizes the Government of the Republic of Indonesia as exercising *de facto* authority over Java, Madura and Sumatra."[252] Writers, in general, agree that the recognition of a rebellious colony by its parent state opens the way to a solution.[253] But this, at first sight, unambiguous text of Art. 1 caused another debate on the nature of recognition. The difference of opinion in this case arose from two interrelated questions:

(a) What is meant by *de facto* recognition?

(b) Who possesses sovereignty over the whole of the country after the *de facto* recognition of the Government of the Republic of Indonesia in part of Indonesia?

The Indonesian interpretation of the Linggadjati Agreement is that it unequivocally recognized the Government of the Republic of Indonesia as a *de facto* government, and further that "in the case of States not already recognized the recognition of the government also implies the recognition of the State." Therefore this Article 1

[249] Oppenheim, *op. cit. supra* note 234, at 121–123 (1948).

[250] Sastroamidjojo & Delson *supra* note 242, at 348.

[251] *Id.* at 349.

[252] Wolf, *op. cit. supra* note 206, at 176.

[253] *Cf.* François, 1 *Handboek van het Volkenrecht* (Manual of International Law) 190 (1949); Hyde, *supra* note 248, at 350; Lauterpacht, *Recognition in International Law* 339 (1947).

establishes the Indonesian government as a *de facto* government and the Republic of Indonesia as an international state.[254]

The Dutch arrived at a different interpretation of Art. 1. It is perhaps best represented in the works of Professor François, who was in fact the legal adviser to the Netherlands Ministry of Foreign Affairs. In his opinion much of the confusion is caused by the inadequate contemporary theories which divided recognition into only two categories, namely those of *de facto* and *de jure* recognition. In addition to these two forms, Prof. François distinguishes a third one, namely, recognition of a *de facto government*. The latter form is said to recognize the fact that the authority claiming to be the government of the territory should indeed be regarded as such, in other words the "facticity" or "efficacy" of that authority is recognized.[255] This third form is said to differ from the *de facto* recognition proper, because the latter is a declaration of intention to enter into (limited) diplomatic and consular relations. François contends that the Linggadjati Agreement only went as far as to confer upon the Government of the Republic the third form, that is the recognition of a *de facto government*, because Art. 1 mentions explicitly the Government of the Republic "as excercising *de facto* authority." There is, however, little appreciation, and consequently little support, for the three-fold division in contemporary literature on international law. Professor Lauterpacht, for instance, says that the term "recognition as a *de facto* government" is conveniently abbreviated to "*de facto* recognition."[256] It seems that such a threefold distinction still does not bring more clarity into the problem. At any rate state practices with regard to the recognition of the Republic of Indonesia showed all marks of a great confusion on the matter of recognition. When the Linggadjati Agreement was only initialled, Afghanistan, Egypt, Iran, Lebanon, Saudi Arabia and Syria recognized the Republic of Indonesia *de facto* and proceeded to grant it *de jure* recognition as soon as the Agreement was signed. On the other hand, other countries, such as Australia, Burma, India, the Philippines, the U.K. and the U.S. granted only *de facto* recognition after the signing of the Agreement.[257]

According to the three-fold recognition theory of Prof. François all above recognitions must have been premature. The first group

[254] Sastroamidjojo & Delson, *supra* note 242 at 350.
[255] François, *op. cit. supra* note 253, at 181.
[256] Lauterpacht, *op. cit. supra* note 253, at 330.
[257] Sastroadmidjojo and Delson, *supra* note 242, at 345.

(Afghanistan and others) has gone furthest by considering the very initialling of an agreement sufficient ground for a *de facto* recognition. The other group (Australia and other countries) seemed to take a middle position between attitudes of the Netherlands and the Afghanistan group.

The second question dealing with sovereignty over the entire territory of Indonesia after the recognition of the Government of the Republic of Indonesia is equally confusing. The Dutch views, as expounded by Mr. Van Kleffens in the Security Council, was of a restrictive nature, at least with respect to the authority of the Republic. Since the *de facto* recognition only referred to Java, Madura and Sumatra, and not to other parts of Indonesia, it did not amount, in their opinion, to a recognition of the Republic as an international state, but only as a state in the nature of a component unit like, for instance, New York, Utah or New South Wales. Therefore, sovereignty over the whole of Indonesia, including Java, Madura and Sumatra, remained with the Dutch Government.[258]

The Indonesians replied that the language as well as the spirit of the agreement suggested a different intention. It was couched in terms, not of a municipal character, but of general international usage,[259] like recognition, cooperation, consultation, and arbitration, all between two distinct parties, the Netherlands Government and the Government of the Republic of Indonesia. Therefore, they say, the agreement indicated the acceptance of the idea of equal, international partnership and not the subordination of a body such as a province to the over-all sovereign authority.[260]

So far the question of formal authority has been dealt with. The matter of effective control is of equal importance. From the very beginning the Indonesian leaders have claimed to be the sole, actual representatives for the whole of Indonesia. They maintained this point of view during almost the entire conflict and simply based this view on the alleged will of the people.[261]

The Dutch position was quite different. Because they were losing

[258] *U.N. Security Council*, Off. Rec., 2nd year, 171st meeting, no. 67, at 1619–1620 (1947).

[259] It is remarkable, though perhaps understandable, that many of the Indonesian counter-arguments are very similar to some opposing views heard in the Dutch Parliament during the debates on the Linggadjati Agreement, *cf.* Ruys de Beerenbrouck, *Souvereiniteitsoverdracht aan Indonesië* (Transfer of Sovereingty to Indonesia) (1950).

[260] Sastroamidjojo & Delson, *supra* note 242 at 352–353.

[261] The Linggadjati Agreement was a concession to this claim. Foster Collins, *supra* note 223, at 122–123.

ground continually it was impossible for the Dutch to take a strong and consistent stand in the debate. Immediately after the Japanese capitulation the Allied powers (not only the Dutch) were apparently unwilling to deal with what they then considered a Japanese "puppet" government, an attitude which soon proved to be untenable.[262] The British occupation forces, for instance, soon changed their mind, since for purposes of the necessary cooperation they had to admit the factual control of the Indonesians.[263] At first the Dutch, falling back upon their formal authority, were unwilling to go that far. However, forced by the weight of facts they gradually gave way. They dealt with the Indonesians first on an informal basis. Then at Linggadjati, they recognized the Indonesian government as exercising *de facto* authority, though in the particular Dutch interpretation[264] and with certain reservations.[265] In the Renville Agreement these principles were confirmed, while at the Round Table Conference at the Hague *de jure* recognition was granted. At this point the circle of arguments was closed and a *status quo* was reached again. Facts had overtaken legal arguments. The rebels had asserted themselves over the legitimate government. Thus, in the recognition *de jure* of the Indonesian government effective control merged again with formal authority.

These, in brief, are the main issues in the legal conflict between the Republic and the Netherlands. Perhaps one more remark may be added here. It does not seem unfair to say that one of the main causes of the dispute springs from a different approach which has characterized many a controversy between the Indonesians and the Dutch in later years.[266] With their great legal tradition and experience, coupled with a high level of scholarship, the Dutch negotiators tend, at times, to become perfectionist and legalistic, an attitude which was not only foreign, but also unappealing to the Indonesians. Having just emerged from a long and painful struggle for independence, the Indonesians were primarily concerned with

[262] Hyde, *supra* note 248, at 956; Wolf, *op. cit. supra* note 206, at 10. In a review of Wolf's book Prof. Vlekke writes, however, that the Dutch have very soon already given up this attitude. Vlekke, in 2 *Indonesië* at 280 (1948–49).

[263] Upon their arrival on Java the British called upon the Indonesian leaders to support them in the exercise of their task. This, according to the Dutch, was an implied recognition of the Indonesian leaders as a *de facto* authority. Van Poll, *op. cit. supra* note 219, at 23.

[264] *Supra* at 105.

[265] Van Mook, *The Stakes of Democracy in Southeast Asia*, 238 (1950).

[266] *E.g.* with respect to the Netherlands-Indonesian Union, and the dispute on Western New Guinea (= Western Irian).

safeguarding their political achievements. Such political results obviously cannot be perfectly represented in a document of legal terms and expressions, which is one reason why throughout this period the Indonesians were rather suspicious of legal documents. In the words of Prof. Van Asbeck, there were "fundamental differences of outlook and attitudes and deep mutual distrust, caused by historical facts, fostered by suspicions and misrepresentations of the partners' views and purposes."[267] Yet, if negotiations are to be successful, they have to be laid down in some document, in spite of all its possible defects. When agreeing to such a document the Indonesians used to insist on its political implications, an attitude which the Dutch were not always willing to go along with. The Indonesian legal arguments, however, stand and fall with their political implications. If one is unwilling to give credit to the political facts and insists on dealing with the agreement strictly on its legal merits as they appear from the text, one cannot escape the conclusion that the Dutch case is a good one. On the other hand, if the Indonesian attitude is accepted, their case is at least equally[268] sound. An examination of the history of the negotiations, they say, testifies to the fact that they always worked on the basis of the above assumption. All through the negotiations the Indonesian attitude was that they regarded themselves as constituting a sovereign state, and they continually made it clear to the other party that there never could be any question of a peaceful solution, if their full sovereignty was questioned.[269] They would never be willing to sign any agreement which would not recognize such a status. This is, for example, clearly demonstrated by their adamant refusal to sign, in

[267] Van Asbeck, "The Birth and Decline of the Netherlands-Indonesian Union," 7 *Y.B.W.A.* 204–227 at 211 (1953).

[268] Even the signing of such an important document as the Linggadjati Agreement took place in a spirit of disagreement. Foster Collins writes: "After an unsuccessful attempt to resolve the differing interpretations, the two governments decided to sign the agreement, agreeing to disagree on the interpretation." Foster Collins, *supra* note 223, at 123.

[269] For an Indonesian point of view, see *e.g.* the article by Miss Rasid, of the editorial staff of the Indonesian newspapier Siasat, which strongly maintained that the main cause of difficulties during the negotiations was the differences of opinion between the Republican and the Netherlands governments as to the nature of the problem, namely whether it was a purely internal question or not. "This fundamental difference in interpretation started all the later difficulties..." Rasid, "Developments in Indonesia," 5 *India* Q. 255–258 (1949). For a Dutch view on the basis of the negotiations and the way they were carried out, see the notes made from the diary of Prof. Schermerhorn, the Chairman of the Dutch Commission-General, which carried on the final negotiations leading to the Linggadjati Agreement. Smit, *Het Akkoord van Linggadjati* (The Linggadjati Agreement) (1959).

later years, the Renville Agreement, and only the oral assertion of Dr. Graham, the U.S. member in the U.N.C.I., that the signing of the agreement would neither harm nor change their established status ("You are what you are")[270] persuaded them to go along with it. The question whether Dr. Graham was authorized to give such an assertion is irrelevant at this point. We are now only concerned with the consistency of the Indonesian attitude with respect to views on sovereignty.

The best example, however, is given by Dr. Hatta, the Indonesian Prime Minister. When he addressed the Round Table Conference at The Hague, which ended the dispute by transferring sovereignty to the United States of Indonesia, he reviewed the Indonesian attitude during the past years and applied such principles as "self-determination" and "the will to freedom" to counter historical and juridical claims of the Netherlands to the sovereignty over Indonesia. He then rejected the argument that the Republic possessed no sovereignty because it had never been recognized by the judicial bearer of sovereignty, the Netherlands Kingdom.[271] He further stated:

> Whatever the juridical arguments of the Netherlands Government, the Indonesian people in the Republic is convinced by experience that its State is a sovereign State, possessing its own Government, its own Army, its own police, its own monetary system, and, last but not least, its own foreign policy and its own representation abroad ... Rightly or wrongly, the Indonesian people in the Republic regards itself as living in a sovereign State. This is the fundamental reason why every agreement... when carried into practice inevitably broke down over the problem of sovereignty. The Netherlands desired that the Republic should surrender its attributes of sovereignty to the Netherlands authorities as the preliminary step toward the creation of a new and sovereign Indonesian State. The Republic contended that the only way to effect the incorporation of the Republican territory into a new Indonesian State was the transfer of sovereignty to an interim Government, which should take over and continue the Republican institutions (army, foreign relations) which may be considered attributes of sovereignty.[272]

The above lines proved clearly that the question of sovereignty under the Linggadjati and Renville Agreements was never con-

[270] This statement of Dr. Graham made at a meeting of the U.N.C.I. with Republican leaders at Kaliurang (near the Republican capital of Jogjakarta) a few days earlier, was apparently reiterated by the Australian member of the U.N.C.I., Mr. Kirby, on board the Renville. Rasid, *supra* note 269, at 255. According to Smit this whole Agreement which was to play an important role in Netherlands-Indonesian relations, was built on a shaky basis. Smit, *De Indonesische Questie* 157 (1952).

[271] Vlekke, "The Settlement in Indonesia – The Final Phase," 6 *The World Today* 32 (1950).

[272] *Id.* at 32–33.

clusively solved. They also proved that no matter how much or little had changed in the Indonesian attitude in the course of these long years of negotiations, at the Round Table Conference they still maintained the same conviction on sovereignty which they always had had and which could not be reconciled with those of the Dutch. The Dutch views, on the other hand, had changed considerably as a result of their growing realization that the hard facts could not be entirely ignored. However, the farhest they were willing to go, until circumstances forced them to abandon sovereignty immediately and entirely at the Round Table Conference, was the Renville Agreement of January 1948. The relevant article (i.e. the first additional principle) dealing with sovereignty, prior to a transfer of that sovereignty, stated:

> Sovereignty throughout the Netherlands Indies is and shall remain with the Kingdom of the Netherlands until, after a stated interval, the Kingdom of the Netherlands transfers its sovereignty to the United States of Indonesia. Prior to the termination of such stated interval, the Kingdom of the Netherlands may confer appropriate rights, duties and responsibilities on a provisional, federal, government of the territories of the future United States of Indonesia. The United States of Indonesia, when created, will be a sovereign and independent state in equal partnership with the Kingdom of the Netherlands, in a Netherlands-Indonesian Union at the Head of which shall be the King of the Netherlands. The status of the Republic of Indonesia will be that of a state within the United States of Indonesia.[273]

The Dutch views on the situation arising from the above quoted article cannot be better explained in brief than Professor Hyde has done. We will, therefore, quote some relevant paragraphs:

> Here was a situation where the character of the statehood of the entity that was coming into being was acknowledged in an arrangement which the Republic found itself obliged to accept through the intervening influence of the UN Comittee. Moreover, the Republic was to content itself by such process with something that acknowledged, for the time being, a certain subordination to the parent state as well as a continued political connection with that state. The agreements were far from declaring that it had become independent and the principles annexed to one of them referred to the retention of sovereignty in the parent state for a specific period after which it was to be transferred to a different entity – namely the United States of Indonesia. There was nothing contrary to such a design in the words of the Linggadjati Agreement, that the Government of the Republic of Indonesia was recognized "as exercising *de facto* authority over Java, Madura and Sumatra." This recognition was quite consistent with an understanding that the Republic was still lacking independence, statehood and enjoyed a control over certain areas of the Netherlands Indies.[274]

[273] *U.N. Security Council, op. cit. supra* note 226, at 97.
[274] Hyde, *supra* note 248, at 960.

The Indonesian viewpoint, as explained by Sastroamidjojo and Delson, did not go into the merits of these principles. It only contended that these principles were accepted as a basis for negotiation, and not as a basis for settlement. Consequently, it did not mean the acceptance of the first additional principle as such. The sovereignty, already possessed by the Republic of Indonesia, could in their opinion not be affected by this principle. So this again proves, that the Linggadjati and Renville Agreements did not produce any solution,[275] a situation which lasted till the Round Table Conference although this meeting did not solve the problems of these two agreements either. Actually it did not matter very much, for the agreement on the status of Indonesia arrived at during the Round Table Conference were to supersede all previous agreements.

In the eyes of the Indonesians their most important achievement at the Round Table Conference (R.T.C.) was embodied in Art. 1 of the Charter of Transfer of Sovereingty which read as follows:

> The Kingdom of the Netherlands unconditionally and irrevocably transfers complete sovereignty over Indonesia to the Republic of the United States of Indonesia and thereby recognizes said Republic of the United States of Indonesia as an independent and sovereign state.[276]

With the conclusion of these R.T.C. Agreements, Indonesia undisputedly reached the end of the road to independence, and entered a new stage in its history, namely, that of a sovereign, independent state of a federal structure.

The R.T.C. also contemplated the creation of a Netherlands-Indonesian Union. Art. 1 of the Statute of the Union dealt with the "Character of the Union" and stated:

> (1) The Netherlands-Indonesian Union effectuates the organized cooperation between the Kingdom of the Netherlands and the Republic of the United States of Indonesia on the basis of free will and equality in status with equal rights.
> (2) The Union does not prejudice the status of each of the two partners as an independent and sovereign State.[277]

However, from the very beginning the parties could not agree on the place which the Union was to occupy in their relationship. The Dutch favoured a "heavy" Union, standing above both parties, and possibly possessing some sovereign rights of its own. The

[275] *Supra* at 106–110.
[276] *U.N. Security Council* (S/1417/Add. 1.), 14 November 1949 at 66 (1949).
[277] *Id.* at 71.

Indonesians, on the other hand, wanted only a "weak" Union with only nominal powers. Thus, this question became another point of disagreement between the Netherlands and Indonesia.[278] But, whatever the correct interpretation of these provisions, it could not detract anything from the status of the Republic of the United States of Indonesia which is, as para. 2 of Art. 1 of the Statute of the Union said, that of an independent and sovereign state.

Some other significant changes followed in subsequent years in the relationship between both parties. Only one year after the transfer of sovereignty to the Republic of the United States of Indonesia,[279] the Indonesian Parliament passed an act which transformed this federal state into a unitary state, called the Republic of Indonesia.[280] The realization of the Netherlands-Indonesian Union remained a great point of dispute. For various reasons resentment against this Union increased in Indonesia in the following years.

Finally, in 1956, Indonesia abrogated the Netherlands-Indonesian Union which provoked a strong protest from its partner who accused the Indonesian Government of violating international law[281]

These are, unquestionably, serious matters and of great legal significance. However, they should be examined in another place. In this chapter we are only concerned with the legal status of the parties. And, whatever the significance of these political developments, they did not change in any way the legal status of the Republic of Indonesia, the successor to the Republic of the United States of Indonesia, which remained that of an independent and sovereign state under international law.

[278] For a brief, but clear description of the differing interpretations of the two parties with respect to the role of the Union in their mutual relationship, see Van Asbeck, *supra* note 267, at 210–211.

[279] Even this period of one year would have been much shorter, if the Federal Republic of Indonesia (U.S.I.) and the Republic of Indonesia (R.I.) had not indulged in the theoretical discussion as to who was to be considered the testatrix of the pending unitary state. Böhtlingk, "De Nieuwe Eenheidsstaat" (The New Unitary State) 4 *Indonesië* 106 (1950–51).

[280] For the ever-present dislike of the federal idea among the leaders of the Republic of Indonesia, see Schiller, *The Formation of Federal Indonesia* 4–5 (1955).

[281] *N.Y. Times*, February 22, 1956.

Cf. Jaarboek van het Ministerie van Buitenlandse Zaken (Yearbook of the Netherlands Ministry of Foreign Affairs), 112 (1955–56).

CHAPTER III

THE ASIAN STATES
IN THE WORLD POWER PROCESS

After having achieved statehood the Asian states could intensify their participation in the world power process. In interactions with members of the world community the decision makers of these new states were constantly faced with conflicting interests and claims of those participants. It is rather obvious that for newly-established states the question of acquisition and allocation of resources has prime importance. In the brief period since independence one can, therefore, find various instances in which these states used all possible means of persuasion as well as coercion either to acquire or to retain resources. Indeed, it seems that the most important conflicting claims which they encountered were concerned with deprivations and threats of deprivations with respect to what they considered their legitimate resources. In order to thwart these deprivations, they naturally appealed to community prescriptions.[1]

An examination of such appeals will show immediately that these new states have commonly referred to community prescriptions which are usually indicated by the traditonal term of "rules of international law." This traditional attitude can easily be explained. Most states in the world today look upon international law as a body of rules or principles which are binding upon states in their mutual relations.[2] During their struggle for independence the Asian nations ran into great authoritative obstacles which all systems of public order will erect to protect the established system. These obstacles were couched in such traditional terms as sovereignty, colonial dependency, domestic jurisdiction and the like. The restrictive influence of these doctrines was obviously intended to prevent nationalist movements from gaining any formal authority. Consequently, the nationalist leaders decided that only through revolution could those traditional legal barriers be effectively broken

[1] See McDougal, "International Law, Power and Policy – A Contemporary Concept" 82 *Hague Recueil* 206 (1953).

[2] Hyde, *International Law, Chiefly as Interpreted and Applied by the United States* 1, note 1 (1951).

and the colonial government be forced to yield to their demands for independence. As seen above, this was ultimately achieved.

However, although they resented the rules used by those who, according to international law, were the legitimate sovereigns, these rules were at the same time the only kind of community prescriptions with which the new states were acquainted. Therefore, it was also to these traditional rules, with all their flaws, that they turned once they had become independent. The question is whether these traditional rules have proved to be adequate means of acquiring and retaining their own resources.

To find the answer to this question an examination of recent practices of international law by the states concerned will be attempted, in order to determine whether or not traditional rules of international law offered a workable instrument for the solution of problems which arose in these states since they achieved independence some fifteen years ago.

Of the numerous possibilities which come into consideration for a closer examination, it is proposed here to consider the following four issues:

(1) The Burmese-Chinese boundary disputes.
(2) The Kashmir conflict.
(3) Sovereignty in the waters of the Indonesian Archipelago.
(4) Peaceful coexistence.

The choice of these subjects requires some further explanation and justification. First of all, they provide us with an opportunity to examine – although only briefly – some practices of Burma, Ceylon,[3] India and Indonesia, separately as well as jointly.

The following considerations have also led to the selection of these issues. In view of the idea of "development of international law" the above choices enable us to review past, present and possible future practices. In the Burma-Chinese disputes, an important aspect of Asian relations can be examined, namely the influence of the past. We will give particular attention here to the influence of historical facts on the solution of the problems since it is sometimes held that historical considerations play a greater part in Asian relations than they do, for instance, in the West, because of the different time-sense of the Asians. The Kashmir case, on the other hand, presents an opportunity to observe the practices of Asian states in an issue which arose in the present time. The case of the

[3] No important example of an international dispute is provided by Ceylon separately.

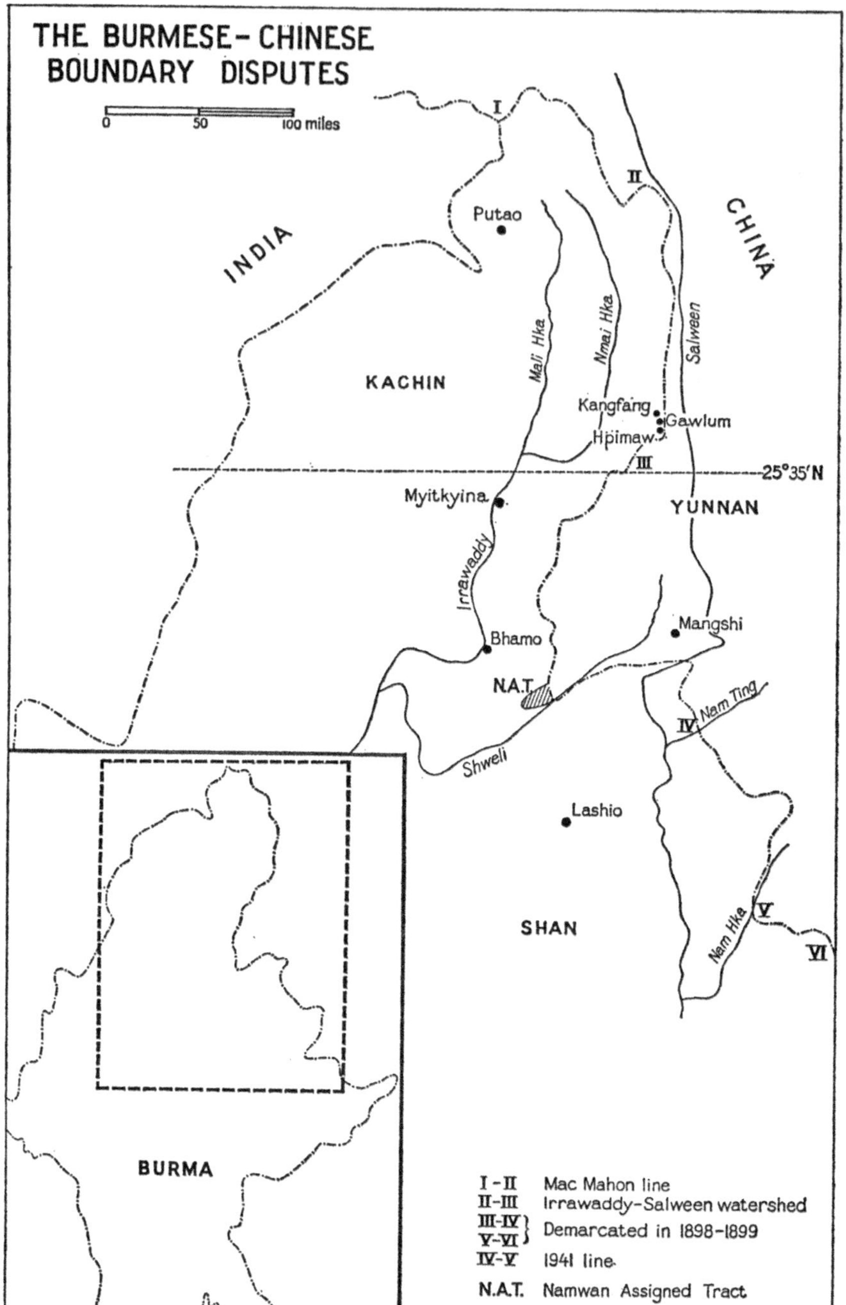
THE BURMESE-CHINESE BOUNDARY DISPUTES
0
50
100 miles
I
II
III
IV
V
VI
INDIA
CHINA
Putao
KACHIN
Mali Hka
Nmai Hka
Salween
Kangfang
Gawlum
Hpimaw
25°35'N
Myitkyina
YUNNAN
Irrawaddy
Bhamo
Mangshi
N.A.T.
Nam Ting
Shweli
Lashio
SHAN
Nam Hka
BURMA
I-II Mac Mahon line
II-III Irrawaddy-Salween watershed
III-IV
V-VI
Demarcated in 1898-1899
IV-V 1941 line
N.A.T. Namwan Assigned Tract

Indonesian Archipelago may enable us to see what future policies of these nations may be like. Finally, some attention will be given to the doctrine of peaceful coexistence, a doctrine which has recently gained much significance. Asians particularly have stated their allegiance to this theory, so that it has been said that, with these practices of peaceful coexistence, they have made an important contribution to the development of international law.

THE BURMESE – CHINESE BOUNDARY DISPUTES

1. The Facts

The border area which has become the subject of conflicting claims between Burma and China separates the North and North-east of Burma from Tibet and the province of Yunnan.[4] At present the Burmese part of the area is administered by the Kachin and Shan States, two component parts of the Union of Burma.

This rugged and inaccessible area is dominated by a mountain range stretching from Tibet in the North southwards into the Malay peninsula. It is intersected by three great rivers, the Irrawaddy, the Salween and the Mekong. The inaccessibility of this barrier is further broken by some important passes linking the plains which stretch on either side of it. These passes have also been the gateways through which several migrations have travelled in the course of history, moving mostly in a southward direction towards Burma.

The migratory peoples, which are today classified as Shans, Kachins, Palaungs and a few other smaller communities, show many ethnic and other characteristics of their neighbours on the Chinese side. Politically, their history has also been closely linked to that of the Chinese provinces across the border, in the sense that they had to resist many incursions from that direction whenever the Chinese felt strong enough to make them. But the Chinese did not constitute the only danger to the border tribes. To the South, in Middle and Lower Burma, the Burmese kingdoms were equally trying to expand their power and of these military operations, some of which went as far as Yunnan,[5] the border peoples were again the victims.

[4] See map of Burma facing this page.
[5] Maung Maung, *Burma in the Family of Nations* 11 (1956).

It is said that the political structure took a more permanent shape in the 13th century when the Mongols conquered China and drove the Shan peoples of Yunnan province deeper into and beyond Northern Burma. Here the Shans established some new kingdoms, but China's mighty arm caught up even with some of these remote Shan states. In the 16th century it was the Burmese who – once more powerful – reconquered the northern part and made the Shans their vassals. These conquests and shifts of power continued during the next centuries.[6] The term "conquest," however, should be understood here in a special sense. The conquered border states were allowed to carry on their own affairs if they only paid tribute to the conquerors who seldom cared about establishing a firmer control over these remote areas. Because of the nominal nature of this vassalage, the border states were not unwilling to pay the tributes even if it gave the impression of submission to the authority of the conqueror. The anomalous nature of the situation was further demonstrated by the frequent occurrences of dual allegiance of the border states to China as well as to Burma.[7] In the light of these facts, it is obviously erroneous to use the term vassalage or suzerainty in the ordinary Western meaning.

The general picture in the next few centuries was one of rivalry, clashes and revolts, alternated with periods of peace and armistice. Yet it is not until the end of the 18th century that we are able to find something resembling a peace treaty. At that time China invaded Burma but she was repeatedly thrown back. The failure of her operations finally forced her to enter into peace negotiations which resulted in the so-called peace treaty of Kaungton near Bhamo. China waived her claims to certain Shan states, while both parties agreed to exchange gift-bearing missions. The treaty also tacitly accepted the dual allegiance of some other Shan states.[8]

With the arrival of the British in Upper Burma a new era began in the history of these border areas. After the conquest of Lower and Middle Burma, the British moved north and occupied first Bhamo and later Myitkyina. But they were not in a hurry and moved about cautiously in order not to arouse Chinese resentment. There was no particular intention on their part to occupy the whole of North Burma immediately. In fact, until 1914 British control only reached

[6] Tinker, "Burma's Northeast Borderland Problems," 29 *Pac. Aff.* 324–346, at 329–333 (1956).

[7] *Id.* at 331–332.

[8] See *infra* at 121.

as far as a point 27 miles north of Myitkyina.[9] China, however, was unwilling to give up her rights to the British occupied areas and the British policy was actually aimed at the conclusion of some agreement. At the Peking Convention of July 1886 such an agreement was reached, but because of its ambivalent nature this did in fact nothing more than to continue the uncertain political as well as legal position.[10] In the struggle for more control in these areas the British finally came out on top. In 1914 they established some administration in the northernmost part of Burma around Putao (Fort Herz) and in subsequent years they extended their authority in the whole area between Putao and Myitkyina.[11] A dispute with China was inevitable now and some border clashes indeed occurred. Subsequently, however, negotiations were opened which led to the establishment of a Joint (Boundary) Commission under the neutral chairmanship of the Swiss colonel F. Iselin who was appointed by the President of the Council of the League of Nations in 1934. The Commission finished its work in 1937 but its findings were not accepted by China until June 1941. The acceptance was apparently not given wholeheartedly, for only a few months later China requested new negotiations on this matter. The outbreak of the Pacific War in December 1941 prevented this proposal from being pursued.

Fighting on the same side, Britain and China did not particularly press for a settlement of this issue during the war years; but the end of World War II immediately brought a renewal of interest. The independent Union of Burma had now taken the place of Great Britain and India in these border questions. China, on her part, expressed the hope of reaching a mutually satisfactory solution,[12] but neither party seemed to be willing to make further concessions. In fact, Burma had already embarked upon a constitutional scheme which was to give the border areas a more permanent place in the Union and she showed little willingness to change these intentions.[13]

In China great changes had also taken place. The Communists had succeeded in wresting power in 1949 from the Nationalist Government (Kuo Min Tang). This had for Burma particularly

[9] Tinker, *supra* note 6, at 334.

[10] *Id.* at 335.

[11] Christian, *Modern Burma – A Survey of Political and Economic Development* 266–268 (1942); Hinton, *China's Relations with Burma and Vietnam* 35 (1958).

[12] Stark Toller, "The Undefined China-Burma Frontier," *Eastern World* 13 (October 1948).

[13] Arts. 154–200 of the Constitution of Burma.

dangerous consequences since a few thousands of these KMT troops, which fled for the Communist forces, crossed the Yunnan borderline and settled afterwards in the Burmese border areas as semi-independent armies. Although requested by the Burmese Government to lay down their arms and be interned, they refused to do so and instead launched counter-attacks on the Communist forces on Chinese territory. The Burmese Government, unable to cope with the problem by force of arms, and seriously worried by these activities because they might provoke an invasion into its territory by Communist forces, finally decided to bring the matter before the U.N. on March 26, 1953. Burma introduced a draft resolution which, *inter alia*, condemned the KMT Government of Formosa for acts of aggression, since the KMT troops on Burmese territory seemed to obey orders or get support from the Nationalist Government at Formosa. The General Assembly finally accepted a compromise Mexican resolution by a majority vote of 59 to 1, with one abstention (Nationalist China).[14] This resolution did not use the term "aggression," nor did it mention the KMT Government by name. It merely condemned the presence of "foreign forces" and declared that they should either be interned or leave the country. A four-nation committee with representatives from Burma, Nationalist China, Thailand and the U.S. was charged with the execution of this task. It succeeded in working out a plan which gave the KMT troops an opportunity to be evacuated to Formosa. Some of them, however, refused to be repatriated and remained in these border regions. The KMT Government in Formosa then disclaimed any responsibility for these elements. Burmese governmental forces still launch occasional assaults on these isolated KMT troops, but apparently not with complete success. A recent report estimated their number at 1330, although their immediate significance seems to have decreased.[15]

The border question with Communist China still retains its impending character. The lasting nature of this problem is demonstrated by the fact that, whatever the political differences of the various Chinese regimes which came to power in quick succession, all had one thing in common, namely that none of them ever relinuished its claims to the disputed border-areas. The Imperial,

[14] For a complete account of the KMT activities, see the publication of the Ministry of Information at Rangoon: *KMT Aggression against Burma* (1953).
[15] *The Times* (London), 10 February 1959.

Nationalist, as well as the Communist regimes, all made it clear from time to time that they maintained their full claims. The present Communist regime gave evidence of the position it took when it became suddenly clear in 1956 that about 5000 of its regular Chinese troops had in fact occupied certain areas in the Wa State (between Nam Ting and Nam Hka rivers) for about three years.[16] These were areas which Burma considered to be clearly part of her territory after the Chinese acceptance of the proposals of the Iselin Committee in 1941. These Chinese military moves underlined once more the great need for fixed boundary lines for the four disputed areas, namely in the extreme north, in the area between the Irrawaddy and the Salween, in the Namwan Assigned Tract, and in the Wa State between the Nam Ting and the Nam Hka.

The importance of this issue for Burma was once again proved in October 1956 when U Nu, the ex-premier and head of the ruling Anti-Fascist People's Freedom League (AFPFL) Party, went to Peking to try to straighten out these matters with Premier Chou En-lai. On November 9 an understanding was reached which seemed to favour the Burmese. The Chinese were willing to withdraw their invading forces behind the 1941 line with the only exception that they intended to stay in the three villages of Hpimaw, Gawlum and Kangfang, as well as in the Namwan Assigned Tract. The significance of these village tracts lies in the fact that they dominate the Hpimaw pass, the main entrance from Yunnan into Eastern Tibet, Assam and Central Burma.[17]

The other claim to which the Chinese stuck tenaciously was the Namwan Assigned Tract, a 100-square miles area near Bhamo which derives its importance from the fact that the main north-south route, linking the Kachin and the Shan states, passes through its territory. By the treaty of 1897 it had been made into a "perpetual lease" to Britain, but the Chinese never considered this stipulation as meaning the termination of their sovereignty and they had made frequent efforts to regain it. Since 1948 the Chinese had also refused to accept the annual rent of R. 1000,— from the Burmese Government so as to express their dissatisfaction with the situation.[18]

In brief, the results of the Peking talks were that, with the ex-

[16] Hinton, *op. cit. supra* note 11, at 53; Tinker *supra* note 11, at 344.
[17] Hinton, *op. cit. supra* note 11, at 53.
[18] *N.Y. Times*, December 11, 1956.

ception of the above-mentioned reservations, China was willing to renounce her rights to the areas in dispute. Delighted about the outcome of his talks, U Nu called the Chinese proposals "fair and just," but at home many disagreed, particularly the border peoples concerned. Part of the press also joined the ranks of the opponents and strong criticism was heard in these circles.[19] As a result no definite solution could be reached. In December 1956, new attempts were made to settle the problems. This time Chou En-lai came to Burma. Together with Premier Ba Swe he visited the border areas and these leaders held a conference in Mangshih on Yunnan territory.[20] By this time, however, the Burmese were asking for more concessions from the Chinese and at first rumours were heard in Burma that the Chinese were willing to renounce their rights to the Namwan Assigned Tract. However, nothing of this kind materialized during the next few years.[21]

2. The Question of Authority in the Disputed Territories

In order to extract from the above events the legal aspects of the case it is necessary to concentrate on two sets of facts. First, one has to determine the territories which are in actual dispute, and secondly the relevant treaties and agreements should be examined.

Following the borderline from the extreme north downwards, the border areas, which form the basis for the conflicting claims, are:[22]

(1) The extreme northern boundary of the Kachin State constituting the eastern part of the Mac Mahon Line of 1914.
(2) The general Irrawaddy-Salween watershed up to the 25^0 $35'$ N parallel including the village tracts of Hpimaw, Gawlum and Kangfang.
(3) The Namwan Assigned Tract, a 100-square miles area near Bhamo in the Southern Kachin State.
(4) The Wa border area between the Nam Ting and the Nam Hka, a stretch of 200 miles (the so-called Iselin-line or 1941-line).[23]

[19] *Ibid.* containing a quotation from The Nation.
[20] *N.Y. Times*, December 15, 1956.
[21] *Id.* December 20 and 21, 1956.
[22] Kozicki, "The Sino-Burmese Frontier Problem," 26 *Far Eastern Survey* 33 (1957).
[23] These are only the most important cases which have made headlines in recent times.

The treaties and agreements which have been concluded in connection with these areas, will be dealt with first in chronological order. They include:

(a) The "Peace Treaty" of Kaungton of 1770.
(b) The Peking Convention of 1886.
(c) The Convention of 1894.
(d) The Convention of 1897.
(e) The 1941-agreement.
(f) The Chou En-lai proposals.

(a) The "Peace Treaty" of Kaungton of 1770

For their historical rights on present Burmese territories the Chinese contend to be able to point back as far as the 3rd century in which time the Kingdom of Szechuan conquered Burma.[24] The subsequent changes of authority in these areas have already briefly been discussed. They are, in general, not backed by written documents. Such a document was not known until the 18th century when the Chinese again invaded Burmese territory. In spite of their numerical strength, they were repelled and later on even surrounded and forced to come to terms. The record says that the Burmese then showed themselves to be wise and tolerant victors by contenting themselves with moderate claims. At the Peace Treaty of Kaungton in 1770 it was laid down in a written agreement that "the Chinese were allowed to withdraw, trade was to be restored and, to prevent misunderstanding, decennial missions were to pass between the two sovereigns."[25] China also renounced all her rights to the Shan States of Mogaung and Mohnyin (Mongkong and Mongyang), but many other Shan states continued to owe allegiance to both Burma and China.[26]

These documents date from the pre-British time and their legal value today poses some problems, for it was not uncommon in those days to formulate a "peace treaty" which was not at all a correct

Burma has other unsettled frontiers, however. In the east there is an undefined frontier with India which has been further complicated by the presence on either side of the Naga people who present a problem to both countries since a separatist movement has developed in this tribe. Fifield, *The Diplomacy of Southeast Asia* 1945–1958, 213 (1958). Another case, yet unsolved, concerns the 21 islands in the Naaf-river which constitutes the boundary between Burma and Pakistan. *Id.* at 216.

[24] Stark Toller, *supra* note 12, at 12.

[25] Harvey, *History of Burma* (1945) quoted in Stark Toller, *supra* note 12, at 12.

[26] Tinker, *supra* note 6, at 332.

representation of the actual outcome of the war. The courteous ways in which a settlement was arrived at might easily lead to a misrepresentation of the real facts. Actually, the Chinese never regarded it as a peace treaty since Burma, which she regarded to be her vassal, could not possibly conclude a peace treaty with her. The Chinese, therefore, regarded the stipulation of decennial gift-bearing missions as a recognition by the Burmese of vassalage.[27]

(*b*) *The Peking Convention of 1886*

The appearance of the British in Upper Burma in 1885 and the resulting territorial disputes with China produced a number of other documents. One would perhaps expect the British not to submit to any commitment couched in terms so ambiguous as those contained in the above-mentioned Kaungton treaty. Yet they did. Perhaps because a stipulation of such a nominal suzerainty of China was established practice and inevitable if one wanted to achieve results in the negotiations. Moreover, such an attitude did not seem to lead to any practical complications, for each of the parties was able to maintain his own contradictory interpretations of the treaty stipulations without being actually forced to come to a showdown. The Peking Convention between Britain and China was a classical example of such an ambivalent document. This convention, which is called "Convention between Great Britain and China relative to Burmah and Thibet" (signed at Peking July 24, 1886, and ratifications exchanged at London on August 25, 1887) stated, *inter alia*, that:[28]

> *Art. I.* Inasmuch as it has been the practice to send decennial missions to present articles of local produce, England agrees that the highest authority in Burmah shall send the customary decennial missions, the members of the missions to be of Burmese race.
>
> *Art. II.* China agrees that in all matters whatsoever appertaining to the authority and rule which England is now exercising in Burmah, England shall be free to do whatsoever she deems right and proper.

[27] Kyaw Thet, "Some Aspects of Sino-Burmese Diplomacy in the Reign of Bodawpaya 1782–1819," in *Burma* (Rangoon) at 1 (July 1951).
[28] 77 *British and Foreign State Papers* 80–81 (1885–1886).

Art. III. The frontier between Burmah and China to be marked by a Delimitation Commission....

The document did not clarify the ambivalent juridical position and China, for example, read into the wording of this document a recognition of her historical rights over Burma. The missions, however, were never sent[29] and in 1894 a new treaty was concluded which was meant to give more attention to the demarcation of the borderline.

(c) *The Convention of 1894*

This document was officially called "Convention between Great Britain and China, giving effect to Art. III of the Convention of the 24th of July 1886, relative to Burmah and Thibet" (signed at London March 1, 1894, ratifications exchanged at London August 23, 1894).[30] However, the delimitation of the border was not completely successful. Although it was possible to define it in considerable detail from latitude 25° 35′ N (just above Myitkyina) southward to the Siamese border[31] the Convention was completely unable to come to an agreement on the part of the borderline north of this point.[32] This fact is of some importance and is laid down in Art. IV which operates to its fullest extent until today:

> It is agreed that the settlement and the delimitation of the portion of the frontier which lies to the North of latitude 25° 35′ shall be reserved for a future understanding between the High Contracting Parties when the feature and condition of the country are more accurately known.

In order to verify the agreed borderline, Art. VI called for a Joint (Boundary) Commission.[33]

China also received some concessions, for Britain recognized China's claim to the Namwan area, ceded, moreover, a portion of the North Hsenwi and the whole of the Kokang state and renounced all suzerain rights over Munglem and Kenghung, but with the condition that the latter two areas would not be ceded by China to a third state without a preceding agreement with Britain (Art. V). In spite of this commitment China did cede part of Kenghung to France in 1895, although apparently under duress. As a result

[29] Christian, *op. cit. supra* note 11, at 266.
[30] 87 *British and Foreign State Papers* 1311–1319 (1894–1895).
[31] Tinker, *supra* note 6, at 335.
[32] Stark Toller, *supra* note 12, at 12.
[33] 87 *British and Foreign State Papers* 1311–1319 (1894–1895).

Britain felt justified to demand a revision of the frontier by a new convention of 1897 which was to replace the 1894 Convention.

(d) *The Convention of 1897*

This new convention ("Agreement between Great Britain and China modifying the Convention of March 1, 1894 relative to Burmah and Thibet," signed at Peking February 4, 1897, ratifications exchanged at Peking June 5, 1897)[34] handed back the North Hsenwi strip and Kokang state to China, in the same way as the 1894 Convention, but the Namwan area was assigned to Britain in "perpetual lease" for an annual payment of 1,000 Rupees.[35] The relevant provisions are to be found in Art. II:

> Great Britain engages to recognize as belonging to China the tract to the South of the Namwan River, near Namkhai, which is enclosed to the West by a branch of the Nam Mak River and the Mawsiu range of hills up to Loi Chow Peak, and thence by the range running in a northeasterly direction to the Shweli River.
>
> In the whole of this area China shall not exercise any jurisdiction or authority whatever. The administration and control will be entirely by the British Government, who will hold it on a perpetual lease from China, paying a rent for it, the amount of which shall be fixed hereafter.[36]

Although the decennial missions were not mentioned here, it seemed that the idea was abandoned from this moment on.[37]

Art. IV of the 1894 Convention was adopted by the 1897 Convention without any addition[38] which meant, of course, that the boundary line north of 25° 35′ N remained undefined. The portion south of this point, however, was demarcated. This situation was confirmed in November 1956 when U Nu stated in a radio broadcast that the Sino-Burmese border north of the conical peak of 25° 35′ N had never been agreed upon and that China accepted the sections south of this point as having a "legal basis," with the exception of the 200-mile strip mentioned below.

Art. VI, which called for a Joint Commission, was indeed put into effect and this body succeeded in setting out a line of demarcation with the exception of the 200-mile stretch between the Nam Ting and the Nam Hka rivers enclosing the Wa State area.[39] Rumours

[34] 89 *British and Foreign State Papers* 25–30 (1896–1897).
[35] See Art. II which only stated that the amount would "be fixed hereafter."
[36] 89 *British and Foreign State Papers* 26 (1896–1897).
[37] Tinker, *supra* note 6, at 335.
[38] For Art. IV see *supra* at 123.
[39] Christian, *op. cit. supra* note 11, at 265.

about the presence of gold mines in this area might have added to the disagreement. Thus, this particular part of the border line was shelved and did not come up again for review until the President of the Council of the League of Nations was asked to nominate a neutral chairman for a new Joint Commission. In 1934 the Swiss Colonel Iselin was appointed to this post. The Iselin Commission[40] then set out to lay down a new border line. Its proposals, if they had been accepted, would seem to have favoured China over Britain. The hostilities between Japan and China, which broke out in 1937, interrupted, however, the work of the Commission.

Moreover, China was at first unwilling to accept the findings of the Commission and only in 1941 did the Chinese Government give its (grudging) approval to the implementation of the Commission's proposals.

(*e*) *The 1941-Agreement*

This agreement came into effect in June 1941 by an "Exchange of Notes between the United Kingdom and Burma with China concerning the Burma-Yunnan boundary."[41] The modifications of the general treaty line, as found by the Iselin Commission, were adopted by the Nationalist Government of the Republic of China, on the one hand, and H.M.'s Government in the United Kingdom and the Government of Burma as the successor in interest of the Government of India, on the other hand.

The Chinese, however, were very unhappy about the solution alleging that it was arrived at under duress. They tried to reopen negotiations on this border-case only a few months later, namely as early as August 1941,[42] but the outbreak of the Pacific War in December 1941 prevented such an undertaking.

After World War II China thought it desirable to make clear on the eve of the creation of the independent Union of Burma in 1947 that it had not waived its claims, an action which seemed understandable in the face of the pending significant changes which were to make independent Burma the successor to Great Britain in the

[40] 139 *British and Foreign State Papers* 165–167 (1935): "Exchange of Notes between the United Kingdom and India, and China regarding the establishment of a Commission to determine the Southern Section of the Burma-Yunnan Boundary," Nanking April 9, 1935.

[41] Stark Toller, *supra* note 12, at 13–14.

[42] –, "The Burma-China Frontier Dispute," 13 *The World Today* 91 (1957); Tinker, *supra* note 6, at 335–336.

case of the border areas. A bill, calling for a settlement of the Burma-Yunnan borderline, was introduced in the Legislative Yuan and is a clear reflection of the Chinese views. The bill stated, *inter alia*:[43]

(1) The undefined border region between the northern section of Burma and Yunnan province has long been occupied and governed by the British Empire. Protests as to its sovereignty were repeatedly made, but these have been unheeded by the British Government. Now that the British have granted autonomy to the Burmese Government, it is time for China to assert herself and ask for a settlement of the issue once for all.

(2) The Burmese Government has just incorporated the region in question together with Bhamo and Myitkyina into the so called Kachin country.

(3) The land in dispute is the gateway to Yunnan, Sikang and Tibet. For national defence purposes a speedy solution is of vital importance.

With the 1941-Agreement we have reached a milestone in the border question. It is, therefore, worthwhile to review at this point the entire situation.

(1) In North Burma the border was constituted by the Mac Mahon line which was the result of a conference between British, Tibetan and Chinese representatives at Simla in 1913–1914. Although Britain and Tibet accepted this line, China refused to sign the agreement and has consistently maintained her historic claims in the area.[44]

(2) The Irrawaddy-Salween watershed has never been accepted by any Chinese government either. Art. IV of the 1894 Convention (which is identical with Art. IV of the 1897 treaty) explicitly stresses the unsettled nature of the border and no agreement could be reached. Britain, however, was very anxious to make the watershed the actual boundary with China but she found China unwilling to give up certain areas west of that watershed, such as Hpimaw, Gawlum and Kangfang. China based her claims on a tribute-relationship, but the strategic importance of this area undoubtedly played a great part in the considerations of either party. Britain then offered to buy out China's rights but the Chinese

[43] Stark Toller, *supra* note 12, at 13.

[44] See Rubin, "The Sino-Indian Border Disputes," 9 *I.C.L.Q.* 96–125, at 97, 105–107 (1960).

understandably refused to accept this offer. Nevertheless, Britain proceeded to occupy these areas in 1913.[45]

(3) The Namwan Assigned Tract, in contrast to the two preceding border disputes seems, at first sight, to have a sound legal basis, namely, the Convention of 1897. However, a closer examination reveals that this document is not free from ambiguities. It contains a recognition of a territory as "belonging to China," a provision which is immediately neutralized, however, by another stipulation which excludes China's "jurisdiction and authority" over the same area. It is hardly conceivable that an independent state would voluntarily consent to waive its sovereignty over a territory of such strategic importance for the surprisingly low sum of R. 1000 a year. Indeed, China has subsequently held that it had signed the treaty under duress. According to international law, however, duress does not necessarily invalidate an agreement, particularly when such an agreement was made in a time when war was still recognized as a legitimate instrument of policy.[46] Nevertheless, the idea that a treaty signed under duress is binding for all time flouts all feelings of justice, and a so-called legislation by treaty will only result in the inevitable renunciation of that agreement at the earliest possible occasion. That moment has not yet arrived but China has now already demanded a renunciation and to express her disapproval of the situation she has since 1948 refused to accept the annual payment.

(4) Finally, there is the 1941-line which has not yet been brought to a satisfactory solution either. The Chinese have agreed, through an exchange of notes in 1941, to accept this demarcation but they have decried this document afterwards as another product of duress, since it was allegedly arrived at when China was involved in an internecine struggle with Japan. There is here a subtle difference, however, from the preceding case of alleged duress in the Namwan Assigned Tract. As has already been stated above, the rational basis of the treaty provisions with respect to the Namwan Assigned Tract, is – to put it mildly – very doubtful. On the other hand, the meaning of the provisions of the 1941-Agreement is perfectly clear. The enforced acceptance of these conditions, although apparently done in a moment of great national emergency, does not at all invalidate the treaty. Immoral though these actions might have

[45] 13 *The World Today, supra* note 42, at 91.
[46] 2 Oppenheim, *International Law* 802–803 (7th ed. 1952).

been, nothing seemed to indicate that China was forced to consent to a legal acceptance. She could have refused to agree. If Britain had then proceeded to implement, on her own initiative, the findings of the Iselin Commission (i.e. the 1941-line), the responsibility would have been entirely hers, and no legal binding force could have been derived from this act. As it was China accepted the 1941-line, probably in order to achieve a better bargaining position *vis-à-vis* Great Britain in her efforts to gain more foreign support for the struggle against Japan. If this is true then it seems hardly correct to give China in this case the benefit of the defence of duress.

(f) The Chou En-lai – U Nu proposals

A later development in this series of events came in October 1956. At that time ex-premier U Nu, in his role of leading Burmese statesman and head of the ruling AFPFL (Anti-Fascist People's Freedom League) Party, visited Peking where he had talks with the Chinese premier Chou En-lai. Among other things they discussed a long overdue settlement of the border issue. The results were very hopeful. China made the dramatic statement that she was willing to renounce all her claims to present Burmese territory with the only exception of the Namwan Assigned Tract and the three village tracts of Hpimaw, Gawlum and Kangfang. This meant, in effect, that China would accept the entire Sino-Burmese boundary line as it had been inherited by independent Burma from the British in August 1947.[47] U Nu endorsed these proposals as "fair and just," and at a press conference he went as far as to say that even without the records and documents relied upon by the Chinese he would be quite willing to cede to them the three village tracts in return for a permanent settlement of the border problem.[48]

As a first step towards the settlement the Chinese troops, which had infiltrated into Burmese territory, would be withdrawn behind the 1941-line, whereas the Burmese troops would be evacuated from the three villages.

At first the Burmese did not seem dissatisfied with the outcome of the Peking talks; their reactions were said to range from "qualified relief to some enthusiasm."[49] Thus, there seemed to be a fair

[47] Kozicki, *supra* note 22, at 35.
[48] *N.Y. Times*, November 11, 1956; *The Nation*, November 11, 1956; see also Kozicki, *supra* note 22, at 35, footnote 9.
[49] Kozicki, *supra* note 22, at 35.

chance that the proposals would be accepted in both countries. Such an acceptance would have permanently disposed of the long-standing border issue. Unfortunately public opinion seemed to have, changed considerably afterwards and U Nu was unable to assure himself of the necessary support to get these proposals through parliament. The Constitution prevents the cession of Burmese territory, however, without the consent of the State Council of the component state concerned. The Kachin State Council, in whose jurisdiction lies the Namwan Assigned Tract as well as the three village tracts, was unable to come to any decision on the issue,[50] which again stalled a possible settlement. Thus, the "fair and just" proposals did not bring the party much closer to the desired solution. Yet it may be said that these proposals have a certain merit, in that they have become a concrete basis for any future negotiations.

3. Decisions by International Courts

It is appropriate in this context to take counsel with cases on border disputes as dealt with by international courts. Unfortunately, they are not of much use for our particular case. For in the first place "as a rule... the two international courts dealt only incidentally with frontier questions when called upon to interpret international treaties or other instruments of an international character.... Thus the Permanent Court of Arbitration and the World Court had but little opportunity to elaborate guiding principles which should govern the actual delimitation of frontiers."[51]

Secondly, the Sino-Burmese border issue is not so much a matter of correct delimitation of the actual frontier as a dispute on the validity of competing territorial claims. From this point of view it is worth quoting from the Palmas case[52] that the "display of sovereignty – if merely in isolated cases – carries greater weight than the contiguity of territory and the existence of natural boundaries."[53] With "sovereignty" is obviously meant here the display of effective control. The mere issue of maps, for instance, on which certain territories are simply annexed – as has frequently been done by these countries – cannot be called a display of sovereignty and is, therefore, without legal effect. In other words, however practical and

[50] *Id.* at 37.
[51] 1 Schwarzenberger, *International Law* 313 (1957).
[52] U. N., 2 *Reports of International Arbitral Awards* 831–871 (1949).
[53] *Id.* at 839.

desirable it may be to introduce a natural boundary – especially in uninhabited and unexplored areas – such a consideration has to yield to evidence of display of actual control in the areas concerned. Therefore, the British actions to create a "scientific" or "natural" frontier by making the Irrawaddy-Salween watershed the eastern boundary line would have been justified only if no such display of sovereignty by others had been made there in the past. However, there has been no lack of such display of sovereignty; on the contrary, the problem is exactly to decide whose display must be regarded as superior, that of the British or of the Chinese. The historical facts are not very clear. They are, moreover, complicated by regional concepts of allegiance, tribute and vassalage. Dealing with another boundary problem, the World Court held in the Mosul case (1925)[54] that the settlement depended in the main on considerations "not of a legal nature." The Court made here the traditional distinction between legal and non-legal matters with the apparent implication that the latter were not suitable for a decision by international law. Such a restrictive view of the function of international law cannot fail to diminish its value as a decision-making process for interactions of participants in the world community. It is very likely that Burma and China, although still adhering to the traditional views on international law, were simultaneously well aware of the limited prospects of a solution when their claims were balanced according to "purely legal" principles only. They have, therefore, shown no inclination whatsoever to submit their dispute to a decision on the basis of traditional international law.

4. Final Observations

In traditional terms a border issue is a case of territorial jurisdiction involving the matter of sovereignty. Yet what stands out in our particular case is the remarkably rare use which is made of the term "sovereignty" in the mutual claims. This is all the more remarkable as, ever since the nationalist movements grew in power, the Asian nations have been talking and thinking in terms of "sovereignty," whatever meaning they may have attached to it. The Burmese have not used it in connection with their border disputes at all. The Chinese only occasionally made a statement

[54] Schwarzenberger, *op. cit. supra* note 51, at 313–314.

on sovereignty. For example, with respect to the Namwan Assigned Tract a direct reference is made to the concept of sovereignty, where it is stated that the existence of a "perpetual lease" is contrary to the dignity of a sovereign state.[55]

Parties have also refrained from attempting to clarify the ever-present phenomenon of suzerainty or vassalage in terms of traditional international law. Probably they sensed the futility of such an effort. Suzerainty, as applied in this part of the world, has a particular meaning, and this Western term of suzerainty has only been used for purposes of convenience to describe as closely as possible a non-Western institution. The actual nature of this regional type of suzerainty is in certain respects quite different from the same term as understood in Western international law. In the latter it usually denotes a relationship between a suzerain state, which represents its vassal in international affairs, and a half-sovereign vassal state with only internal independence.[56] In our case the more symbolic nature of the Chinese tribute system flouts any attempt to fit it perfectly into the Western concept of suzerainty. The Asian type of suzerainty, namely, a suzerain power which contents itself with periodical gifts of its vassal who, but for that, is entirely independent, has no place in the system of modern international law. This does not mean that the case is to the parties entirely devoid of legal significance. Parties have even stated at one time that they were willing to settle the dispute on the "legal basis" of existing treaties.[57] In general, however, parties have approached the problem on a broader basis which seems to agree with the meaning, though not with the wording, of the holding of the World Court that settlement of disputes of this nature depended in the main on considerations "not of a legal nature."[58] This statement apparently concedes that international law, as it is applied here, is not capable of solving community problems with important factual implications of a historical, cartographical, topographical and anthropological nature.

Historically, the claims put forward by both parties relied principally on the relationships established as a result of the tributary payments of the border peoples to China.[59] The Chinese

[55] See further the bill introduced in the Legislative Yuan, *supra* note 43.

[56] 2 Oppenheim, *op. cit. supra* note 46, at 188–190 (8th ed. 1955).

[57] Kozicki, *supra* note 22 at 35; *The World Today*, *supra* note 42, at 90.

[58] See Schwarzenberger, *op. cit. supra* note 51 at 313.

[59] With respect to Burma: *The World Today*, *supra* note 42, at 36; for China, see Stark Toller, *supra* note 12, at 12.

contend that the tributary payments have established the allegiance of the border areas to her authority. This, however, seems to give China the benefit of all the Western implications of the term "suzerain" which, as already pointed out above, had only been used for descriptive purposes and not with the intention of equating Asian suzerainty with the concept as used in Western countries. The real nature of this institution is better represented by the following description:

> The Manchus afterwards regarded this settlement (=the "Peace Treaty" of Kaungton)[60] as an admission of regular tributary or vassal states of the Manchu Empire and much subsequent Chinese policy toward Burma has been based on the assumption that this view is correct....
>
> The Burmese kings, however, did not regard themselves as vassals; if they understood the Chinese attitude, they probably considered that it would be unnecessary and perhaps unwise, to make an issue of it. It was on this ambiguous basis that the first Burmese effort, at least in modern times, to maintain regular foreign relations began.[61]

The influence of historical facts is further reflected in cartographical evidence. The maps of both parties show all the effects of confusion, prematureness and arbitrariness. It should again be stated, however, that – contrary to the impression in many sources – the arbitrariness was not an exclusively Chinese characteristic. The preceding pages have tried to show that they had good cause to stand firm on some of their claims. It is true that some Chinese maps – even those issued by authoritative bodies – show clearly that China had rather prematurely included disputed territories into her territory.[62] On the other hand, English maps, including the official map of the Burma Railways of 1935, seemed to have recognized certain Chinese claims, for example, with respect to the area east of the Nmai Kha, a mistake which was soon thereafter rectified.[63]

Topographically, the desirability of natural boundaries in such inaccessible areas has already been discussed above.[64] As has been explained, such a practical solution had to yield to the stronger argument of display of sovereignty.

Anthropological considerations also contribute to the problem. It is generally contended that the origin of the Burmese people lies in Southwest China, and such a statement is generally followed by

[60] *Supra* at 121.
[61] Hinton, *op. cit. supra* note 11, at 32.
[62] *Id.* at 40.
[63] Stark Toller, *supra* note 12, at 12.
[64] See *supra* at 130.

the observation that culturally, however, not China, but India and Ceylon have had the greatest impact on Burmese society.[65] Whatever the truth of this statement, it would perhaps be better to examine the opinions and sympathies of the border peoples themselves *vis-à-vis* the Chinese and Burmese. Here, however, we run again into the general difficulty of lack of sufficient and relevant information. As far as we can judge from the scant material which is available, it seems that most border peoples are happy with the present situation, that is to say, they favour their inclusion in the Union of Burma. The ruling government party is apparently working hard to convince the Kachin border peoples that a cession of the village tracts of Hpimaw, Gawlum and Kangfang, and of the Namwan Assigned Tract, in return for a permanent border line is an inevitable sacrifice, but the Kachins have not taken so easily to this idea. Especially those now living in the territories claimed by China were said to have resisted the move and have expressed the wish to be evacuated to other Burmese territories in case the cession would be carried out.[66]

A review of all these relevant facts points out that Communist China's claims are not totally devoid of some justification. Statements denying this, which have found easy acceptance, should be viewed with some reservation. One such statement has been put forward by a writer who says bluntly that the Chinese Communists "have employed the Chinese Nationalists' technique of claiming territory not through conquest, colonization or negotiation, but simply by drawing the desired boundary on a map."[67] This statement does not give due consideration to the factual background of the case. For if one does, then it cannot be denied that China has some good claims to certain territories.

It is characteristic of the Burmese views that they themselves do not go as far as some of the foreign authors by accusing the Chinese of arbitrary practices in setting out the border lines. In fact the Burmese leaders have stated on various occasions that the problem only resulted from the fact that the border was not precisely defined[68] and that there was no question at all of Chinese aggression.[69]

[65] Hinton, *op. cit. supra* note 11, at 29–30.
[66] Kozicki, *supra* note 22 at 35–37.
[67] Hinton, *op. cit. supra* note 11, at 40.
[68] *The World Today*, *supra* note 42 at 86; Kozicki, *supra* note 22, at 35.
[69] The problem of subversion by an increasing number of Chinese immigrants, however, has the Burmese authorities very worried.

Summarizing it can be said that both parties were well aware that traditional international law considered itself incapable or unauthorized to deal with "non-legal" matters. However, since in their eyes these so-called non-legal matters weigh heavily they seem unwilling to submit the dispute to a decision based on such a restrictive interpretation of international law. What they needed was a settlement by a process which gives due consideration to all relevant facts and events. Only then will a decision be reached which parties will regard as both authoritative and controlling. The most suitable way to arrive – under the present circumstances – at a reasonable solution appears to be the use of the policy instrument of diplomacy. Recently (February 1960), this has indeed resulted in an agreement which struck a balance between the conflicting claims. It was decided to establish a joint boundary commission which would determine the northern border (Mac Mahon line). Burma would retain the Namwan Assigned Tract, while the three village tracts of Hpimaw, Gawlum and Kangfang would go to China, as well as part of the Wa Area along the 1941 line.[70] If the joint boundary commission would be able to agree on the delimitation of the borderline, the prospects of a peaceful and final solution are bright.

THE KASHMIR CONFLICT

Kashmir did not become an international issue until the Indian sub-continent was divided into the two new dominions of India and Pakistan in 1947.[71] Prior to that time the State of Kashmir and Jammu (conveniently abbreviated here to Kashmir) carried on its existence in a more peaceful way as one of the five hundred odd princely or native states which were scattered over the Indian subcontinent. It would most probably have been able to continue that peaceful existence if the passing of powers could have been made to only one all-embracing new state. However, when the pro-India and pro-Pakistan populations of this British dependency came to accept the idea of partition as an inevitable event they unknowing-

[70] *The Observer* (London), February 7, 1960, p. 5, col. 1. For the significance of the Chinese-Burmese frontier agreement for India, see *The Guardian* (Manchester), February 1, 1960, p. 9.

[71] See Prem Nath Bazaz, *History of the Struggle for Freedom by Kashmir* (1954); Birdwood, *Two Nations and Kashmir* (1956); Brecher, *The Struggle for Kashmir* (1953).

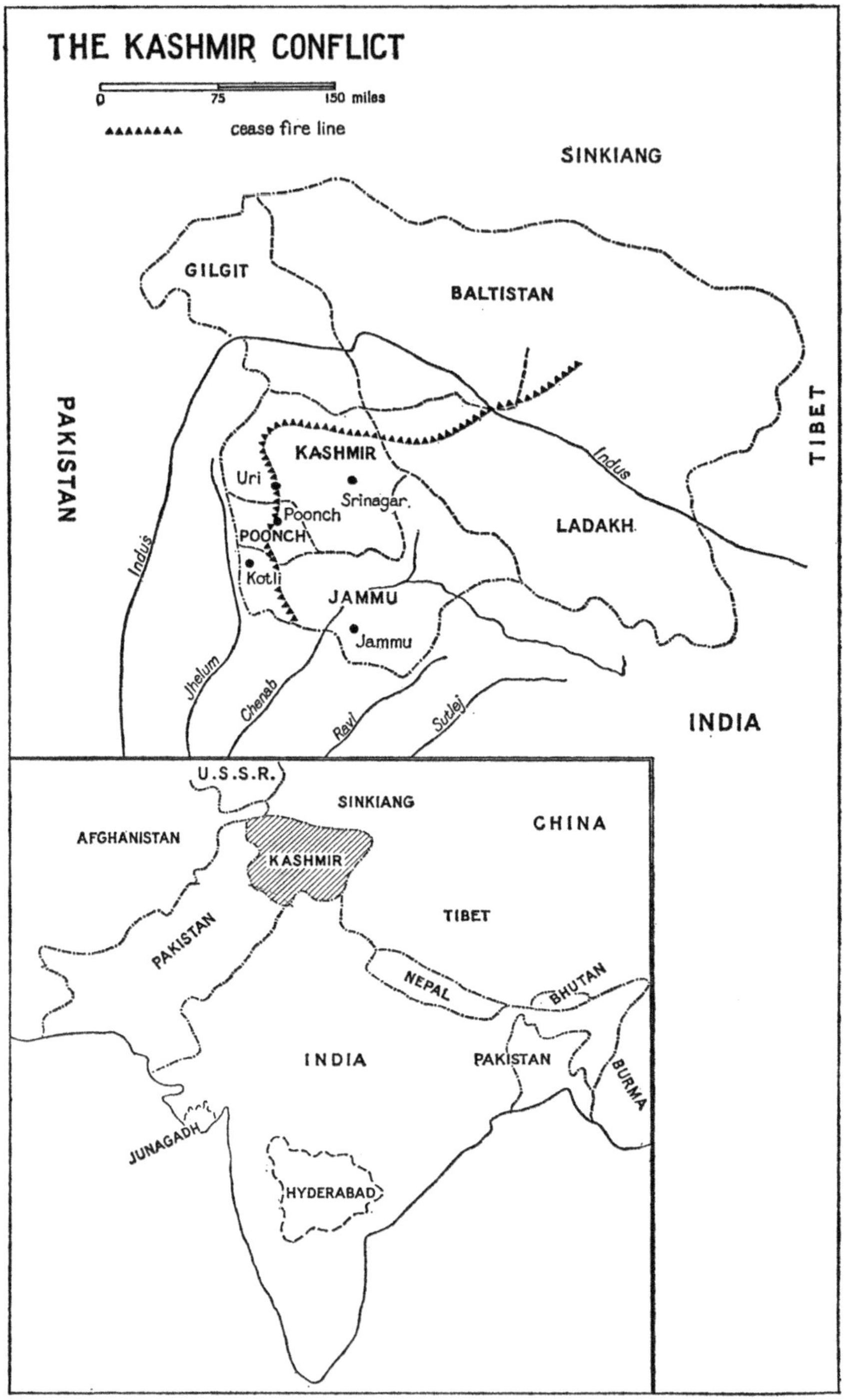
THE KASHMIR CONFLICT
0
75
150 miles
cease fire line
SINKIANG
GILGIT
BALTISTAN
PAKISTAN
TIBET
KASHMIR
Uri
Srinagar
Poonch
POONCH
Kotli
LADAKH
JAMMU
Jammu
Indus
Indus
Jhelum
Chenab
Ravi
Sutlej
INDIA
U.S.S.R.
SINKIANG
CHINA
AFGHANISTAN
KASHMIR
TIBET
PAKISTAN
NEPAL
BHUTAN
INDIA
PAKISTAN
BURMA
JUNAGADH
HYDERABAD

ly set the stage for some of the bitterest conflicts which have raged in this part of the world in recent times. Although the projected solution for the Princely States in the new political structure of the area seemed, theoretically at least, sound and guaranteed a prosperous future as integrated parts of either dominion, subsequent events did not entirely fulfil those expectations.

Today, thirteen years after partition, relations between Pakistan and India are still very much strained as a result of violent clashes which took place after the transformation of this dependency into the two independent, sovereign states. These relations are not likely to improve very soon, in spite of the clear and undeniable interdependence of both countries in many fields. Kashmir is perhaps the most important cause of the cool political relationship between the two countries and an improvement can only be achieved if both parties are willing to compromise their present rigid positions.

The significance of the Kashmir state is enhanced by the important fact that, on or near its borders, India, Pakistan, Russia, China and Afghanistan meet each other, thus making it perfectly clear that the issue has more than just local significance. It is not imaginary that an armed dispute between India and Pakistan will develop into a conflict of world proportions.[72]

The Kashmir conflict will be discussed here by giving due attention to claims and counterclaims of the contending parties. It has one important difference from the Burma-Yunnan border dispute discussed above. Whereas the latter is strongly linked to old, historic rights, the Kashmir problem is not dominated by historic arguments. Since it is entirely the result of the recent inception of the parties, it also represents their contemporary views on matters of international relations and law.

1. Genesis of the Kashmir Conflict

The State of Jammu and Kashmir, which leans against the great Himalayan mountain range, is bordered to the north by China (Sinkian), the U.S.S.R. (Turkestan) and Afghanistan, on the west by West Pakistan, on the south by India and on the east by Tibet.[73] The territory of the state comprises the province of Jammu, the

[72] Zafrullah Khan, *The Kashmir Question* 5 (1950); Potter, "Principal Legal and Political Problems Involved in the Kashmir Case," 44 *A.J.I.L.* 362 (1950).

[73] See map of Kashmir, facing this page.

province of Kashmir, and further the administrative districts of Ladakh, Baltistan, Gilgit and Poonch Jagir.[74] With its 84,471 square miles (approximately equal to Great Britain) it is the largest and one of the most important of the Princely States. It was ruled by a Maharadja who was very unpopular with the Moslem majority of the four million population.

The effects of World War II and its aftermath, which brought about such violent and thorough changes on the political map of Asia, did not bypass the Indian subcontinent (and thus Kashmir). Under strong Indian nationalistic pressure Britain finally decided to grant independence to the two major groups in this territory and in 1947 the Indian Independence Act was passed dividing British India into the two new Dominions of India and Pakistan.

The Act also dealt with the Princely States. In the British time the relationship between these states and their overlord, the British Crown, used to be described by that peculiar term "paramountcy," a term which defies any clear-cut definition since "it epitomized a whole complex of shifting relations,"[75] though it worked perfectly well in regulating the mutual relationship of the Crown and the native states. Rather than trying to explain this vague concept of paramountcy, it may be worthwhile to cite an authority on the subject who describes it in the following way:

> Broadly speaking, it meant on the one hand that the Crown was bound to protect the rulers and their dynasties from external aggression and internal revolt, while ordinarily abstaining from interference in the domestic government of their territories; on the other, it meant that the rulers acknowledged the suzerainty of the Crown, involving its right to conduct their foreign relations..., requisition military forces..., regulate disputed successions, conduct minority administrations, and intervene in their internal affairs in cases of gross misrule. These mutual obligations resulted in a peculiar position in which the ultimate sovereignty had passed to the British power, yet no British or British Indian authority could make laws for any state. The territories of the Indian Rulers had not become British territory, nor were their inhabitants British subjects.[76]

Although in many cases the mutual relationship was defined by way of treaties or other agreements, there were other examples (especially in the case of smaller states) where it was not substantiated by any document; in these cases it had become based on "usage and sufferance."[77]

[74] Mayfield, "A Geographical Study of the Kashmir Issue," 45 *Geographical Rev.* 181, note 3 (1955).

[75] Lumby, *The Transfer of Power in India 1945–47*, 203 (1954).

[76] *Id.* at 203–204.

[77] *Id.* at 204.

The Independence Act of 1947 had the peculiar effect of terminating the suzerain power of the British Crown without explicitly defining the new status of the Indian states. As a result a controversy arose as to whether the lapse of paramountcy re-established the former sovereign position of the native states, or whether it resulted in the passing of that same sovereign authority to the newly created states of India and Pakistan as the successors to British authority.[78]

The Act, however, did mention the right of the Princely States to accede to either Pakistan or India or, if they so desired, to continue their existence as independent states outside either dominion.[79] It was this possibility to remain independent which subsequently gave rise to some delicate problems concerning the extent of freedom enjoyed by the States in making their final choice. For, theoretically, it would have been quite possible that of the 562 states a fair number would decide to stake its claim in the status of an independent, sovereign state. Such an unfortunate decision would undoubtedly have caused political chaos. The controversy, however, was never actually decided on its own merits for other considerations were taken into account which provided an easier and more practical solution.[80]

Anticipating the problems which would arise from such a difficult choice, Lord Louis Mountbatten, the last Viceroy, tried to set up some principles which were to guide the princes in making their decisions. Although he explicitly admitted the complete freedom of the Princely States to opt for an independent existence, he advised them to accede to India or Pakistan. In their decisions they should not ignore certain compulsions and considerations. They were:[81]

(1) Geographical compulsions or geograpical contiguity.
(2) Communal composition of the state.
(3) Economic and strategic considerations.

Taking these factors into consideration, few states would have difficulties in deciding their future. Yet in many instances the decision was not made enthusiastically. There were many delaying

[78] See *infra* note 114 & 115.

[79] Diwan, "Kashmir and the Indian Union – The Legal Position," 2 *I.C.L.Q.* 338–339 (1953).

[80] Prime Minister Attlee advised the Princely States not to isolate themselves from the rest of India; see Diwan, *supra* note 79, at 339.

[81] Nawaz, "The Kashmir Problem," 2 *I.Y.I.A.* 184 (1953).

activities and much procrastination. Giving up as cherished a privilege as sovereignty has seldom been done enthusiastically by any ruler and in this case the Indian Rulers finally got a chance to reconquer a long lost prerogative. Therefore, their enthusiasm to subject themselves to the over-all authority of the Indian Government was not always very great. Some of the princes tried to make a bargain with the dominion governments in order to retain as many privileges and benefits as possible.[82] In fact, the implementation of these provisions of option would have been far less successful if the states had been left entirely free to make up their minds. Instead, however, the obvious choice was often "tactfully suggested" and by a "mingled process of coercion and persuasion" almost all states made a decision and signed an Instrument of Accession to one of the Dominions.[83] The subtle pressure, which was exerted by the dominion governments, was in a sense not unreasonable in view of the impossible situation which would have arisen had the states in fact made use of their right to remain independent, regardless of any practical compulsion. The weight of these factors, especially the communal composition and the will of the majority of the population, facilitated a choice in all cases except three, viz., with respect to the State of Junagadh, Hyderabad and the present case of Jammu and Kashmir. The issues involved in the first two states bear not only much similarity to those in Kashmir, but they have at the same time been used as a precedent for the latter case. Their connection with the Kashmir case, therefore, justifies a brief examination of the developments in those two states.

Junagadh, situated close, but not immediately adjacent, to the Pakistan border was ruled by a Moslem prince and populated by a majority of Hindus. Using his legitimate right of option, the Moslem ruler unwisely ignored the wishes of his people and acceded to Pakistan. The accession was accepted by this dominion but the resentment of the Junagadh people took such a violent character that the ruler fled to Pakistan. The representative body of Junagadh then requested India to take over the maintenance of law and order which was actually done. After this the accession of the State of Junagadh to India became only a matter of time and organization and it mattered little that afterwards a plebiscite was organized which clearly and unequivocally confirmed the desire

[82] Diwan, *supra* note 79, at 340.
[83] Birdwood, *op. cit. supra* note 71, at 39.

of the Junagadh people to accede to the Union of India.[84]

The case of the state of Hyderabad was of a more complicated nature, since it was situated in the heart of the Indian Dominion. It had a Moslem ruler and a majority population of Hindus. The Moslem Nizam, however, used his right of option by stating that he would remain independent, thus disregarding the pressure from the Hindu majority of his people for an accession to India. India did not consent to his act, but instead it was willing to sign a Standstill Agreement with Hyderabad for one year. Whether the choice of the Nizam was the principal cause for ensuing troubles, or whether there was also considerable agitation from outside the state territory is hard to tell. It is a fact, however, that, as a result of the chaos which threatened the State of Hyderabad, India felt justified to take a "police action" and moved its troops into the territory of Hyderabad. Subsequently, the Nizam acknowledged "his misgovernment and the violation of the (Standstill) Agreement by some of his ministers," and consented to accession to India.[85]

The case of the State of Jammu and Kashmir was in so far exceptional that the factual compulsion did not apply so directly as in the preceding states. On the basis of her geographical position, it might well have been possible for Kashmir to enjoy an independent status if she would only have been allowed to do so, but – as we will see – she was not given that opportunity. This resulted in the famous Kashmir dispute which will be the subject dealt with here.

The Maharadja of Kashmir, a Hindu prince, did not immediately decide to join either dominion. Instead he stated on August 12, 1947, that he would approach the governments of both Pakistan and the Union of India and offer them to sign a Standstill Agreement which, in effect, would continue the pre-partition status-quo with regard to its post, telegraph and railways communications till such a time that Kashmir would be able to decide its future.[86] India rejected the proposal for the Standstill Agreement fearing that this would only encourage a policy of independence by the Maharadja. Pakistan, which had by an earlier agreement provisionally taken care of the communications of Kashmir, was

[84] Nawaz, *supra* note 81, at 185; Lumby, *supra* note 75, at 244; Zafrullah Khan, *supra* note 72, at 6, 9–10.

[85] Das, "The Status of Hyderabad during and after British Rule in India," 43 *A.J.I.L.* 71–72 (1949); Nawaz, *supra* note 81, at 185; Zafrullah Khan, *supra* note 72, at 9.

[86] Griffith, *Modern Burma* 140 (1957); Symonds, *The Making of Pakistan* 157 (1950); Birdwood, *op. cit. supra* note 71, at 40.

equally anxious for Kashmir to make her decision and she exerted pressure on Kashmir in the form of an economic blockade. When riots broke out in the Moslem district of Poonch, they were ruthlessly suppressed by the Hindu state-troops. This, in turn, provoked Moslem tribes from beyond the Pakistan border in the North West Frontier Province to "come to the rescue" of their Kashmir kinsmen.[87]

The next development was the creation by the Moslem population of an Azad (Free) Kashmir Government which managed to drive the State troops out of Poonch and threatened to launch another invasion in the province of Kashmir in which lies the capital of Srinagar. The Maharadja, in panic, appealed to the Indian Government for military support; and when it was not directly granted, he offered to accede to India in return for the necessary military support. India now accepted the offer and the very next day troops were flown to Kashmir which managed to put an end to the tribal invasion in the centre of the Kashmir state.

India's acceptance of the Maharadja's accession was made on the condition of a subsequent plebiscite, for Lord Louis Mountbatten, then the first Governor General of the Union of India, made it very clear in his reply to the Maharadja on 27 October, 1947, that:

> In consistence with their policy that in the case of any state where the issue of accession has been the subject of a dispute the question of accession should be decided in accordance with the wishes of the people of the state, it is my government's wish that, as soon as law and order have been restored in Kashmir and its soil cleared of the invader, the question of the State's accession should be settled by a reference to the people.[88]

Prime Minister Nehru repeated this wish for a plebiscite; and since such a plebiscite had always been one of Pakistan's main conditions, it became the main point of agreement between the two countries during the entire duration of the dispute.

Meanwhile the Indian troops had succeeded in driving back the tribes behind the Kotli-Poonch-Uri line, but they had to stop there lacking the service of good roads beyond that line.[89] Pakistan troops also crossed the border and joined the Azad Kashmir forces. An all-out war was imminent. Fortunately, however, both parties seemed

[87] Mayfield, *supra* note 74, at 182; Diwan, *supra* note 79, at 341.
[88] Birdwood, *op. cit. supra* note 71, at 214, App. V.
[89] Griffith, *op. cit. supra* note 86, at 150. See also map of Kashmir, facing p. 135.

to avoid an open clash and the stalemate was later on to be sealed by a cease-fire agreement. The waiting was now for the promised plebiscite, but this was the only part of the agreement that could not be implemented to the satisfaction of both parties. The crux of the matter was the question as to who was to govern Kashmir during the plebiscite. India maintained that Kashmir had become constitutionally a part of the Indian Union after the Maharadja had signed the Instrument of Accession and that she thus had the duty to exercise her authority. Pakistan objected to this, maintaining that a plebiscite under such Indian supervision would not be free and impartial and would make a farce of the whole plebiscite.

Not being able to come to any compromise, both parties considered taking the case to the United Nations. Finally, it was India which referred the Kashmir dispute to the Security Council of the United Nations where she charged Pakistan with violation of her sovereignty by assisting the tribes in their invasion. India accused Pakistan under article 35 of the Charter of committing aggression and asked the Security Council to call upon Pakistan to cease assisting the tribes in any way. Pakistan, on the other hand, still infuriated by the accession of the Maharadja to India, retorted by questioning the legality of the Maharadja's act as being based on fraud and violence; and she, in turn, invoked article 35 of the Charter to charge India, *inter alia*, with breach of international agreement and incitement to revolution.[90] Pakistan further requested the Security Council to appoint a commission of investigation and to prepare for a plebiscite. Such a commission (United Nations Commission for India and Pakistan, or UNCIP) was established on January 20, 1948.[91] The Commission, after having arrived on the scene, made a study of the situation and passed a resolution on August 13, 1948, calling for a cease-fire agreement which was finally concluded on January 1, 1949.[92] East of the cease-fire line India took possession of Kashmir territory, whereas the western part was occupied by Pakistan forces and administered by the Azad Kashmir Government.

The Commission also called for a demilitarization of Kashmir and a confirmation by both parties of the plebiscite principle.[93] When both sides accepted these proposals the UNCIP proceeded to

[90] Nawaz, *supra* note 81, at 187.
[91] *U.N. Security Council* (S/654), January 20, 1948.
[92] For the text of this agreement, see *U.N. Security Council* (S/955), August 13, 1948.
[93] Birdwood, *op. cit. supra* note 71, at 217, App. VIII.

pass a second resolution on January 5, 1949[94] which made provisions for the accession of Kashmir to India or Pakistan "through the democratic method of a free and impartial plebiscite." To this end it was proposed that the Security Council should nominate a Plebiscite Administrator who would be formally appointed by the Government of Kashmir. The general principles of the plebiscite, as laid down in this resolution, were again accepted by both parties, but further implementation again failed to materialize,[95] mainly because of a difference of interpretation regarding the withdrawal of troops. This deadlock has continued to exist till the present day, in spite of the appointment of Admiral Chester Nimitz of the U.S.A. as Plebiscite Administrator and the subsequent efforts by two U.N. mediators (Sir Owen Dixon of Australia, and Dr. Frank Graham of the U.S.A.).[96]

Internal political development in Kashmir did not contribute to a quick solution. After the accession to India in October 1947, the Maharadja charged Sheikh Abdullah with the formation of an administration. Sheikh Abdullah, a Moslem, and originally a member of the Muslim League of Kashmir, left the party in 1938 to form the National Conference which became the strongest political party in Kashmir. Owing also to his friendship with Nehru and his great influence on the people of Kashmir, he became the accepted leader of this state. In the first years after having taken office he clearly showed pro-Indian sympathies but a few years later his enthusiasm for India dropped and he leaned more and more to the idea of Kashmir as an independent state. In 1953 he was arrested and put in jail. His successor, Bakshi Ghulam Mohammad, was known for his pro-Indian sympathies. Subsequently, the trend in Kashmir became clearly one of a greater integration with India and it was even officially stated that accession was no longer a problem since Kashmir had acceded for good to India, an opinion which received public approval of Prime Minister Nehru.[97] Ignoring Pakistan's angry protests, India and Kashmir went ahead and on January 26, 1957, the constitution of Kashmir converted this state into a component unit of the Union of India, although reserving for itself certain autonomous privileges. India then de-

[94] *U.N. Security Council* (S/1192), Jan. 5, 1949.
[95] Nawaz, *supra* note 81, at 189; Zafrullah Khan, *supra* note 72, at 27–32.
[96] Birdwood, *op. cit. supra* note 71, at 221, App. X; Nawaz, *supra* note 81, at 190.
[97] Griffith, *op. cit. supra* note 86, at 152.

clared that she regarded the Kashmir question as closed,[98] an attitude greatly resented by her Pakistan neighbour.

For her part Pakistan had meanwhile concluded defence agreements with some other countries, e.g. with Turkey and the U.S. (in 1954). She also joined the collective security agreement of the South East Asia Treaty Organization in September 1954 and the Baghdad Pact in September 1955, thus building up her military power. The inevitable result of these military measures was that India regarded these actions as an effort not for defence purposes, but to increase the offensive power of the Pakistan forces in order to impose eventually a military solution of the Kashmir dispute. Consequently, India felt justified in reconsidering her views on the validity of the earlier concluded agreements.

2. *The Origin of Authority in the Kashmir Conflict*

As in any other territorial dispute, the Kashmir case centers around matters of formal authority and effective control. In traditional terms this means that it concerns matters of sovereignty as well as non-legal considerations.[99]

All problems arising from the position of the Princely or Native States during the formation of the new states of India and Pakistan rest on the nature of authority *vis-à-vis* the British Crown, for it is from this relationship that the right to choose their post-partition destiny is derived.

Before partition came into force on August 15, 1947, India consisted administratively of British India and the Princely States.[100] The Indian Independence Act of 1947 transformed British India into the two dominions of Pakistan and the Union of India and gave the Princely States the choice of acceding to either dominion or to remain independent.[101]

It is in this right to remain independent that the seed for possible future conflicts has been sown, for the possibility of an independent position is understandably a very attractive status for some of the larger states of the Indian continent which had much reason to remember their once powerful position before being reduced by the

[98] *Ibid.*

[99] *Cf.* Eagleton, "The Case of Hyderabad before the Security Council," 44 *A.J.I.L.* 277 (1950); Potter, *supra* note 72, at 361.

[100] Keith, *The Governments of the British Empire* 25 (1935).

[101] Diwan, *supra* note 79, at 334–339; Nawaz, *supra* note 81, at 183–185.

British to states of a lesser nature. In fact, Indian princes have made frequent efforts in the past to have their exclusive authority (as opposed to the inclusive authority exercised by the British Crown) explained in terms of a direct relationship with the British Crown in order to avoid a direct responsibility to the Government of India. This contention is not borne out, however, by an examination of the actual nature of the relationship which – as already explained above – is indicated by the term paramountcy. The general opinion is that, whatever the exact position of the Crown in its relationship of paramountcy with the States, paramount power rested in fact with the British Government in India.[102]

In this situation the Indian Independence Act of 1947 brought the most recent and final change by providing in the famous section 7b:

> As from the appointed day (August 15, 1947) ... the suzerainty of His Majesty over Indian States lapses, and with it all treaties and agreements in force at the date of passing of this act between His Majesty and the rulers of Indian States, all functions exercisable by His Majesty at that date with respect to Indian states, all obligations of His Majesty existing at that date towards Indian states or the rulers thereof, and all powers, rights, authority or jurisdiction exercisable by His Majesty at that date in or in relation to Indian states by treaty, grant, usage, suffrage or otherwise.[103]

From this provision arose the legal controversy as to what the subsequent relationship was between the new Government of India and the Princely States. Professor Das explains the Indian view in the following words:

> By the Independence of India Act the Government of India was divested of paramountcy. To meet this new unworkable situation, the Government of the Union of India approached the Indian Princely States to accede to the Union in terms according to which the Princely States would enjoy the rights of being an integral part of the Union. Paramountcy was thus replaced by partnership.[104]

Although he did nowhere expressly state so, Professor Das seemed to imply that India and Pakistan became the successors to the paramount power of the British Crown.[105]

Professor Eagleton, on the other hand, took an entirely different view. After having reviewed the Hyderabad case he came to the conclusion that the above-mentioned section 7b of the Indian Independence Act did only state that the suzerainty of the British

[102] Das, *supra* note 85, at 57.
[103] Nawaz, *supra* note 81, at 183.
[104] Das, *supra* note 85, at 70.
[105] Nawaz, *supra* note 81, at 184, n. 3.

Crown lapsed at the time of partition and nothing more or less. With regard to the theory of succession to the paramount powers of the British Crown he is explicit in stating:

> India had, and could have, no jurisdiction or claim whatever over Hyderabad, for the simple reason that there was no India, as a state, before 1947. Hyderabad, was part of a geographical area known as India, but she was not part of a non-existent state of India; nor could the newly created state of India claim to have had rights or paramountcy over Hyderabad before India existed as a state; nor could India claim by right of succession rights which were not transferred to her by the previous ruler.[106]

These are the opposing views arising from the lapse of British suzerainty over the Indian Princely States. They must perhaps principally be attributed to the unintended, but nevertheless inevitable, result of the remarkable British ability to administer their dependencies by unwritten, vague and yet workable concepts. The legal relationship between the Crown and the Indian native states is one such example of that British tradition. It served its purpose well, as long as it was applied in the sphere and spirit of British colonial administration. Lord Curzon has very aptly described this relationship in 1903 by explaining that "the political system in India is neither feudalism nor federation; it is embodied in no constitution; it does not always rest upon treaty – the sovereignty of the Crown is everywhere unchallenged. It has itself laid down the limitations of its own prerogative."[107]

No sooner, however, did the British suzerain withdraw or the certainty and stabilizing influence of his presence disappeared too, not the least in the legal system. The particular feature of British colonial policy has further been illustrated by a certain hesitation or reluctance to be forced into an express pronunciation of its exact intentions at the time of the creation of the Indian Independence Act. The then Prime Minister of Great Britain, Mr. Attlee, stated on July 10, 1947:

> With the ending of treaties and agreements the states regain their independence. But they are part of geographical India, and their rulers and people are imbued with a patriotism no less great than that of their fellow Indians in British India. It would, I think, be unfortunate, if owing to the formal severance of their paramountcy relations with the Crown they are to be islands cut off from the rest of India.[108]

[106] Eagleton, *supra* note 99, at 281.
[107] Quoted by Das, *supra* note 85, at 64.
[108] Eagleton, *supra* note 99, at 283.

Fortunately, most Princely States saw the wisdom of Mr. Attlee's advice and, although many rulers only acted after much hesitation and procrastination, they all acceded to one of the two newly created dominions, India and Pakistan.[109] Most of the states, but not all, however. Junagadh, Hyderabad and Kashmir[110] were the three dissenters which gave the projected partition plans a thorough testing. Junagadh and Hyderabad attempted to exercise such a policy of procrastination by expressing their wish to remain independent,[111] a right which India never denied.[112] But in the case of Hyderabad, India objected to such a policy decision by the Nizam of Hyderabad. There may have been various reasons for the Indian objection, geography and religion being only two of them, but one wonders how the explicit and intended guarantees to the states, as masters of their own fate, who would be free to choose whether they wanted to associate themselves with one or the other of the dominions or even to stand alone, could be ignored in favour of accidental and – in the case of Kashmir – not insoluble geographical and religious compulsions.[113] At any rate, when the case of Hyderabad was taken before the Security Council of the United Nations, the Indian contention was that Hyderabad had no legal status under international law and that, therefore, any intervention of the Security Council would amount to a violation of the principle of domestic jurisdiction. [114]

Professor Eagleton, being of an entirely different opinion, rejected this view, since it seemed perfectly clear to him that the British Government had guaranteed the right of the Princely States to remain independent. He concluded, therefore, that "Hyderabad assumed (if it had never been independent) or resumed (if it had been independent) the position of sovereign state; in any case it was a political entity disconnected from either Britain or India."[115]

The Hyderabad case is still on the agenda of the Security Council but no further discussion of the case seems to be forthcoming since

[109] See for the different varieties of states in the Indian Federation, Diwan, *supra* note 79, at 334–335.

[110] *Supra* at 138.

[111] *Ibid.*

[112] Eagleton, *supra* note 99, at 284 & n. 18.

[113] See the other statements to this effect from *e.g.* the British Government, Lord Listowell (Secretary of State for India), Mr. Churchill and Lord Mountbatten, in Eagleton, *supra* note 99, at 281–284.

[114] Das, *supra* note 85, at 72; *cf.* opinion of Sir Benegal Rau, quoted in Eagleton, *supra* note 99, at 285.

[115] Eagleton, *supra* note 99, at 285.

the accession of this state to the Union of India is a *fait accompli.* Therefore, no answer has been given to the interesting question whether Hyderabad, which brought its case before the Security Council by a request of its own government, should be regarded as a state under international law.

In this respect the Kashmir conflict is of a slightly different nature. The case was introduced into the Security Council not by the Government of Kashmir itself, but by one of the two contending parties, India and Pakistan. Therefore, the question as to the status of Kashmir under international law was in this instance irrelevant. The activities of the Security Council have already been reviewed above.[116] They have, in general, relatively little legal importance with the exception of the main question, whether Pakistan committed an act of aggression in Kashmir.

The Indian position in this respect[117] has been that from October 26, 1947 (the date of Kashmir's accession to India), the defence of Kashmir became the responsibility of India. In the exercise of these duties India responded to the urgent appeals of the Maharadja of Kashmir for military assistance by sending troops into the areas threatened by tribal attacks from the direction of Pakistan. On the other hand, so the Indians say, Pakistan acted entirely without justification, and by aiding the tribal invaders, as well as ordering later on her armed forces into Kashmir, she committed an act of aggression contrary to international law.

In defence, Pakistan contended, *inter alia,* that she had sufficient evidence to prove that the military activities of India were designed to launch a general offensive in order to occupy all important parts of the state of Jammu and Kashmir. Economically, as well as socially, this would have resulted in the total disruption of the Pakistan nation which was so vulnerable from the Kashmir side. It might have put an end to the viability of the Pakistan state as a sovereign and independent nation.[118] In order to prevent such a national disaster the Pakistan army was ordered to move into Kashmir in execution of the legitimate right of self-defence.

There is another point of formal authority which has always been contested by Pakistan. She has never considered the accession by the Maharadja of Kashmir to India as a valid act since it was

[116] *Supra* at 141.
[117] Nawaz, *supra* note 81, at 191.
[118] Korbel, *Danger in Kashmir,* 137–140 (1954).

based on "fraud and violence" as well as "duress of circumstances,"[119] and had been implemented against the will of the majority of the people. To support her claims Pakistan also repeatedly referred to the cases of Junagadh and Hyderabad where, so she said, India acted exactly in the opposite way. Therefore, as long as no free and impartial plebescite had been held in the Kashmir state, no accession could have any permanent consequences.

In reply India explained that the accession was voluntarily requested by Kashmir and accepted as such by India. Once it had been effectuated by an Instrument of Accession it was "complete in law and in fact,"[120] and not open to doubt or challenge. Furthermore, a unilateral secession by Kashmir from the Union of India was not possible anymore.[121] The permanent character of the accession has subsequently been confirmed by the entry of state representatives of Kashmir to the Constituent Assembly of India and by the constitutional incorporation of the State of Jammu and Kashmir as a component unit of the Union of India.

It is true that the Government of India, through the Governor General of the Union (Lord Mountbatten) and through its Prime Minister (Mr. Nehru), declared that the accession would have to be confirmed afterwards by a plebiscite, a most remarkable declaration in view of the fact that it was unasked for, nor required by any treaty or agreement. This Indian gesture sprang from her belief in, and commitment to, the principle of self-determination, and "once made, and noted by Pakistan and other countries likewise, it has become more or less binding."[122] How binding it was, is not clear, however, in view of the earlier statement that the accession was regarded as complete in law and in fact, and that no unilateral secession was possible anymore. Does this mean that a future plebiscite which will return a pro-Indian result would only be considered as a confirmation of the existing situation? On the other hand, suppose the result would be in favour of an accession to Pakistan, could such a decision of the people invalidate an accession which was – as India said – complete in law and in fact? The solution would probably be that, if such a plebiscite would indeed be organized, the Indian position would first have to be clarified or

[119] Diwan, *supra* note 79, at 346.

[120] Nehru's speech in Parliament on August 7, 1952, in *Kashmir 1947–1956 – Excerpts from Prime Minister Nehru's Speeches*, 33 (1956).

[121] Diwan, *supra* note 79, at 347.

[122] Potter, *supra* note 72, at 361.

modified, so that in case of a pro-Pakistan result the accession could be carried out without legal objections from the Indian side.

Finally, the inevitable question arises whether any solution acceptable to both parties can be expected from a balancing of the legal claims of the parties concerned. If we were to take the narrow view that this involves only an examination of the "simple issue"[123] whether Pakistan committed an aggression and violated international law by sending her troops across the border, then perhaps a quick answer can be given by any decision-maker by simply stating his preference for any legal facts under consideration.

It could, for instance, be held that the Burma-Yunnan boundary dispute, dealt with above, could be decided on the merits of formal authority, for much is dependent there on the determination of the correct borderlines on the basis of treaties and agreements, and although any decision would bring some hardship on some of the peoples involved, they are small in number and can, therefore, easily be evacuated and resettled without too many difficulties. Indeed these borderpeoples have expressed such a wish repeatedly.

In an issue of such a complex nature as the Kashmir conflict, however, in which both sides advance claims of all sorts, involving the lives, property and other interests of millions of people, the question cannot only be decided on the strict legal issue whether one party is the aggressor and must therefore see all his claims fail as a result of that act. This would make the fate of millions of people dependent on the construction or application of a simple rule. Such can never have been the real purpose of any legal prescription. Rather it should be taken into account that both parties have put forward their own exclusive claims which must then be balanced against one another, as well as reconciled with existing inclusive claims of the regional or global community. Such exclusive claims and counterclaims of the parties, in terms of resources, people and institutions will be discussed below.

3. Claims and Counterclaims

It has perhaps already become clear that it is rather optimistic to expect that a balancing of considerations of effective control would give more hope for a reconciliation than was possible in the case of formal authority. The preceding historical and legal account

[123] Nawaz, *supra* note 81, at 191.

of the conflict may have already exposed the enormous complexity of the problem, and there does not seem to be any justification for an optimistic expectation. Actually, since the beginning of this dispute subsequent happenings have made the issues increasingly complicated; the case is further aggravated by the often biased accounts of writers from both sides. If an attempt is now made to examine the competing claims, it is only because there is no alternative for an outsider trying to form an opinion but to take the arduous path of comparing claims and counterclaims.

The present dispute is remarkable for the fact that from the very beginning the matter of control has played a great part in the process of balancing claims; these aspects were explicitly indicated and emphasized by no one less than the Viceroy of British India, Lord Mountbatten. The importance of his statement is clearly reflected in the central position which it has been given in almost any discussion of the Kashmir conflict. When partition was about to be implemented, Lord Mountbatten addressed a conference of rulers and other representatives of the Princely States at Delhi on July 25, 1947. In his speech he confirmed the complete, technical and legal freedom of the states which would result from the impending lapse of British paramountcy. He then advised the states to link their future with either Pakistan or India since there were certain geographical and other factors which could not possibly be ignored. These factors have already been mentioned. They include geographical composition and geographical contiguity, communal composition of the state, and economic and strategic considerations. It is perhaps best to make these factors the basis of the examination of the claims, since they have been used by both parties to prove the strength of their case. It is proposed here to discuss briefly the following factors in succession: Population and culture, geographical position, communications, strategic considerations, trade and economic situation.

(a) Population and culture[124]

Of the approximately four million people of the State of Jammu and Kashmir, 77% was Moslem and it was therefore very likely that if a free plebiscite had been held just before or after partition, the

[124] Mayfield, *supra* note 74, at 184–186; Zafrullah Khan, *supra* note 72, at 13; Human Relations Area Files (HRAF), *Area Handbook on Kashmir*.

Moslem population by sheer weight of numbers would have made the accession of Kashmir to Pakistan inevitable.

The most important parts of Kashmir are the Vale and Jammu. Jammu in the south-west has been the seat of strong Hindu sympathies since it is the only Hindu majority area. On the other hand, the Vale (constituting the greater part of Kashmir province) was for 90% Moslem.

If the more remote parts of the state are considered, we have to deal with Gilgit, Baltistan and Ladakh which together cover approximately three-quarters of Kashmir's total area of about 84,000 square miles. These border areas are very thinly populated, containing only about 300,000 people. Gilgit is inhabited by nomadic Pathan tribes which, while herding their cattle, frequently cross the undemarcated borderline between Pakistan, Afghanistan and Kashmir. Although having close relations with their kinsmen on the Afghanistan side, they have often given active support to the case of Pakistan. Baltistan, having a Moslem Indo-Aryan population, is also closely affiliated with Pakistan. The Ladakh population, on the other hand, presents an entirely different picture. Being of Mongoloid stock with a Tibetan language and Buddhist religion, they have strong links with Tibet and the Dalai Lama whose leadership they recognize. The political sympathies of the Ladakh people, in so far as they can be determined, seem to favour an accession to the secular state of India rather than to the theocratic Pakistan state. A comparison of the population, cultural and religious factors, therefore, clearly point to the desirability of an accession to Pakistan. One author also makes the observation that "the demographic and cultural heterogeneity of Kashmir precludes the establishment of a preferential claim to the state on such grounds by either Pakistan or India. Political determination based on these factors would involve Afghanistan, China, Pakistan and India in a piecemeal division of the state."[125] Though it is perhaps a correct geographical evaluation of the situation, it is obviously not true politically. The question with which we are concerned presents a choice between only India or Pakistan. The other countries do not come into consideration at all, whatever the strength of their links with the Kashmir territories, and regardless of the feasibility or desirability of such a solution, for at present it is inconceivable that either Pakistan or India would recognize any territorial claims of those states to part of Kashmir.

[125] Mayfield, *supra* note 74, at 186.

(b) Geographical position[126]

The state of Jammu and Kashmir which formed the extreme northwestern part of pre-partition India, is bordered in the south by India and in the west by Pakistan. The border with India is formed by an almost continuous range of high and inaccessible mountains. The boundary between Pakistan and Kashmir, on the other hand, runs over plains and across several rivers which carry the waters from the watershed areas into Pakistan. The most important parts of the state, the Vale and the southwest, show all the signs of a geographical integration with Pakistan. Only the eastern part of Kashmir (Ladakh) again forms the exception to the rule, in the sense that there is no direct geographical connection with Pakistan. In general it can, therefore, be said that the geographical factors point in the direction of Pakistan as the most obvious and plausible choice for an accession of Kashmir.

(c) Communications[127]

It follows from the geographical structure of the state that the communication system is also mainly dependent on Pakistan. Roads, railroads and rivers represent the logical means of communication in the plains of the border areas. The Vale, the centre of communication for the whole of Kashmir, clearly faces toward Pakistan for its communications. Here too the balance sheet points to Pakistan, at least at the present time. Unlike the geographical position, and to a lesser degree the population and cultural factors, communications do not represent a permanent and unchanging element in the structure of the state. In spite of the geographical disadvantage of India with respect to her boundary with Kashmir, the handicap is not completely insurmountable and with the present technical know-how better means of communications could be introduced. In this respect it should be noticed that even in spite of her geographical difficulties India has been the more active side in embarking upon the construction of roads. This might well slowly but gradually diminish Pakistan's priviliged position with regard to surface traffic.

(d) Strategic factors[128]

These factors are obviously also closely related to the geographical

[126] See *id.* at 186; Zafrullah Khan, *supra* note 72, at 10.
[127] See Mayfield, *supra* note 74, at 187–188.
[128] See Zafrullah Khan, *supra* note 72, at 12–13; Mayfield, *supra* note 74, at 191–192.

position of the area and, in view of the geographical connection between Kashmir and Pakistan, the latter is most anxious to have her claims recognized. Without Kashmir, so Pakistan contends, no adequate defence of West Pakistan is possible, since the whole northwestern part of Pakistan lacks any natural boundary between herself and her Indian neighbour. Another Pakistan argument is designed to win her the support of the Western nations particularly, a fact which is understandable taking into account that Pakistan has already committed herself to the Western bloc. Kashmir, an area where Pakistan, India, China and Russia face each other, is of such great strategic importance that it would be wise to have her join that state which is strategically best suited for such a task in this case, i.e. Pakistan.[129]

The relativity of both arguments lies in the fact that they are based entirely on the assumption of the presence of India as a perpetual enemy and the improbability of any possible fraternization. That no such eternal factors exist in the field of international relations needs no further elaboration. Moreover, the presence of the U.N. and the commitment of both nations to the Charter of this organization and, most of all, the realization of the folly of any military action in Kashmir, make an all-out war improbable. It is often forgotten that nothing could have stopped these two nations from starting a war, if they had desired to do so in the past twelve years. Actually, both have shown a remarkable military restraint during that time, as well as an inclination to avoid large scale military clashes. Finally, it should be remembered that, if they would today decide to launch such military operations, no mountain ranges or rivers would give any effective protection against an invader who would have at his disposal modern means of transportation and long range weapons.

These obvious facts are, of course, no news to the parties concerned and their actual claims have been less demanding than would appear at first sight. Pakistan has not seriously pressed her claims for the whole of Kashmir. She has never explicitly maintained that she also wanted the remote district of Ladakh which, with its Mongoloid and Buddhist population, is of more importance to India. On the other hand, India never showed a real desire for the northwestern part of the Kashmir state, the affinity of which is clearly directed towards Pakistan. It seems, therefore, that with

[129] Kusun Nair, "Where India, China and Russia meet," 86 *For. Aff.* 335 (1957–58).

regard to strategic considerations the attitudes of the two countries are very much conditioned by psychological factors – fear and distrust being the most important ones. Judging all these facts on their merits, one could perhaps go as far as to say that these considerations are on the whole more in favour of Pakistan. However, unless it is possible to establish the imminent nature of a possible Indian military invasion even in the present structure of the organized world community, little weight should be attached to strategic factors when it comes to deciding the future status of Kashmir. Finally, it seems rather strange that the possibility of a Pakistan invasion into India is seldom discussed or even alluded to. Apparently the parties agree that such an undertaking is at present a chimera. Whether the situation would always remain this way is, of course, open to question.

(e) Trade and economic situation[130]

Kashmir's most important products are timber, fruits and vegetables, woollens and carpets, produce of the cottage industry and silk work. Timber, the number one article, is transported by way of the rivers and streams to West Pakistan where it is marketed and sold. India has tried to present an alternative to this transportation today by using trucks, but that has not been very successful yet.

Fresh fruit and vegetables are sold in many Indian cities, but Pakistan is still the principal market. The same holds true for woollens and carpets. As far as the products of cottage industries and silk works are concerned, both countries have tried to appeal to Kashmir; Pakistan with plans of large scale industrialization, and India with the establishment of co-operative and protected markets in India. In this case, there might be an even greater attraction in Kashmir for the Indian projects than for those of Pakistan.

Exports as well as imports seem to be mainly dependent on Pakistan, and particularly Karachi as the natural and principal outlet.[131] India claims that Kashmir, being an agricultural state, needs the supplies of the industries of India and she will point to the cotton textiles and sugar products which constitute two of Kashmir's most important import articles. Pakistan, on the other hand, can point to the import of leather goods and grains from Pakistan which

[130] Dhar, "The Kashmir Problem – Political and Economic Background," *India Q.* 142–160 (1951); Mayfield, *supra* note 74, at 189.

[131] Zafrullah Khan, *supra* note 72, at 11.

is not very far behind on the list of leading import articles.[132] The subject of agriculture brings up the question of land reform which is of special importance in a country with such a long feudal history. Although both countries have propagated and also started to implement their plans for land reform, the Indian efforts seem to have been carried out more energetically and successfully.[133]

Tourism, another source of income especially in the beautiful Vale, seems to depend largely on people from the Indian-held areas although they used to enter the Vale from the more accessible Pakistan side. This, however, is again only the contemporary situation and it is not inconceivable that India would be able to establish a better entry into the Vale from the Indian side of the state.[134]

An examination of economic factors cannot overlook the importance of the great and small rivers for Kashmir and the neighbouring territories. The area is intersected by the Indus and her five main tributaries (the Jhelum, Chenab, Ravi, Beas and Sutlej). With the Jhelum and Chenab, the Indus forms the western water system, while the Ravi, Beas and Sutlej constitute the eastern system. The Indus has its source in Tibet, the Jhelum and Chenab in Kashmir; the Ravi and Sutlej begin in Kashmir and flow through parts of India and Pakistan, while the Beas runs entirely through Indian territory.

Partition and the subsequent division of Kashmir caused the present borderline to cut across the rivers and canals. The occupation by Indian troops of the territories intersected by these rivers meant that Pakistan agriculture and economy was left to the discretion of the Indian authorities. Pakistan's fears of a permanent hold by India on these rivers are therefore clear. Besides the problem of a fair division of the expenses involved in the maintenance of the irrigation system, as well as the payment of seniorage (the price of the supplied water), there is the fear that India might decide to cut off the water supply in times of bad relations or that she might favour her own territory in a year of drought; finally, she might develop new areas needing irrigation, thus certainly leaving Pakistan with a smaller supply.[135] Experts of the World Bank, which have tried to assist the parties in their search for a solution, have put

[132] Korbel, *supra* note 118, at 7–8.
[133] Mayfield, *supra* note 74, at 189.
[134] *Ibid.*
[135] Griffith, *op. cit. supra* note 86, at 154–155.

forward their own projects. These plans give Pakistan the exclusive use of the western rivers (except in Kashmir) and India the same rights with regard to the eastern waters.[136]

It would be a hazardous undertaking to say which side has a better claim to control over the waters. Fortunately, that may not even be necessary, for the answer should perhaps be found in a fair distribution of all available water resources. It seems that the chances for creating such a fair distribution of waters are present, but much will depend on the spirit in which these proposals are approached by both parties. The real problem is therefore more of a psychological than of a material nature. To the people in the area concerned the dangers are imminent. As long as no permanent solution is found they will continue to have an interest for their personal welfare only, regardless of the claims of the other party.[137]

So far we have dealt with two major factors which have poisoned the relationship between the two states on the subcontinent, namely, the struggle for the State of Kashmir and the problem of the river waters. There are two other factors which should be mentioned. Firstly, there is the question of trade relations and secondly, the difficult problem of the hundreds of thousands of refugees and their former property.[138] Like the question of the river waters, the trade relations do not seem to present an insurmountable problem, and today they are carried out as well as is possible under the present conditions. The chances for the refugees, to recover some of their property, however, are not very bright. Although negotiations have been carried on between the parties, no settlement has as yet been reached, nor can it be expected very soon.

It would have been very useful if we could have given a clear-cut answer to the question of what a balancing of all relevant factors would show. It will be clear, however, that such an expectation must remain wishful thinking, not only because the factors considered here were not at all indisputably in favour of one and the same party, but also because not all of the facts which support the claims can at present exactly be established. The two countries see these facts too much from their own narrow point of view. Thus, there is no justification for the hope that, if we could only

[136] Birdwood, *op. cit. supra* note 71, at 224–225.

[137] Recently (September 1960) a solution was found for the problem of the division of waters when India and Pakistan signed a treaty containing an Indus Basin Settlement Plan. See *Keesings Historisch Archief* 16015 (1960).

[138] Griffith, *op. cit. supra* note 86, at 162; Symonds, *op. cit. supra* note 86, at 162.

expose all facts, it would be the first step to a reasonable solution.

To illustrate the difficulty of establishing the value which should be attached to the above facts one such example may be given here. One of the perhaps inevitable consequences of the disturbances in 1947 was the great number of women which were abducted by both groups. Later on social workers on both sides were allowed to trace them back. According to certain figures the Indian workers managed to recover about eleven thousand Moslem women, whereas their Pakistan colleagues only found half that number. The Indian reaction was obviously that Pakistan did not deal seriously with this problem, but Pakistan retorted that the figures only proved that fewer women were abducted in Pakistan than in India. This is but one of the many instances in which the parties arrived at opposing interpretations of the very same facts. This then leads us to the final question: What are, at this stage of the conflict, the prospects of a solution of the Kashmir conflict as viewed in the light of authoritative as well as non-authoritative considerations?

4. Prospects of a Solution

Since the beginning of the Kashmir conflict enough time has passed and sufficient efforts have been made to justify a statement to the effect that all possible solutions have in the course of the dispute been discovered and discussed. Yet they have not brought us closer to the needed solution. A review of the whole Kashmir case leaves the observer with the strong impression of a hopeless deadlock. Several reasons can be given for this situation, and a search for a possible way out of it has to take full consideration of these facts.

There is firstly the tenacity (some call it intransigence) which each party has displayed at certain times and particularly when crucial points of the dispute were under discussion. This is not to say that the parties have never showed any sense of responsibility or reasonableness. On the contrary, but the Kashmir case is notorious for its complexity – its involvement of so many factors of varying nature that any party may find among them a few which can be advanced to support its claims. This is what in fact has happened, and it is, therefore, difficult to state which side was "right" or "wrong." The question is more one of emphasis. If the geographical situation was at one time advantageous to one of the parties, it would often build it up so strongly that its claim in this respect would become almost indisputable. The other party, however, might seize upon the legal side of the case to show the strength of its title. If this were the only difficulty involved in studying the issue, the picture perhaps would be distorted but it could not be said that such an attitude of the parties concerned was unreasonable. There is, however, another peculiarity in the case which, although perhaps not unnatural, is of a more serious character. Both parties have made a remarkable shift of their positions in the course of the dispute.

In the first years of the Kashmir conflict India, lacking strong arguments of a physical and cultural nature, concentrated understandably on what seemed at that time her strongest weapon, namely the legal aspects of the case. She has stressed continuously and emphatically (e.g. in the United Nations) the legal nature of the accession of the Maharadja of Kashmir, as well as the illegal character of Pakistan's act of aggression. Pakistan, on the other hand, looked to the "non-legal" factors for supporting material, which she therefore equally emphasized, arguing in the Security Council, for instance, that to understand the real implications of the conflict one has to look at the whole background and the sequence of events.

Today the situation has changed considerably. Pakistan, which is much in favour of the resolutions of the United Nations Commission for India and Pakistan of 13 August, 1948, and of 5 January, 1949,[139] now makes those documents the legal basis of her claims. India's attitude, on the other hand, has been influenced by recent events which have caused a gradual shift to a less legalistic approach, and Indian statesmen have explicitly come out with statements to this effect. They refer to a number of events which, in their opinion, cannot fail to affect the whole picture of the Kashmir dispute. They point to such facts as: Pakistan's acceptance of military aid from foreign countries; her accession to the Baghdad Pact and the South East Asia Treaty Organization;[140] the discrimination against Hindus of East Pakistan which resulted in a flow of Hindu refugees into India; the economic progress and integration of Kashmir with India; as well as some more authoritative considerations, such as Kashmir's constitutional incorporation into India in 1957, and the pro-India results of the general elections in Kashmir of 1957. Thus, both parties have adopted attitudes almost the reverse of the initial

[139] Respectively *U.N. Doc. No.* S/955 and S/1192.

[140] Korbel, "New Hope for Kashmir?," 34 *For. Pol. Bull.* 89 (1955).

stands taken. At that time they both used to speak of a "simple question" involving only a determination of "right" or "wrong." Today they give more weight to complicated considerations and it does not look as if they are going to change that position very soon.

One fact should, therefore, be made perfectly clear, namely that the question is, on the contrary, far from simple.[141] From the balancing process of claims and interests reviewed earlier, it should have become clear that there is no single factor or combination of factors which carries so much weight as to enable us to come to a decision with respect to which of the competing claims should deserve preference. Keeping these considerations in mind, we should now proceed with a review of the solutions which have been suggested in the course of the dispute.

The possibility of accession of the whole state of Kashmir to either Pakistan or India is at this stage of the conflict extremely small, since neither has shown a willingness to give up the territories now held under its authority. The remaining possibilities, which are worth considering, may follow here:[142] an independent Kashmir; the acceptance of the cease-fire line as a permanent solution; an independent Vale. It is also possible that a plebiscite will after all be resorted to which might produce a preference for one of the parties concerned. Finally, it is conceivable that a more restricted question amounting to a choice between any of the above-mentioned alternatives, will be put before the people.

The first-mentioned alternative , i.e. an independent Kashmir, does not seem to be a very viable one. Firstly, there is the strong Indian objection to discontinuance of the already implemented integration of Kashmir into the constitutional structure of the Union of India. To become independent at this time would mean that Kashmir would have to secede from the Indian Union. According to Diwan[143] such a secession can no longer be carried out unilaterally. Though it is regrettable that such legalistic arguments are made the crux of the whole matter, it would be unwise not to take this argument seriously. The Indians do take it very seriously and, therefore, this alternative has at present no chance. In fact, it

[141] Not only Indian or Pakistan writers have made this mistake. Foreign authors too have made superficial remarks which they then reversed afterwards; see Kirkpatrick, "A Claim Disproved," *New York Post*, May 30, 1948.

[142] *Cf.* Mayfield, *supra* note 74, at 194–196.

[143] Diwan, *supra* note 79, at 346.

is generally thought that even the government of the beloved leader, Nehru, might not survive, under the present conditions, a decision to allow Kashmir to secede in any way from India.[144] Be that as it may, the reasoning behind Diwan's above-mentioned contention is worth mentioning. This author took the view that the State of Kashmir, like any other Princely State, became an independent state after partition came into force and, therefore, the negotiations between Kashmir and the Union of India were carried out on a footing of equality and full sovereignty of both states. Therefore:

> the Instrument of Accession was nothing but a treaty between two states.... Thus even according to the principles of international law the State (of Kashmir) or its Constituent Assembly is not competent to abrogate the Instrument by a unilateral act, provided the situation does not materially change. The declaration of independence by the State (of Kashmir) ... would amount to a breach of treaty.[145]

It is worth noting that this view rests in general on the theory which Professor Eagleton had expounded in order to prove that the state of Hyderabad, for instance, was an independent state at the time of the passing of power in India.[146] Professor Eagleton's views were diametrically opposed to those of Professor Das who defended the position that the Indian states did not become independent states as a result of the termination of British suzerainty, and that Hyderabad, not being a state under international law, could not be heard in the Security Council. It is remarkable that Diwan has in this case adopted Professor Eagleton's view rather than the Indian opinion of Professor Das. Only by taking Eagleton's position was he able to hold that a secession by Kashmir must be viewed as a breach of an international obligation.

There are, however, other factors which raise considerable doubt as to the viability of an independent Kashmir. The absence of a strong unifying factor, the inability to defend herself adequately, the lack of sufficient economic and financial resources have been mentioned as some of the reasons.[147] It is difficult to determine whether these factors make the idea of an independent Kashmir really illusory, but coupled with the earlier mentioned legal obstacles, the idea does not seem to have much chance of realization.

[144] Ter Laan, *Kashmir, de heksenketel in India* (Kashmir, the cauldron in India) 3 (The Hague, 1957).
[145] Diwan, *supra* note 79, at 346.
[146] Eagleton, *supra* note 99, at 281.
[147] *Id.* at 195.

The alternative of the cease-fire line presents a more viable idea, if it would be accepted as the final *status quo*. Religious, economic and agricultural difficulties do not seem to be so insurmountable as to eliminate, *a priori*, all chances of a solution.[148] Since the cease-fire line follows approximately the religious boundaries of the Kashmir state the acceptance of such a solution would apparently be identical to a partition of the country along religious lines. It was said, however, that such a plan would find little support with either party since India is committed to a support of the Kashmir Government in the Vale, while Pakistan is adamant on the control of the river Chenab.[149]

A third possibility, i.e. an independent Vale is suggested as a face-saving device for both claimant parties.[150] The viability of this plan would depend greatly on the ability and willingness of the parties to work in close cooperation for the furtherance of the common interest. It seems unlikely, however, that a problem of such a complex nature can be solved by a simple face-saving device.

There is, finally, the possibility of a plebiscite which has been accepted by the parties as the only device which comes closest to a fair representation of the people's views and desires. It has always been the main point of agreement, but unfortunately this agreement ended as soon as the organization of the plebiscite was discussed. An examination of the relevant facts gives the impression that Pakistan was, in general, more willing to iron out all disagreements in order to arrive as soon as possible at the desired goal of a plebiscite. India, on the other hand, was less enthusiastic in this respect and her reactions sometimes showed a very ambivalent character.

According to some sources, Prime Minister Nehru himself has sometimes indulged in controversial statements on this point. His opinion on the right of self-determination of the Kashmir people seemed to deviate in 1956 from the position taken earlier.[151] Others in India have also expressed some doubts on the fairness of the proposed plebiscite, if it is influenced by an appeal to religion.[152] It is not very clear by what appeals a plebiscite should, in their opinion, be influenced, in order to deserve the qualification "fair."

148 *Ibid.*
149 Symonds, *op. cit. supra* note 86, at 161.
150 Mayfield, *supra* note 74, at 196.
151 Palmer, "The Changing Scene in Kashmir," 22 *Far Eastern Survey* 158 (1953); *cf.* Griffith, *supra* note 86, at 152.
152 Griffith, *op. cit. supra* note 86, at 151.

One might perhaps venture the suggestion that it would be worthwhile to hear what the Kashmir people themselves think of the prospects of a plebscite. This point, however, like all others is faced with several difficulties. Firstly, the disturbances in 1947 have led to the exodus of thousands of the original population and since then many "outsiders" have entered the state. The determination of who are to participate in voting poses a great number of problems, for many Kashmir refugees now live outside the state. It is also apparent that there is some degree of apathy among the population, at least in so far as they have been exposed to all pressures of both claimant states. Moreover, the Indian policy of pouring money into Kashmir could not and did not fail to impress some parts of the Moslem population. Under such conditions one may perhaps wonder whether a plebiscite is indeed the correct answer for the Kashmir dispute. A European author made a point which is worth noting when, writing about his talks with Sir Zafrullah Khan, he said:

"I told him about the discouraging experiences we had in Europe with plebiscites which had turned into mere instruments of propaganda, pressure and falsification, and I cited those conducted by Hitler and by the Communists. He realized all this, but insisted that it was up to the U.N. to secure conditions conducive to a free plebiscite in Kashmir."[153] With such a discouraging picture of the possible means of solving the conflict, even in the case of a basically sound and democratic instrument as a plebiscite, it is understandable why no further progress has been made.

It has been suggested at times that a change of leadership may well bring about a switch in the policies. Such a change has indeed taken place in recent times when the military leaders of Pakistan took over the government of their country. What this means in terms of the Kashmir question is not yet clear. Here again only time will bring the answer. In matters of such a complex nature as the issue here under consideration, one is indeed tempted to leave everything to time, in the hope that a lapse of a sufficiently long period would blunt the edges and soothe feelings which had temporarily been excited. On the other hand, time has not always played the role of the great healer. In the Kashmir case, at least, it has been proved that every year the issue has grown in complexity, since the dynamic happenings of our time have linked up the issue

[153] Korbel, *op. cit. supra* note 118, at 136.

with new considerations of a military and economic nature. Therefore, the issue may not be helped at all by shelving it for so long a time.[154] What could be very helpful, however, is a willingness of the parties to give up some of their claims for the benefit of a quick solution. The problem is to find the first party which is willing to make a great gesture.[155] Unless such a more agreeable attitude is adopted, the prospects of a settlement remain very small.[156]

The international significance of the Kashmir dispute has already been stressed above when dealing with its geographical position. The interest of the neighbouring countries in the events in the State of Kashmir was sufficiently clear. Afghanistan's claims are connected with the Pathan tribes which live in the border areas.[157] Russia has occasionally indulged in historical arguments by launching attacks on British imperialism with respect to "small portions of Tibet, such as Ladakh, Sikkim and Bhutan."[158]

Until recently China has not made any comment on the Kashmir situation, nor on her interests in the other Indian regions bordering the Himalayas,[159] though it is commonly known that the border line is disputed and that the Ladakh population shows many cultural links with the people of Tibet.[160] In the autumn of 1959 reports were heard about clashes between border patrols on the Sino-Indian frontier in Ladakh, Northeast Kashmir. It then turned out that such border clashes had happened for some time already.[161] The Indian, as well as the Chinese government, accused each other of having its frontier guards cross the border line. Suddenly the exact delineation of the Ladakh border became of the greatest importance. Then again – as in the Burma-Yannan border dispute – the well-known argument was heard that the boundary was "fixed from ancient times."[162] In spite of diplomatic activity no settlement has as yet materialized in this matter.

Finally, some attention should be given to the efforts of the

[154] *Cf.* Birdwood, *op. cit. supra* note 71, at xvi.

[155] Symonds, *op. cit. supra* note 86, at 162.

[156] After the clashes on the Chinese border following the Tibet troubles, it was rumoured that closer ties between India and Pakistan would be established. *Cf.* N.R.C. 2 September 1959, p. 1, col. 1).

[157] Tikekar, "The Durand Line," 6 *India Q.* 326–331 (1950); Tyler, *Afghanistan* 296 (1953).

[158] Feer, "India's Himalayan Frontier," 22 *Far Eastern Survey* 137 (1953).

[159] *Ibid.*

[160] Kachru, "Ladakh," 6 *India Q.* 58–67 (1950).

[161] *Manchester Guardian*, 24 October 1959, p. 1, col. 1.

[162] *The Times* (London), 20 November 1959, p. 10, col. 5.

Security Council to settle the dispute. As is well-known they did not result in any concrete solution in spite of the exertions of the UNCIP, the nominated Plebiscite Administrator (Admiral Chester Nimitz) and the two U.N. Representatives in Kashmir (Sir Owen Dixon and Dr. Frank Graham). The arguments during the debates in the Security Council were long and irreconcilable. To illustrate this point a few arguments will be discussed here.

The Indian position, as it developed in the course of time, is based on the theory that since the formal accession of Kashmir to India, sovereign powers are vested with the Union of India. In the opinion of India, these sovereign powers did not only apply to the India-held eastern part of the state, but to the state as a whole, including the western part under Pakistan supervision. Having once taken this position, she refused to enter into an agreement which would recognize in any way a Pakistan authority and thus jeopardize her position.

Therefore, when the parties accepted the UNCIP resolution of 13 August 1948[163] India was very careful to point out at that time that this should in no way be interpreted as a deviation from her previously adopted attitude. In particular she pointed to paragraph A. 3 of Part II of the above resolution which states:

> Pending a final solution, the territory evacuated by the Pakistan troops will be administered by the local authorities under the surveillance of the Commission.[164]

Although accepting the resolution, India pointed out very clearly through a letter of Mr. Nehru:

> That paragraph A. 3 of Part II of the resolution should not be interpreted, or applied in practice, so as (a) to bring into question the sovereignty of the Jammu and Kashmir Government over the portion of their territory evacuated by Pakistan troops;
>
> (b) to afford any recognition of the so-called "Azad Kashmir Government," or
>
> (c) to enable that territory to be consolidated in any way during the period of truce to the disadvantage of the state.[165]

India's hesitancy and caution was evoked by the fear that an acceptance of the resolution would accord a legal status to the Azad Kashmir Government under international law. Such a fact would not be to the advantage of the Kashmir Government in Srinagar

[163] *U.N. Security Council*, (S/955), Aug. 13, 1948.
[164] Birdwood, *op. cit. supra* note 71, at 218.
[165] Zafrullah Khan, *supra* note 72, at 36.

which she recognized as the only legitimate government of the territory. To avoid this difficulty the UNCIP refers on the one hand to the Government of the State of Jammu and Kashmir, while on the other hand it speaks of "the local authorities" instead of the Azad Kashmir Government. Whereas India regarded the relevant paragraph A. 3 as a confirmation of her views, Pakistan, on the other hand, pointed out that the term "the local authorities" was merely adopted by the UNCIP in order to avoid the term "Azad Kashmir Government" which was so much resented by India. However, no conclusion should be drawn from this term, so Pakistan contended, certainly not that the Commission had recognized in this parapraph the sovereign authority of the Kashmir Government over the whole of the state. According to the Pakistan interpretation, all that the Commission was trying to do was to give provisions which would apply to the whole of the state, regardless of the actual administering authorities and without taking any position with respect to the question as to whom sovereignty actually belonged.[166]

The same legalistic controversy arose from the other UNCIP resolution of 5 January 1949[167] where it was stated in paragraph 3 (b): "The Plebiscite Administrator shall derive from the State of Jammu and Kashmir the powers he considers necessary for organizing and conducting the plebiscite and ensuring the freedom and impartiality of the plebiscite." India again saw in this provision a recognition of the authority of the Government of Jammu and Kashmir over the whole of the state. For, without possessing itself such a state-wide authority, it would have been impossible for the Kashmir Government to confer authority in the whole of the state to a Plebiscite Administrator. Pakistan, on the other hand, refers to the remark of the Commission that it had no intention whatsoever to recognize with this provision the state-wide authority of the Government of Jammu and Kashmir. According to Sir Zafrullah Khan the provision only meant that the Plebiscite Administrator should be deemed to have derived his powers, as a matter of legal technicality, from the State of Jammu and Kashmir. No mention was made of the Government of Jammu and Kashmir; the State of Jammu and Kashmir was meant here as a legal entity.[168]

[166] *Id.* at 37.
[167] *U.N. Security Council* (S/1192), Jan. 5, 1949.
[168] Zafrullah Khan, *supra* note 72, at 38.

In view of the diametrically opposed attitudes it is understandable that no plebiscite could materialize. As the efforts of negotiators and mediators were unsuccessful, the alternative became to submit the conflict to arbitration. This would seem especially suitable since apparently Asians are very well acquainted with, and thus in favour of, settlement by arbitration. India's constitution, for instance, states explicitly in art. 51 that India encourages settlement of international disputes by arbitration. The Pakistan delegate in the Security Council obviously quoted this article and further pointed out that since in the Indonesian question India herself suggested the establishment of an international arbitration commission,[169] she should herself submit her disputes to arbitration. The Indians, however, rejected the idea of arbitration here. Prime Minister Nehru declared in New Delhi that, since he had offered a no-war declaration (i.e. non-aggression pact) to Pakistan, this would, if accepted, by itself create an atmosphere favourable to the settlement of any dispute. On the other hand, India was unwilling to have the no-war declaration be made powerless by a stipulation that the signing must be tied to the condition that the Kashmir case be settled by arbitration.[170] Nehru gave his views on the matter in the following words:

> Having had nine years of this Kashmir affair in changing phases which have affected the people of Jammu and Kashmir State and India in a variety of ways, affecting our Constitution, sovereignty and vital interests, am I to be expected to agree to some outside authority becoming an arbitrator in this matter?[171]

This statement illustrates at the same time an important point. Many Asian leaders still use the term sovereignty with the implied meaning of a mystical, supreme authority which cannot in any way be impeded. However, the Kashmir case proved that at other times they were less legalistic and more inclined to give greater weight to so-called non-legal matters if they are of vital importance. In spite of their adherence to traditional international law, it cannot be said that the present Asian decision-makers have been consistent in the application of that traditional system.

Summarizing, it appears that the process of balancing claims has run into serious difficulties as a result of three factors: 1. the

[169] M. M. R. Khan, *The United Nations and Kashmir* 176 (1954).
[170] *Id.* at 43.
[171] From a statement in Parliament, March 29, 1956, in "*Kashmir 1947–1956. Excerpts from Prime Minister Nehru's Speeches,*" 44 (1956).

lack of clarity of the claims; 2. the shifting of claims; 3. the continual addition of claims.

The first reason has already been touched upon above. There is a great stress on such legal technicalities as sovereignty, permanent accession, impossibility of secession. Parties also seem to look upon strategic and economic claims as invariable elements.[172] Moreover, there was an unrestrained use of vague accusations which were never proved.

The shifting of claims occurred when one party, which had built up its position on a legalistic argument, switched to one of non-legalistic nature, while the other party made the reverse move.[173]

Finally, the parties seem to add more claims as time progressed. One important new claim, as advanced by India, is that U.S. military aid has changed the entire situation. Nehru stated on this subject:

> Now the whole issue has to be considered from an entirely different point of view when across the border, across the cease-fire line on the other side, large additional forces are being thrust from outside in Pakistan and put at the disposal of Pakistan. It does make a difference.[174]

Pakistan, however, contends that U.S. military aid will only be used for defence purposes and thus it should in no way prevent India from settling the dispute in a peaceful way. In Pakistan's view:

> Peace can be secured in the world, not by insisting that a particular country refrain from reinforcing its defences, but by settling all the disputes which cause bitterness and conflict between the parties concerned.[175]

The futility of such arguments and counterarguments is fairly clear. Every new addition of claims immediately invites a counter-claim. The outlook for a speedy solution remains therefore bleak.[176] The only bright spot in this matter is perhaps that, after the origin of this conflict, parties have been exemplary in avoiding the outbreak of real hostilities which might have great repercussions for the whole region, if not for the world. Nehru has described this attitude in the following words:

[172] *Supra* at 152–157.

[173] *Supra* at 158.

[174] Statement in Parliament, March 1, 1954, in *Kashmir 1947–1956, op. cit. supra* note 171, at 39.

[175] M. M. R. Khan, *op. cit. supra* note 169, at 177.

[176] A recent article stated that in the last few months the Indo-Pakistan relations have

... I do think that since both Pakistan and we agreed that on no account should we go to war with each other, we should settle our problems peacefully though they may not be settled for some time. It is better to have a problem pending than to go to war for it.[177]

INDONESIA AND THE LAW OF THE SEA

One glance at the map of the Indonesian archipelago is sufficient to prove the important place which the sea occupies in this area.[178] The greater part of the archipelago belongs to the Republic of Indonesia while smaller territories are administered by the U.K., the Netherlands and Portugal. The archipelago is comprised of the five main islands of Sumatra, Java, Borneo, Celebes and New Guinea, surrounded by a host of smaller islands. Whereas some of the latter are of extremely small size, the main islands belong to the largest in the world. The following comparison may perhaps provide a useful illustration of their sizes:[179]

Sumatra: equals the combined territory of the states of Virginia, North and South Carolina and Georgia;

Java: approximately the size of the state of New York;

Borneo: (of which the northern part is British) is slightly larger than the state of Texas; it is the third largest island in the world;

Celebes: 1,5 times Java;

New Guinea: the second largest island in the world the eastern part of which is administered by Australia, whereas Western New Guinea (called Western Irian by the Indonesians) is under Dutch administration, but claimed by Indonesia. This

taken a turn to the better, especially with regard to the division of waters, commercial and financial relations. But "nothing at all has so far been done about Kashmir" which still constitutes an "almost measureless gap." "Indo-Pakistani Relations," *The Round Table*, no. 198, at 163 (1960).

[177] From a statement made in Parliament, March 29, 1956, in *Kashmir 1947–1956*, *op. cit. supra* note 171, at 44.

[178] See folding map of the Indonesian archipelago, facing this page. This appendix is a reproduction of the map attached to the Indonesian Act No. 4 of 18 February 1960 (U.N. Doc. A/CONF. 19/5/Add. 1) supplied by the Indonesian Government as an Addendum to the Supplement to Laws and Regulations on the Regime of the Territorial Sea (U.N. Legislative Series). Permission for reproduction was kindly granted by the U.N. Publications Board.

[179] Cressey, *Asia's Land and Peoples* 527 (1952); Stamp, *Asia - A Regional and Economic Geography* 434–450 (1957); Vlekke, *Nusantara – A History of the East Indian Archipelago* xi (1944).

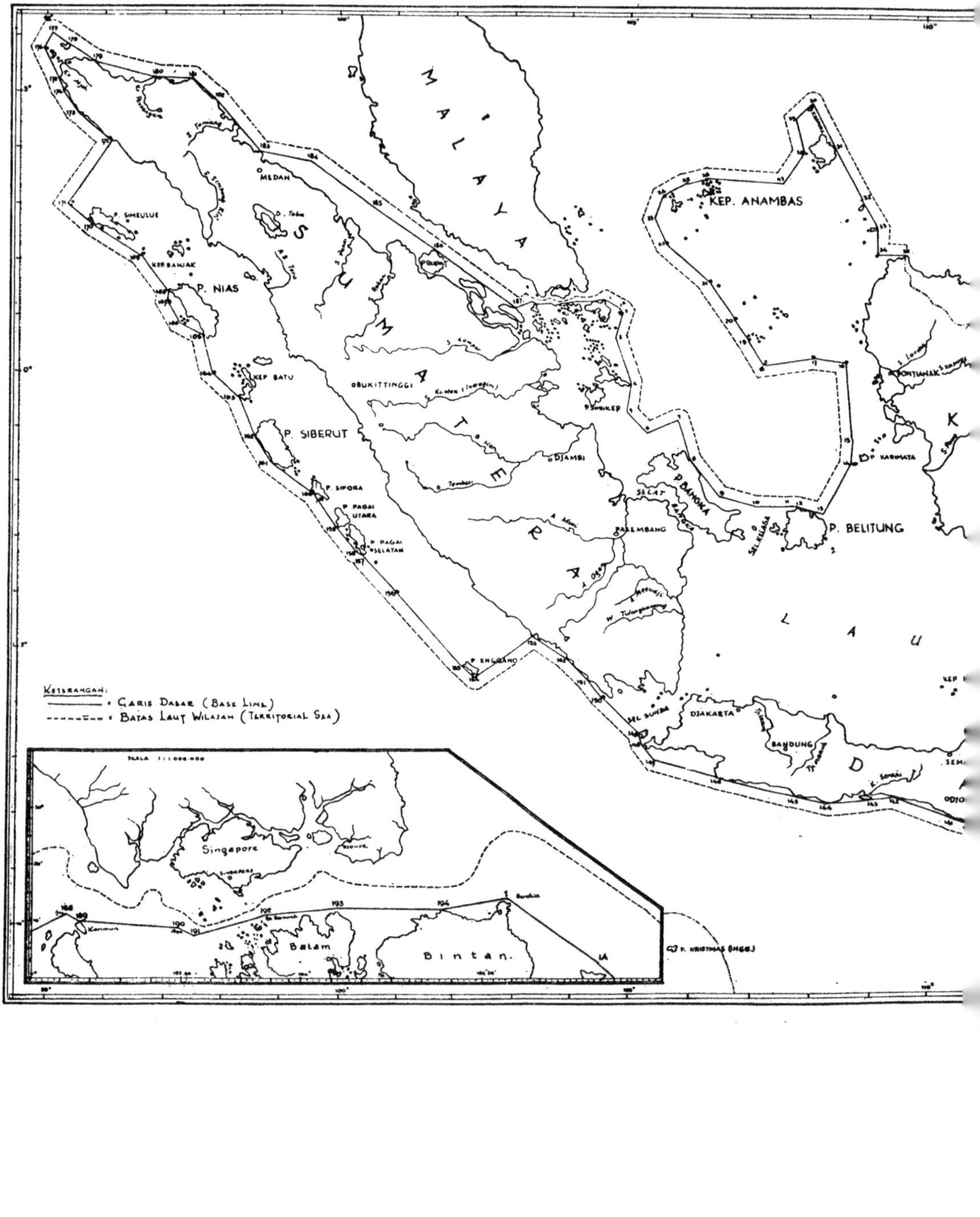

M A L A Y A
S U M A T E R A
KEP. ANAMBAS
P. SIMEULUE
P. NIAS
KEP BATU
P. SIBERUT
P. SIPORA
P. PAGAI UTARA
P. PAGAI SELATAN
P. ENGGANO
MEDAN
BUKITTINGGI
DJAMBI
PALEMBANG
SELAT BANGKA
P. BANGKA
P. BELITUNG
PONTIANAK
P. KARIMATA
SEL SUNDA
DJAKARTA
BANDUNG
L A U
K
D
KETERANGAN:
= GARIS DASAR (BASE LINE)
= BATAS LAUT WILAJAH (TERRITORIAL SEA)
Singapore
Karimun
Batam
Bintan.
P. KRISTMAS (INGG.)

BASESLINES OF THE INDONESIAN WATERS

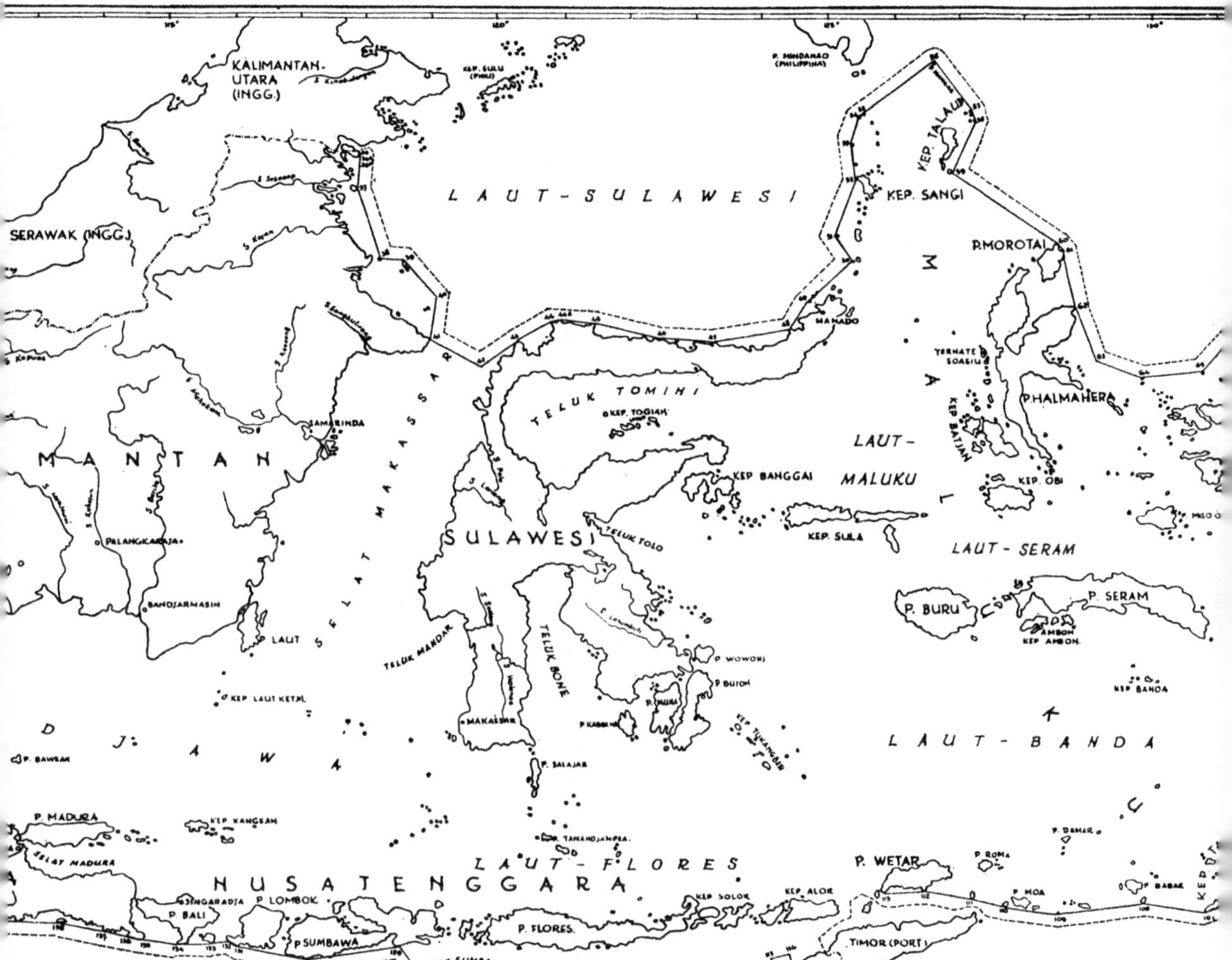

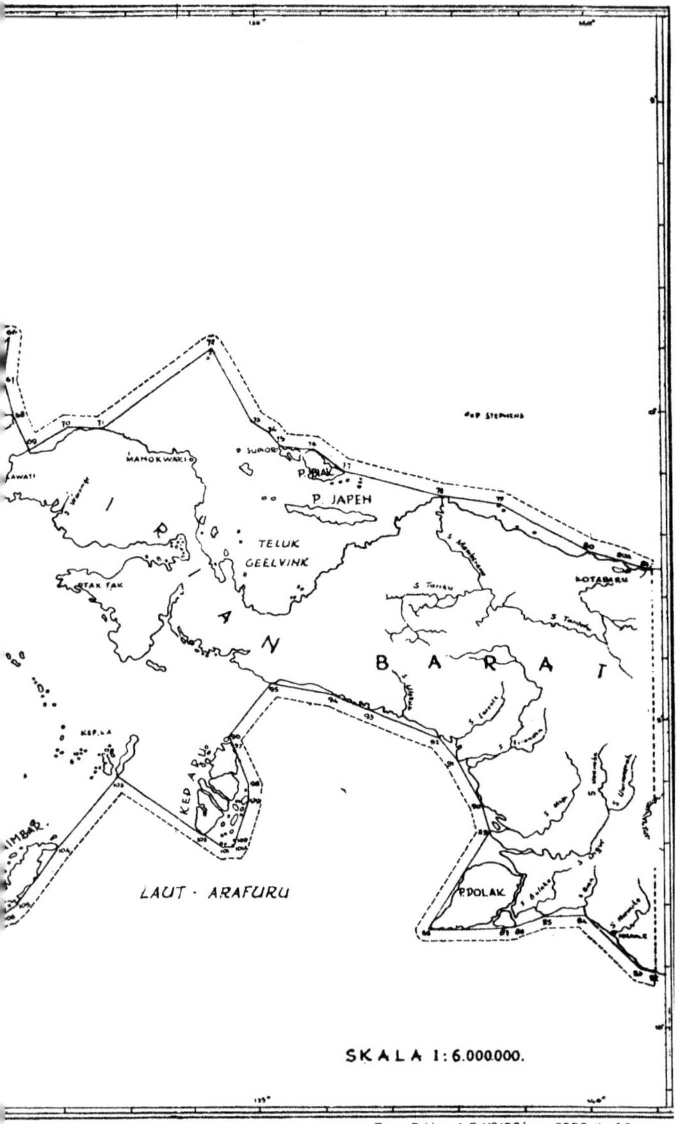

Repr Dittop A D N°100/c J-2000 lb/60

western part has the size of the combined territories of Wisconsin, Illinois and Indiana.

Of the total area of more than three million square miles only about 730.000 sq. miles comprise land area, i.e. ¼ of the territory of the United States. The maximum length of the archipelago is 2.750 miles (equal to the distance San Francisco – Bermuda Islands) while the maximum width is 1.150 miles (Buffalo, N.Y. to Key West, Florida).[180]

The strategic importance of Indonesia lies in her position as a bridge between the Asian and Australian continents and the fact that it is surrounded by most of the important waters of Asia. In the east it is bordered by the Pacific, in the west by the Indian Ocean. In the north it is separated from the Asian mainland by the Strait of Malacca and the South China Sea, and from the Phillippines by the Sulu Sea, while in the south the Indian Ocean and the Arafura Sea separate it from Australia. The commercial and maritime importance of this area is enhanced by the many lines of world communication which pass through these waters, most of them being concentrated on a few important straits, such as Sunda Strait, Strait of Macassar and Torres Strait.

Geologically, Indonesia is considered to be the extension of, and the bridge between the two neighbouring continents. The connection with these continents is further demonstrated by the presence of large continental shelves. The Sahul shelf in the east constitutes the undersea extension of Australia, New Guinea and the islands around it. In the west the same is true of the Sunda shelf with the islands of Sumatra, Java and Borneo. Both shelves are covered with shallow waters from 10 to 200 metres. Between these shelves the sea reaches considerable depths, occasionally of five and seven thousand metres.

The topographical structure of Indonesia is therefore one of a complex archipelago of a few large islands and thousands of smaller ones. They are the remainder of a once continuous area which was broken up by movements of the sea and the earth crust. In spite of the brokenness the area still shows clear and striking features of its former interconnection. The mountain range of the South East Asian mainland, which runs through the Malay Peninsula southwards, finds its oversea extension in the mountain range of Sumatra, Java, the Lesser Sunda Islands, eastwards to the crescent of islands around the Banda Sea. In fact there are many such crescents of

[180] Cressey, *op. cit. supra* note 179, at 527.

islands which make up the Indonesian Archipelago. In other words, the uniqueness of the Indonesian Archipelago, the largest archipelago in the world, is due to its peculiar shape and the varied composition of the archipelago with some of the largest islands in the world as well as innumerable smaller and tiny islands separated by very shallow, as well as some of the deeper, waters of the world, and with widths ranging from a few to some hundreds of miles.

The geography of Indonesia received much attention when, on 13 December 1957, the Indonesian Government issued a declaration stating that it intended to change the maritime laws obtaining in the archipelago to the extent that in essence all waters, surrounding, between and connecting the islands constituting the Indonesian state were to become internal waters, while the breadth of the territorial waters must be considered to be twelve miles.

This intention was finally realized by Act no. 4 of 18 February 1960. The nature and implications of these regulations will be the subject of the following section.

1. The Facts

(a) The Laws of the sea in the Netherlands Indies period

Before World War II Indonesia, then the Dutch colony of the Netherlands Indies, applied in general the same principles of the law of the sea as the Dutch mother country. The main laws and regulations of that period are laid down in the "Territoriale zee en maritieme kringen ordonnantie" (Territorial sea and maritime districts ordinance) of 1939.[181] This ordinance embodied principles of the law of the sea as applied in the Netherlands and contained definitions of several expressions which are generally used in laws of the sea. It may be worthwhile to examine this ordinance because certain sections still apply in the present Republic of Indonesia.

Art. 1 started with defining the expression "Netherlands Indies territorial Sea" which for the purposes of this ordinance is defined as:[182]

(I) The sea area extending to seaward to a distance of three nautical miles from the low water mark of the islands or part of

[181] *Staatsblad van Nederlands Indië* (Official Gazette of the Netherlands Indies) 1939, no. 442, translated by the Secretariat of the U.N. and printed in "Laws and Regulations of the Regime of the Territorial Sea," *U.N. Legislative Series* 193–201 (ST/LEG/SER. B/6) (1957).

[182] *Id.* at 194.

islands, which belong to Netherlands Indies territory, subject to a few other provisions.

(II) The sea area situated to seaward of the area defined in para. I but lying within specific anchorage limits.

The ordinance then proceeded to define the following expressions:

Netherlands Indies sea territory (territorial waters): the Netherlands Indies territorial sea and, in addition, those parts of the coastal waters and the water areas of bays, arms of the sea, river and canal mouths which are situated to landward of the territorial sea.

Netherlands Indies internal waters: all waters situated to landward of the Netherlands Indies territorial sea, including all rivers, canals, lakes and pools in the Netherlands Indies.

Netherlands Indies waters: Netherlands Indies territorial sea including Netherlands Indies internal waters.

Maritime districts: those parts of Netherlands Indies waters designated, or to be designated, as such by the Governor General.[183]

Art. 1 also laid down the Netherlands Indies position with respect to other matters on the law of the sea. In the case of a bay, for example, if the opening of the bay does not exceed ten miles, the territorial waters are measured from a straight line across the opening of the bay. If the opening is more than ten miles the same line shall be drawn as close as possible to the entrance at the first point at which the width of the opening is not more than ten nautical miles.[184]

With respect to a group of two or more islands (apparently alluding to an archipelago), the three-mile limit is to be measured from straight lines "connecting the outermost points of the low water marks of the islands on the outer edge of the group, at the point where distance between these points is not more than six miles.[185]

In the case of straits with a width not exceeding six nautical miles, connecting two areas of the high seas of which the Netherlands Indies is not the sole coastal state, the dividing line between the territorial waters of both states will be drawn through the middle of the straits. Where the Netherlands Indies is the sole coastal state "the part of the straits enclosed by two lines drawn between the two shores at either end of the straits, as close as possible to the high

[183] This was done in *Staatsblad van Ned. Indië* 1939, no. 452.
[184] *Staatsblad van Ned. Indië, supra* note 181, art. 1, para. IA.
[185] *Id.* art. 1, para. IB.

seas at the first point where the breadth of the straits does not exceed six nautical miles, shall be deemed to be territorial sea, even if at other points within the two lines the breadth of the straits should be greater".[186]

Other well-known principles which have found a place in the said ordinance are the right of visit and the right of hot pursuit.[187] Some specific provisions are given with respect to fishing rights. In the maritime districts fishing is prohibited to all but the indigenous population[188] and persons with a licence from the naval commander.

(b) Laws and Regulations in the Republic of Indonesia

On December 29, 1949 the Dutch Government transferred sovereignty over the Netherlands Indies to the independent Republic of the United States of Indonesia. The question now arises whether the former Netherlands Indies provisions of the laws of the sea still apply in the newly created Indonesian state. This is indeed the case since transitional measures provided that existing laws and regulations at the time of transfer of sovereignty would remain in force until such time that they would be expressly revoked. This provision has been laid down in one of the documents of the Round Table Conference at The Hague of 1949, namely art. 8 of the Agreement on Transitional Measures which states that:

> All provisions in existing legal regulations and administrative ordinances inasmuch as they are not incompatible with the transfer of sovereignty... remain in force without modification, as regulations and ordinances of the Republic of the United States of Indonesia... as long as they are not revoked or modified by the competent organs.

Subsequently this provision was adopted by the constitution of the United States of Indonesia (art. 192) and since 1950 it has become art. 142 of the provisional constitution of the Republic of Indonesia.[189]

The above-mentioned "Territorial sea and maritime district ordinance" was not revoked and thus remained the basic document with respect to the laws of the sea in Indonesia. It should be noted

[186] *Id. art.* 1, para. 1C.
[187] *Id.* art. 15, 16 and 17.
[188] *Id.* art. 3 and 4 (para. 1).
[189] Engelbrecht, *De Wetboeken, Wetten en Verordeningen, benevens de Voorlopige Grondwet van de Republiek Indonesië*," (The Code Books, Statutes and Ordinances including the Provisional Constitution of the Republic of Indonesia) 17, 33, 67 and 95 (1956).

that these laws now remain in force not as Netherlands Indies enactments but as purely Indonesian laws.

On the other hand, the adoption of these maritime laws by transitional legislation did not imply that Indonesia thereby adhered permanently to all those principles of Netherlands Indies laws. By definition, transitional legislation is of a tentative nature and the adopted regulations are therefore subject to subsequent modification or revocation. Thus the temporary continuation of the applicability of the Netherlands Indies maritime rules did not imply the unqualified adherence of Indonesia to the principles embodied therein. It meant no more, and no less, than what was laid down in the above-mentioned art. 8 of the R.T.C. Agreement of Transitional Measures, namely that the provisions are applicable in so far as they are "not incompatible with the transfer of sovereignty" and may be revoked by subsequent legislation. Such a revocation finally came in the much publicized, and equally criticized, Indonesian declaration of December 13, 1957, which revoked in so many words some parts of the "Territorial sea and maritime districts ordinance" of 1939. This then leads us to the present situation created as a result of that decree.

(c) The present situation

The Government declaration of December 13, 1957, did not, revoke the entire Dutch ordinance; several of the provisions are still in force. One of the most important parts, however, namely art. 1, paragraph 1, dealing with Netherlands Indies territorial sea, was expressly revoked and replaced with provisions of a very different nature. The announcement stated:[190]

GOVERNMENT DECLARATION
CONCERNING THE WATER AREAS
OF THE REPUBLIC OF INDONESIA

The Cabinet, in its session of Friday 13 December 1957, discussed the problem of the water areas of the Republic of Indonesia.

The geographical composition of Indonesia as an archipelago consisting of thousands of islands has its own particular characteristics.

For the purposes of territorial unity, and in order to protect the resources of Indonesia, all islands and the seas in between must be regarded as one total unit.

The delimitation of the territorial sea as laid down in the "Territorial Sea and

[190] Translation of the Indonesian text as published in the Indonesian law journal "*Hukum*," vol. 1958, no. 5–6, Annex I. This same declaration as printed in an Indonesian newspaper article (*Keng Po*, 14 December 1957) includes also the following line: "From time immemorial the Indonesian archipelago has formed one unit."

Maritime Districts Ordinance of 1939," (Official Gazette, 1939, no. 442, Art. 1, par. 1) is no longer in accordance with the above-mentioned considerations (as it divides the land territory of Indonesia into separated sections, each with its own territorial waters).

On the basis of these considerations, the Government declares that all waters, surrounding, between and connecting the islands constituting the Indonesian state, regardless of their extension or breadth, are integral parts of the territory of the Indonesian state and, therefore, parts of the internal or national waters which are under the exclusive sovereignty of the Indonesian state. Innocent passage of foreign ships in these internal waters is granted as long as it is not prejudicial to or violates the sovereignty and security of Indonesia.

The delimitation of the territorial sea (the breadth of which is 12 miles) is measured from baselines connecting the outermost points of the islands of Indonesia.

The above-mentioned provisions will be enacted as soon as possible.

This Government position will be maintained at the International Conference on the Law of the Sea which will be held in Geneva in February 1958.

The outstanding features of this declaration can be summarized as follows:

(1) Indonesia is an archipelago and must therefore be treated as one unit.

(2) All waters surrounding, between and connecting the islands of the archipelago, regardless of breadth are to be considered as internal waters.

(3) The breadth of Indonesian territorial sea is twelve miles, to be measured from baselines connecting outermost points of the islands at the fringe of the archipelago.

(4) Innocent passage is guaranteed.

(5) All other provisions of the Territorial Sea and Martime Districts Ordinance of 1939 remain in force, e.g. those with respect to fishing, search of vessels, hot pursuit and protection of cables, pollution of sea water and other regulations for the purpose of ensuring orderliness and safety.

As could be expected the declaration evoked much comment from other members of the community of states; their reactions can be divided into three categories. Firstly, there was the group of states which strongly criticized the Indonesian actions as being contrary to the rules of international law.[191] As one might easily have predicted, these objections came principally from the big maritime nations whose interests were directly affected by the

[191] Besides the Netherlands other countries have protested against the Indonesian intentions, e.g. U.K. *N.R.C.* 20 Dec. 1957, U.S. and Japan, *id.* Jan. 14, 1958, Australia and France, *The Times*, London, Jan. 16, 1958, and New Zealand, *N.R.C.* 20 Jan. 1958.

restrictions imposed by the Indonesian decree. Secondly, there was the great majority of states which did not react in any way and were thus either indifferent or tacitly approved, or disapproved, of it. Finally, there were also a few states (e.g. Russia)[192] which unequivocally came out in favour of the Indonesian claims which they considered to be fully in accordance with the rules of international law.

Those who had expected that the Geneva Conferences on the Law of the Sea of 1958 and 1960 would lead to a solution of the Indonesian case were disappointed by the results and the problems are still awaiting a solution. Fortunately, the situation has not been aggravated since Indonesia – as well as the contesting states – has been very careful not to carry their claims too far. Hence, no serious conflict has as yet arisen out of this issue, but on the other hand neither side has relinquished its full claims. In fact, Indonesia has proceeded to realize the enactment called for in the Government declaration of 13 December 1957. On 18 February 1960, Act no. 4 was passed containing virtually the same principles as the abovementioned declaration:[193]

THE PRESIDENT

OF THE REPUBLIC OF INDONESIA

CONSIDERING:

(1) that the geographical configuration of Indonesia as an archipelagic State which consists of thousands of islands has its own characteristics and peculiarities,

(2) that since time immemorial the Indonesian archipelago has constituted one entity,

(3) that in the interest of the territorial integrity of the Indonesian State all the islands and the waters lying between those islands should be regarded as a single unit,

(4) that the delimitation of the territorial waters as provided for in article 1 paragraph 1 of the Territorial Sea and Maritime Circles Ordinance of 1939 (Government Gazette 1939 No. 442) is not in accordance with the above considerations, as it divided the territory of Indonesia into separate parts having their own territorial sea,

(5) that it is therefore deemed necessary to enact an Act concerning the Indonesian waters in accordance with the above considerations,

HAVING REGARD TO:

Article 5 paragraph I of the Constitution of the Republic of Indonesia

HAVING HEARD:

The deliberations of the Cabinet of Ministers of 20 January 1960.

DECIDES TO ENACT:

[192] *Manchester Guardian*, Febr. 13, 1958.

[193] This English text of Act no. 4, 1960 is published in *U.N. Doc* A/Conf. 19/5/Add. 1, p. 3–4. (1960).

ACT CONCERNING INDONESIAN WATERS

Article 1

(1) The Indonesian waters consist of the territorial sea and the internal waters of Indonesia.

(2) The Indonesian territorial sea is a maritime belt of a width of 12 nautical miles, the outer limit of which is measured perpendicular to the baselines or points on the baselines which consist of straight lines connecting the outermost points on the low water mark of the outermost islands or part of such islands comprising Indonesian territory with the provision that in case of straits of a width of not more than 24 nautical miles and Indonesia is not the only coastal state the outer limit of the Indonesian territorial sea shall be drawn at the middele of the strait.

(3) The Indonesian internal waters are all waters lying within the baselines mentioned in paragraph (2).

(4) One nautical mile is one sixtieth of a degree of a meridian.

Article 2

On the map annexed to this Act is indicated the position of the points and baselines mentioned in article 1 paragraph (2).

Article 3

(1) Innocent passage through the internal waters of Indonesia is open to foreign vessels.

(2) The innocent passage as mentioned in paragraph 1 shall be regulated by Government Ordinance.

Article 4

(1) This Act comes into force on the date of its promulgation.

(2) Article 1 paragraph 1 sub-paragraph 1 to 4 of the Territorial Sea and Maritime Circles' Ordinance of 1939 is no longer valid as from the date mentioned in paragraph 1.

In order that the Act be known to everybody whomsoever it is instructed that this Act be promulgated by publication in the Government Gazette.

Done at Djakarta on 18 Februari, 1960.

Promulgated at Djakarta on 18 February, 1960.

Minister of Justice
sd. (SAHARDJO)

President of the Republic of Indonesia
sd. (SOEKARNO)

We will now proceed with a further discussion of the claims involved in this controversy.

2. *The Interplay of Competing Claims*

The Indonesian efforts to assert her authority in sea territories over which other states claim concurrent authority, are neither a novel nor a rare event in the interactions of participants in the process of claim.[194] Claims and counterclaims are made continually in all fields of international contact. In fact, viewed from a functional perspective, international law owes its place in the world community to the function which it is supposed to fulfil as an instrument for the achievement of a fair balance between conflicting claims of one state *vis-à-vis* another state or the world community.

With respect to the oceans and other waters of the globe, which constitute one of the main resources for mankind, it can be said that the laws of the sea which are applicable have been created as a result of the following process:

> Through several centuries of interaction, of particular claim and general community acceptance or rejection, a body of principles and process of decision were thus developed which achieved a compromise between demands of coastal and noncoastal states, roughly corresponding to exclusive and inclusive claims, effectively internationalizing in the common interest a great resource covering two-thirds of the earth's surface.[195]

The claims which were advanced with respect to the oceans and other waters originated, of course, from states which are land-based. This relationship between land and water gave rise to the well-known but not precisely defined concept of coastal contiguity or propinquity which is basic to the understanding of the prescriptions which have been developed for the solution of claims in the laws of the sea. It also follows from the nature of the relationship of contiguity that the comprehensiveness and intensity of the claims made by land-based states are strongest nearest the land-base and tend to decrease the further one moves away from the coast.[196]

Since the applicability of the principles of the laws of the sea is in general not questioned here, it is not attempted either to review all these rules and concepts. The increased attention which is given to-day to the changing nature of international relations is well taken care of by various contemporary authors of international law.

[194] McDougal and Burke, "Crisis in the Law of the Sea. Community Perspectives Versus National Egoism," 67 *Yale L.J.* 539–589 (1958).

[195] *Id.* at 540.

[196] At the Geneva Conference on the Law of the Sea in 1958 it appeared from the discussions in the Third Committee (High seas, fishing, conservation of living resources) that there were two different approaches to the problem of conservation on the high seas. The minority opinion maintained that there was complete freedom of navigation and fishing on the high seas. The majority of states, however, put the interests and rights of the coastal states first. Ministerie van Buitenlandse Zaken, *De Conferentie van de Verenigde Naties over het Zeerecht* (Neth. Ministry of Foreign Affairs, The U.N. Conference on the Law of the Sea) 59 (1958). As is suggested above, claims and counterclaims must be seen in their relation to and distance from the land-base.

One such article[197] is chosen here as a basis for the discussion of the Indonesian position, in order to see where Indonesia's claims agree with, or deviate even from progressive contemporary theories.

Therefore, a categorization of such claims into groups according to comprehensiveness and intensity coincides with a similar series of possible conflicts which become the more serious, the more comprehensive and intense the claims. The interrelation of the asserted claims and their concomitant controversies have been categorized in the following groups:[198]

(a) Internal waters.
(b) Territorial sea.
(c) Boundary between internal waters and the territorial sea.
(d) Breadth of the territorial sea.
(e) High seas areas regarded as contiguous to the claimant state.
(f) High seas areas not regarded as contiguous to the claimant state.

It will be attempted below to examine the specific exclusive claims[199] of Indonesia in the order of these categories. By balancing these claims against the competing inclusive claims of one or all other states concerned we may be able to arrive at a fair appraisal of their validity.

One point should be made clear beforehand, however. It is undoubtedly true that ultimately states are better served to-day by an attitude of "mutual restraint and tolerance which inhere in a recognition of common interest."[200] But this is a choice to be made by each state on the basis of its long-term policies, which are designed to encourage and increase "effective capacity for the fuller enjoyment of their existing common right," rather than to destroy "their equality of access to inclusive uses of the oceans."[201]

Unfortunately, many of the newly established Asian states find themselves in the desperate and unenviable position of needing an

[197] McDougal and Burke, *supra* note 194.
[198] *Id.* at 551–555.
[199] For an explanation of the terms "exclusive" and "inclusive" claims, see McDougal & Burke, *supra* note 194, at 539, n.l.
[200] *Id.* at 589. Statements to that effect were frequently heard at the Geneva Conference of 1958, e.g. during the debate in the 1st Committee, by the representative of the Philippines, *Summary Records of the 1st Committee*, U.N. Doc. A/Conf. 13/39 at 5 (1958), of India *id.* at 15 and of Ceylon, *id.* at 27.
[201] McDougal & Burke, *supra* note 194, at 589.

improvement of conditions in the shortest possible time.[202] They often repeat the argument that there will not be any question of a long-term policy if the state cannot survive the present initial stage of its development.[203] This holds true to a great extent for Indonesia and, therefore, a discussion of the Indonesian claims has to be pursued in the light of these considerations. This thesis, which pretends to represent as much as possible the views of the Asian states, cannot evade this task.

It seems rather unrealistic to expect a new country like Indonesia to exercise any restraint on what she considers matters of vital importance, only for the benefit of common world interest, which to her is often too vague and idealistic a concept. Paradoxically, practice has shown that these young states do have a surprisingly great trust in international conferences, perhaps even to an unwarranted degree. This shows that they are willing to give consideration to common world interest if only it can be done on a multilateral basis. Resolutions passed at such conferences would, therefore, carry greater weight with them than views of individual, or groups of, states.

In the case of Indonesia, however, this does not mean that she will have no consideration for the inclusive claims of other states. Not being a major power, Indonesia cannot afford to ignore the counterclaims of bigger nations some of which belong to the group of states which joined issue with the Indonesian intention of enlarging her authority in the waters of the Indonesian Archipelago. The balancing of Indonesia's exclusive claims will, therefore, have to be carried out *vis-à-vis* the inclusive counterclaims of objecting parties as well as the entire world community, but it should always be kept in mind that in the balancing process Indonesia draws support from another group of states, and from the tacit approval of states of a third group which adhere to similar practices.[204]

[202] The Indian representative in the Third Committee of the Geneva Conference of 1958 illustrated this point when he stressed the importance of protection of the interests of the coastal state in the living resources of the high seas; especially to the "underdeveloped areas with their expanding populations and increasing dependence on the sea for food." *Summary Records, 3rd Committee,* U.N. Doc. no. A/Conf. 13/41, at 4 (1958).

[203] Such statements, made in many Asian countries, were obviously the result of strong nationalistic feelings prevalent in these new states at the time. However, subsequent developments on the domestic scene have demonstrated that the basic issue was indeed to survive the mounting problems of political, economic and social nature.

[204] *Supra* at 175.

(a) Authority in internal waters

Over these waters, also called inland waters, interior waters or national waters,[205] coastal states make the most comprehensive authoritative claims[206] since the area is situated closest to the land territory. In fact, there is no particular difference between the comprehensive nature of these claims and the authority which the coastal state exercises over its actual land territory.[207] Although not physically equivalent to each other, for purposes of law, internal waters are put on the same level as land territory.[208] The exclusive claims which coastal states advance in this zone of water are usually expressed in terms of sovereignty, independence and jurisdiction. Their opponents, although conceding the comprehensive authority of the coastal state, put forward another set of doctrines which purport to establish rules which derogate from the general principle; for example, with respect to entry, distress, trade.[209] Any accommodation of both sets of claims cannot overlook the fact that the practice of extensive state control over such internal waters has become firmly established now and is regarded as reasonable. This is understandable if it is taken into consideration that control of such waters, which because of their close connection with the coast is regarded as land territory proper, is a necessity for the protection and development of the territory and interests of the coastal state, and for the protection of access to and exit from the territorial base.[210] The only reservation which is made to this all comprising right over internal waters is that the exclusive demands of the coastal state should not be exercised in an arbitrary and unreasonable manner.

The declaration of the Indonesian Government has been severely criticized for its transformation of extensive sea areas into internal waters. The relevant paragraph in that document states: "The government declares that all waters surrounding, between and connecting the islands constituting the Indonesian state, regardless of their extension or breadth, are integral parts of the internal or national waters which are under the exclusive sovereignty of the Indonesian state." In Act no. 4 of 1960 the counterpart of this

[205] 1 Oppenheim, *International Law* 460 (8th ed. 1955).
[206] McDougal & Burke, *supra* note 194, at 551.
[207] *Cf.* 1 Oppenheim, *op. cit. supra* note 205, at 487.
[208] *Id.* at 460–461.
[209] McDougal & Burke, *supra* note 194, at 561.
[210] *Id.* at 574.

provision can be found in Art. 1. After having first established the baselines "which consist of straight lines connecting the outermost points on the low water mark of the outermost islands," para. 3 of this article states that the Indonesian internal waters are all waters lying within these baselines. Having thus established the area of internal waters, Indonesia proceeded to make the most comprehensive claims which are commonly attached to such internal waters and which in traditional terms are called "exclusive sovereignty."[211] However, this rigid provision is immediately followed by the concession of innocent passage if neither prejudicial to nor violating the sovereignty and security of Indonesia.[212] The International Law Commission, in its draft articles of 1956, had incorporated exactly the same rule. It had opened the possibility to a state to incorporate vast areas into its internal waters, while on the other hand the Commission gave enough weight to the interests of other states to recommend the recognition of a right of innocent passage through waters which previously had been used for international navigation.[213]

It is true, as is sometimes contended, that the acceptance of such a view would considerably blur the dividing line between internal and territorial waters which were previously clearly distinguished by the right of innocent passage. This right was only accorded to foreign ships in territorial waters, but not in internal waters.[214] Since the Indonesian regulations do guarantee the right of innocent passage in *internal* waters, one might contend that the regulations incorrectly speak of internal waters instead of territorial waters. It is suggested here, however, that this might well be correct in the Indonesian example. Territorial waters are closely connected with the idea of a belt of waters *around* (or in front of) a land territory. Therefore, the term seems only correct for the waters around the

[211] *Supra* at 174. The Act No. 4 of 1960 does not use the term "exclusive sovereignty," but the Explanatory Memorandum which accompanies this Act explicitly mentions Indonesia's exclusive sovereignty over her internal waters. See *e.g.* Circular No. H. 248 of the *Commercial Advisory Foundation in Indonesia* (CAFI) of which an annex contains the Explanatory Memorandum.

[212] The question of innocent passage in "areas which previously had been considered as part of the territorial sea or of the high seas," is dealt with in art. 5, para. 3 of the draft-articles of the International Law Commission (Doc. A/3159). At the Geneva Conference in 1958, it appeared that the meaning of "innocent" was essentially: "a passage which is not prejudicial to the security of the coastal state." The meaning of the word "security" was not clearly explained, however. Min. v. B.Z., *op. cit. supra* note 196, at 21. The Indonesian decree seemed to be in agreement with these views.

[213] McDougal & Burke, *supra* note 194, at 574.

[214] *Ibid.*

outer islands of the Indonesian archipelago and not for the waters which are in fact surrounded themselves by large and small islands. For example, the term territorial waters would be meaningless if the Java Sea in its entirety is considered as such, for the Java Sea could be regarded not as a belt of water *around* (or in front of) land, but actually as a water surrounded by land.[215] Furthermore, the idea of territorial waters is closely connected with a certain breadth, a characteristic which is foreign to the idea of internal waters. If, therefore, the Java Sea as a whole is called territorial waters, then the basic element of breadth loses its meaning. In this particular respect it is, therefore, possible to say that although the term "internal waters" is perhaps not fully justified[216] since the Indonesian form shows little difference from the concept of territorial waters, yet it seems a more correct terminology here in view of other above-mentioned considerations. Of course, other cases may exist where these considerations do not apply, and where the meaning of internal waters and territorial waters very much more resemble each other. In such cases one may indeed hold that the functional distinction between these two marine zones is no longer valid and rather obliterates than clarifies the situation.

(b) Authority over territorial waters

To-day the territorial waters are still clearly distinguishable from the above-mentioned internal waters. With respect to the comprehensiveness of the claim, it can be said that the authority asserted by claimant states over this zone which in coastal contiguity comes next to internal waters, is not very much smaller than that exercised in the preceding zone. To substantiate their claims over territorial waters, states indeed employ the same terms of sovereignty, independence, and jurisdiction as are used to claim internal waters,[217] since the territorial sea is regarded as an extension of land territory and therefore of sovereignty.[218]

In terms of asserted claims and counterclaims the concept of territorial waters gives rise to two competing sets of doctrines. On

[215] The question is somewhat different, however, in such "closed seas" as the Black Sea and the Baltic where more than one state possesses the coast. Although one could then still claim the existence of a special regime, a certain breadth of the territorial sea still has sense here. See the discussion on closed seas in *Summary Records, 2nd Committee,* Doc. A/Conf. 13/40 at 37–40 (1958).

[216] *Ibid.*

[217] *Id.* at 561.

[218] Colombos, *The International Law of the Seas* 66 (3rd rev. ed. 1954).

the one hand, the coastal state for reasons of the security of the lives and property of its subjects as well as for commercial, fiscal, political and economic considerations,[219] feels itself justified to make exclusive claims over the marginal belt. It has become generally accepted that in these cases the competing interests of other states have to yield to those of the coastal states with the exception of the right of innocent passage, which, unless applied in a manner prejudicial to the coastal state, cannot be considered to hurt the legitimate interests of that state in its territorial waters.[220] It is also worth noting that in contrast to the right of entry in internal waters innocent passage is recognized without an express agreement. It is furthermore of special significance in the case of international waterways, i.e. historical straits connecting two open seas, a matter which obviously applies to an archipelago such as that of Indonesia.[221]

In the preceding section on internal waters it has been observed that the Indonesian decree establishes a regime in its waters which allows for little distinction between internal and territorial waters. Indonesian waters have been proclaimed internal waters but the exclusive sovereignty has been tempered by expressly according the right of innocent passage to foreign ships unless their behaviour is detrimental to the security of the state. Security consideration is precisely the reason why foreign war ships have not been given this right, although opinions differ on the exact rule applicable to men-of-war in territorial waters.[222] Here then again the difference between internal and territorial waters is of some importance. In the latter the right is rather undefined, whereas with regard to the former it seems clear that such a right does not exist and a foreign war ship is entirely dependent on a permission from the coastal state to enter national waters.[223]

Thus, the authority which the Government of Indonesia has conferred upon itself is a far-reaching one. It would apparently imply

[219] *Ibid.*

[220] See Briggs, *The Law of Nations*, 354 (1952).

[221] At the 1958 Geneva Conference the Indonesian delegate stated in the 1st Committee that in the absence of an independent organ of arbitration the only practical possibility was to maintain a subjective criterion, *e.g.* that of art. 17, para. 1, with respect to suspension of exercise of the right of innocent passage in its territorial sea. This, according to the Indonesian representative, was the basic rule. Therefore, he rejected a proposed amendment which would establish the right of innocent passage through straits which connect a part of the high seas with the territorial sea of a particular state. Such a rule would be an infringement on the basic right of art. 17, para. 1, in its own territorial sea, he said. *Summary records, 1st Committee,* A/Conf. 13/39 at 93–94 (1958).

[222] Colombos, *op. cit. supra* note 218, at 99.

[223] *Id.* at 192; 1 Oppenheim, *op. cit. supra* note 205, at 461.

that all "internal waters," i.e. all waters between the islands of the archipelago, could be closed to foreign war ships at any time, and to merchant vessels if they are considered to endanger the security of the state. This provision has understandably aroused much protest from other sea-faring nations, but here – as is so often the case – it is not the letter but the spirit of the regulation which is of importance. The above stipulation obviously cannot be intended by the Indonesian government to mean that it could close its internal waters to foreign men-of-war or even merchant vessels arbitrarily. Such an act would ignore the legitimate claims of other interested parties and disregard community practices which have been arrived at after a centuries' old process of balancing of claims and counter-claims. On the other hand, there cannot be any valid objection to a temporary limitation of passage of a foreign ship if the security of the state is at stake.[224] The particular configuration of Indonesia as an archipelago with innumerable islands, extensive waters and enormous coast length, might very well justify a quicker use of its sovereign authority to prevent any passage of a foreign ship than is allowed to countries with a solid land-base. Domestic as well as external events may present greater problems of security and military defence in an extensive archipelago than in ordinary countries, especially if the archipelago belongs to a country with only a small number of security forces. These problems have been dealt with in the Explanatory Memorandum to Act no. 4, 1960. The section of "General Explanation" mentioned as a disadvantage of the traditional system that

> the air space over a territory with such a structure (i.e. of an archipelago) would automatically not have a homogeneous character either. Pockets of high seas in the midst of or in between the land-territories (islands) of Indonesia were putting functionaries in a difficult situation as they had to observe all the time whether they were finding themselves in national waters or on the high sea, because their rights of taking any step depended on their present position.
>
> In case of war between two parties, with their battle-fleets moving to and fro on the high seas between Indonesian islands, our unity would be threatened.[225]

The test of legality with respect to Indonesia's exclusive claims can therefore not lie in the apparent meaning of a few prescriptions but in the question whether her activities can stand the test of

[224] The history of art. 24 of the ILC draft, which article was dropped from the Convention on the Territorial Sea and the Contiguous Zone, seems to support the Indonesian attitude with respect to passage of warships. See *Summary Records, 1st Committee, op. cit. supra* note 200, at 127, 129–131.

[225] CAFI, *Supra* note 211.

reasonableness. The result can only be arrived at after a fair balancing of all relevant factors.

(c) Boundary between internal and territorial sea

The delimination of the boundary between the two zones nearest to the shore does not generally give rise to any problem if the coastline is only slightly indented. Gulfs, bays, estuaries and other indentations cause some difficulties in determining the dividing line between these zones and therefore also in dealing with the corresponding authoritative claims. In recent years, there has been a tendency to move the dividing line away from the shore and thus bring under the authority of the coastal state great expanses of sea territory as internal waters.[226] The extensive claim of the coastal state has been met by counterclaims which contend that the arbitrary enlargement of authority violates the long-established principles of the freedom of the seas with all its implications. To support their claim, decision-makers in the coastal state invoke a set of prescriptions on archipelagos, gulfs, bays, ports, and the like, whereas their opponents advance equally well-known concepts of "each island its own territorial waters,"[227] low water mark, ten, twelve or fifteen miles closing line.[228]

The technical side of this controversy centres around the methods of determining the base-lines for the measurement of the breadth of the territorial waters. Whatever the correct method[229], it is useful to keep in mind that, thus far, the accepted traditional prescriptions are inclined to restrict the freedom of the coastal states to make arbitrary extensions of their internal waters to the detriment of the inclusive rights of other members of the community of states. The traditional prescriptions have proved their value if we look at the conviction which prevails to-day that it is in the common interest of any state to honour these rules,[230] unless it is able to prove that certain special and *unique* features of the particular country justify a deviation from established practices.[231]

226 McDougal & Burke, *supra* note 194, at 552–553.

227 *Cf.* International Law Commission, Report U.N. Gen. Ass., Off. Rec. 10th sess., Supp. No. 9, art. 10 at 18 and comment.

228 McDougal & Burke, *supra* note 194, at 562.

229 See Evensen, *The Anglo-Norwegian Fisheries Case and its Legal Consequences*," 46 *A.J.I.L.* 609–630 at 621 (1952).

230 McDougal & Burke, *supra* note 194, at 575.

231 The consequences of the adoption of straight baselines connecting the outermost points of the Indonesian Archipelago are fairly clear. Alll waters within such baselines

The archipelago in the law of the sea. It is, therefore, in the unique characteristic of her territory that Indonesia has sought the principal justification of her exceptional, exclusive claims. Her uniqueness rests on her geographical composition as an archipelago of thousands of bigger and smaller islands which nevertheless form one single unit. Historically, though not politically, this area has constituted one unit from time immemorial.[232] Economically too, the interdependence of the various islands is clear, for none of them is sufficiently self-supporting to be regarded as a separate unit. The significance of the sea in the lives of the people, is reflected in the ancient fishing rights of the population which have already been recognized during the Dutch period.[233] The main part of the Indonesian argument, however, remains the geographical composition of her territory as an archipelago, i.e. "a formation of two or more islands (islets or rocks) which geographically may be considered as a whole."[234]

Traditional doctrines have as yet not developed any well-established rules for the delimitation of the waters of an archipelago. In fact the striking feature of these prescriptions on archipelagos is their complex and uncertain nature which is in turn reflected in the provisions of the recent draft of the International Law Commission.[235] Evensen, while making a survey of all possible sources of international law on this topic, reviews first the studies of international bodies.

become internal waters. The Philippine delegate brought this up at the Geneva Conference of 1958. His proposal (Doc. A/Conf. 13/C1/L98) was later withdrawn. *Summary Records, 1st Committee, op. cit. supra* note 200 at 148.

For the ring of straight baselines around the Indonesian archipelago, see map facing p. 168.

[232] See Act. 4, 1960, *supra* at 175.

[233] Staatsblad van Ned. Indië (Official Gazette of the Neth. Indies) 1927 no. 145 on "General Regulations of April 29, 1927, for the hunting of whales within three nautical miles of the coast of the Netherlands Indies" (printed in "Laws and Regulations of the Regime of the Territorial Sea," *op. cit. supra* note 182 at 535) which speaks in art. 2 of the right of the indigenous population to hunt whales "insofar they have been accustomed from time immemorial to carry on such hunting."

[234] Evensen, "*Certain legal aspects concerning the delimitation of the territorial waters of archipelagos*," U.N. Gen. Ass., A/Conf.13/18 at 5 (1957). During the general debate in the 1st Committee of the Geneva Conference of 1958 the Indonesian representative expressed the hope that art. 10 of the ILC draft concerning islands would be supplemented so as to regulate the question of "groups of islands as a single geographic or economic unit, and covering cases in which such groups were situated in the middle of an ocean" *Summary Records, 1st Committee, supra* note 200 at 15. However, the Conference was unable to succeed where the ILC had failed. Efforts by Yugoslavia (Doc. A/Conf. 13/C. 1/L. 59), the Philippines and Indonesia to have a provision adopted regulating the special regime of an archipelago did not receive enough support. See *Summary Records, 1st Committee, op. cit. supra* note 200 at 161–163.

[235] Evensen, *supra* note 234, at 13.

He shows the varying attitudes of those organizations which range from a restrictive attitude which refuses to consider the archipelago as a single unit for the above purposes (e.g. the Drafts of the Institut de Droit International (1892, 1894) and the Harvard Research in International Law (1929)) to that of a broad view as taken by the Alvarez draft of the International Law Association (1924), the Schücking draft of the Hague Codification Conference (1930) and the draft no. 10 of the American Institute of International Law of 1925. The present proposals of the International Law Commission take a middle course between the above two extremes.

A subsequent examination by Evensen of the works of various leading authors proves that they have paid little attention to archipelagos, and the above discussions moreover show many diverging views. Here, however, the usual attitude is to "look upon such archipelagos as units with the ensuing legal implications as far as the delimitation of territorial waters is concerned."[236]

An examination of the practices of the various states does not bring us much further either since no uniformity can be found.[237] There is, however, one interesting point which should be made. In the case of the Philippine Archipelago, Evensen comments on the relevant provisions for delimitation of the territorial waters of this country as being "somewhat unique." The uniqueness is represented by the Philippines' views on internal waters which hold that: "All waters around, between and connecting different islands belonging to the Philippine Archipelago, irrespective of their width or dimension, are necessary appurtenances of its land territory, forming an integral part of the national or inland waters, subject to the exclusive sovereignty of the Philippines."[238] A similar provision extends the regime of the territorial waters over other extensive areas without giving a clear recognition of the international status of straits in those regions. The case of Indonesia clearly

[236] *Id.* at 13.

[237] The question of the territorial sea of islands has another important aspect to which the Burmese delegate at the Geneva Conference of 1958 drew the attention. He pointed to the position of an island situated in the territorial sea of another state. He stated that, if such an island were to have its own territorial sea, it would also be entitled to its own contiguous zone and continental shelf and the result would only be an intolerable conflict of jurisdiction since the "median line" only solves the problem on the landward side of the island. *Summary Records, 1st Committee, op. cit. supra* note 200, at 161. The representative of Thailand saw this statement as directed towards some Thai islands off the Burmese coast. In his opinion the matter could best be solved by bilateral negotiations. *Id.* at 162.

[238] Evensen, *supra* note 234, at 17.

bears a very great resemblance to that of the Philippines, and the use of identical terms is very striking.

A comparison of these two similar cases leads to at least two observations:

(1) The case of the Philippines has not been received with so much protest and criticism as that of Indonesia. The reason is perhaps mainly that the Indonesian Archipelago occupies a more central geographical position in South East Asia. As a result every alleged limitation of international navigation in this area will be greatly resented by other countries.

(2) The Philippines constitute a unique example of archipelago in the sense that it has two large centres (Luzon and Mindanao) surrounded by thousands of islands and separated by relatively broad waters.[239] In this respect Indonesia is even more unique since there is not one or two centres, but at least four main parts, namely Sumatra, Java, Borneo and Celebes. The significance of numbers and size becomes clear if we consider the attitude of those countries which oppose the "archipelago one-unit" concept. It is, for example, perfectly understandable and correct, that the Alaskan Archipelago is treated by the U.S. in the restrictive way of giving every island its own territorial waters. So is the U.K. attitude towards her own archipelagos; here however, the process of balancing of interests and claims is not very difficult. Those archipelagos are minor, non-vital parts of the main country. A total loss of these islands does not constitute a disaster for the whole country. In Indonesia, however, the whole state apparatus and development might be seriously upset if one of those four islands would, for some reason, be cut off from the others. In other words, the interdependence of the various parts of the archipelago necessarily results in the rejection of the simple theory of "each island its own territorial waters" without giving special consideration to the above-mentioned facts. It is, therefore, on the great degree of interdependence that Indonesia has built its case for the contention that the archipelago is one single unit. The Explanatory Memorandum[240] to Act no. 4, 1960 states that

> The main objection against the way of fixing the boundary of the territorial sea mentioned above is the fact that this method took little or no account at all of the special nature of Indonesia as an archipelago. According to this old method

[239] *Cf.* the examples of New Zealand and Japan which differ also in this respect that they are less centrally situated than Indonesia and the Philippines.

[240] *Supra* note 211.

of measuring the territorial sea, i.e. starting from a baseline in the form of the low-water line, each island in Indonesia would theoretically have its own territorial sea (The Indonesian archipelago consists of about 13.000 islands of which about 3000 are inhabited).

These considerations seem to justify a deviation from traditional world prescriptions, if it is only kept within reasonable limits. Here too, the test is again the fair balancing of the comprehensive interests of the Archipelago-state in asserting its authority and the general interests of the world community and the special states concerned. The prescriptions developed by traditional international law represent a fair interpretation of both interest groups as a result of centuries of a balancing process. The specific interests of the Indonesian Republic as laid down in the new regulations are said to set aside established community prescriptions to a considerable extent. They are only justifiable if, in the words of the World Court in the Anglo-Norwegian fisheries case, there is "a more or less close relationship existing between certain sea areas and the land formations which divide and surround them,[241]" although a state must also be allowed "the latitude necessary in order to be able to adopt its delimitations to practical needs and local requirements."[242]

To support her case Indonesia has relied in these regulations only on a theoretical statement of general principles of international law, and of the law of the sea in particular. That alone cannot be enough to establish her peculiar position. It should be supplemented by detailed relevant historical, economical, geological and other data which will be able to prove the contention that the country is one territorial unit and should be regarded as such. Although such a factual account does not seem to be very difficult to arrive at, it will depend on a careful selection of supporting evidence whether the Indonesian claims can be sufficiently substantiated.

(d) Breadth of territorial waters

Few principles of the laws of the sea are so well-known and seem to be so generally accepted as the breadth of the territorial sea; yet this same notion has in fact continually been attacked as not representing the correct situation. It has already been said in the preceding section that the exclusive claims of the coastal state to its waters are made in order to secure and protect the various

[241] Evensen, *supra* note 234, at 33.
[242] *Ibid.*

interests of its subjects, whereas the counterclaims of other states, which try to do the same for their own subjects, retort that any extension of such authority beyond the three-mile limit is an unwarranted and unnecessary extension of control in what is essentially territory under the regime of the high seas.[243] Yet recent history has shown that the three-mile limit, whatever its binding force in the past, is rapidly losing its alleged general application. The fact is that the three-mile rule has never in recent times achieved the general or even predominant acceptance which is claimed for it. It is the frequent reference to this so-called traditional rule which has caused so much confusion. State practice up to the end of the 18th and the beginning of the 19th century showed that European nations, among whom were the staunchest supporters of the three-mile limit, were making all sorts of extensive claims to the seas around Europe.[244] Some of these states have afterwards for technical, economic and political reasons adopted the restricted 3-mile zone of territorial waters, but many other nations never did so.

Great Britain and the U.S., for instance, have changed their views when their interests changed. "From the time when England silently dropped her claim to jurisdiction over the seas surrounding her coasts ... she has persistently contended for the emancipation of all the oceans from the claim of any state to domination"...[245]

Apart from incidental drafts by international associations[246] a general review of state practices came at the Hague Codification Conference of 1930 after the League of Nations had thought the time ripe for a codification of the laws of territorial waters in order to conclude a general convention on this subject.[247] After a proposal for the adoption of three miles as the maximum limit had failed, the members were asked to express their views as to the limit of territorial waters, without a vote being taken. Of the 42 states less than half (20) agreed to 3 miles, 12 states said 6 miles and 4 claimed 4 miles. To-day the camp of three-mile supporters is rapidly losing its former majority position; the great influx of newly created states seems to strengthen the side which favours a wider zone.

If we examine the opinions of the leading writers we will also

[243] McDougal & Burke, *supra* note 194, at 553, 562–563.
[244] Colombos, *supra* note 218, at 40.
[245] *Id.* at 50.
[246] Evensen, *supra* note 234, at 6–18.
[247] Colombos, *supra* note 218, at 80.

find the same disagreement. Before 1930 many of them claimed the existence of such a three-mile limit as an established rule of international law.[248] To-day the attitude is a more cautious one[249] and the general opinion seems to be that there is no unanimity and too little agreement to establish an indisputable rule.[250]

Summarizing the above material in order to arrive at an answer to the question whether the Indonesian regulations with respect to territorial waters would be valid according to the present prescriptions applied by the community of states, two points stand out:

(1) The state practices on territorial waters have never been sufficiently consistent to warrant an assertion of the three-mile limit. This concept has undergone considerable changes from a period of extensive, exclusive claims of coastal states some centuries ago to one of a more limited character and now back to one of a more extensive nature. It is, therefore, erroneous to speak of an established "traditional" three-mile limit of the territorial waters.

(2) Moreover, there is a wide-spread dissatisfaction with existing doctrines of maritime jurisdiction in general.[251] It is now more or less admitted that under modern conditions the three-mile zone is not wide enough for all the legitimate interests of the shore state.[252] As the concept of territorial waters is now in a state of flux, it would be quite erroneous to take a rigid attitude with regard to the question of what the exact width should be. Most of all, it seems unrealistic to resist any extension of the territorial waters, as a matter of principle, as has sometimes been attempted by some states.[253] The delimitation of this breadth is not a matter of principle but one of higly practical nature. The above-mentioned changing state-practices clearly demonstrate this point; in fact, it should be

[248] Jessup was of the opinion that the three-mile limit was an established rule in 1927. Jessup, *The Law of Territorial Waters & Maritime Jurisdiction* 66 (1927). See also Harvard Research in International Law, Draft Convention on Territorial Waters, arts. 2–7, in 23 *A.J.I.L.* (Supplement) at 250–262, 275–280 (1929).

[249] At the 1958 Geneva Conference art. 3 of the ILC draft was not discussed successfully. Of the many proposals only a few survived the first stages. They were taken to the Plenary meeting of the Conference, but all failed to receive the necessary 2/3 majority. Indonesia had co-sponsored the Mexican proposal (A/Conf. 13/L. 34).

[250] Dean, "The Geneva Conference on the Law of the Sea – What Was Accomplished," 52 *A.J.I.L.* 608–616 (1958); Smith, *The Laws and Customs of the Sea* 13 (1948); 3 Gidel, *Le Droit International Public de la Mer* 123 (1934).

[251] Young, "Recent Developments with Respect to the Continental Shelf," 42 *A.J.I.L.* 857 (1948).

[252] Smith, *supra* note 250, at 17.

[253] Colombos, *supra* note 218, ta 83.

considered an advantage rather than a disadvantage of this doctrine that it has been possible to adjust it to the changing needs of time.

But one runs into difficulties if one tries to make it a matter of principle. For example, two such opinions which are sometimes advanced in support of the three-mile limit, contend that it was accepted by maritime nations possessing nearly eighty per cent of the world's effective tonnage,[254] while the coastline of maritime nations accepting the three-mile zone is very "impressive." If the strength of the three-mile zone should depend on such arguments it could hardly have chosen a weaker basis. There is no reason, why the claims of effective tonnage should be a decisive factor if balanced against the counterclaims of security, conservation of fisheries and other exclusive claims of the coastal state. And the principle of percentage of coastline is not only less convincing but also no longer correct. It may have been true in the years before World War II, but today a measurement of the coastline may very well favour the nations opposing the three-mile limit. A more cautious, and less doctrinaire, attitude is necessary and desirable. Today such an attitude is indeed more and and more adopted even in the ranks of ardent supporters of the three-mile zone.[255]

What can be said in positive terms is that "world community policy should continue to be heavily weighted in terms of accepting only a very narrow width of waters as territorial sea."[256] This is quite correct as a general principle, and it should be up to the particular state to prove that its particular circumstances justify an exceptional exclusive claim.

What then can be the supporting arguments for the Indonesian claims to a zone of territorial sea of twelve miles, measured from straight base lines which connect the outermost points of the islands of Indonesia? Obviously, Indonesia will fall back on the main argument that as an archipelago, and thus a single unit, the delimination of the territorial sea as laid down in the Territorial Sea and Maritime Districts Ordinance of 1939 (art. 1, para. I) is no longer in

[254] *Id.* at 81.

[255] *Cf.* the more cautious and thus more correct view in D.H.N. Johnson, "Control of Exploitation of Natural Resources in the Sea off the U.K.," 4 *I.L.Q.* 447 (1951) where it was stated that territorial waters mean in general "such parts of the sea adjacent to the coast of the U.K. as is deemed by international law to be within the territorial sovereignty of Her Majesty".

[256] McDougal & Burke, *supra* note 194, at 578.

accordance with the above-mentioned consideration.[257] In support Indonesia can point to several facts. Firstly, there is the Anglo-Norwegian Fisheries case; although it is in general not very relevant to the Indonesian example it is in so far correct to cite it here since it proves the fallacy of looking at doctrines as being almost sacrosanct, and the rejection by the World Court of this contention also meant the rejection of the British view that the laws of territorial domain were a fixed and inflexible set of rules governing all states and all situations.[258]

Like many other states, Indonesia looks for support of her claims to such proponents of a more progressive view as Judge Alvarez and it need not therefore surprise anyone if the Indonesian arguments would heavily rely on Judge Alvarez' views as propounded in his separate opinion in the Anglo-Norwegian Fisheries case in which he spelled out what principle should be created in the absence of existing general principles. They may briefly be stated as follows:

(a) There is no uniform rule possible with regard to territorial waters, owing to the great variety of geographical and economic conditions.

(b) Each state has a right to determine the extent of its maritime domain, "provided that it did so in a reasonable manner ... that it did not infringe upon the rights acquired by other nations and did not harm the general interests or commit an "abus de droit."" Judge Alvarez further emphasized, when dealing with the contiguous zones, that such exclusive claims receive more weight if established by a group of states, and especially by all states of a continent.[259]

These considerations, which must be regarded as supporting the legitimate claims of the coastal state, undoubtedly carry great weight. Whether one agrees with them or not, the impact of a numerical majority is demonstrated by the draft of the International Law Commission[260] which incorporates the desire for extensive claims, made by so many states belonging to all parts of the world. Yet it cannot be too much emphasized that the very interests of these states are ultimately also dependent on the well-being of the whole community of states of which they form an inseparable part, at a time when the interdependence is (at least materially) constantly increasing. Here then we have to fall back again on the answer

[257] *Supra* at 174.
[258] Evensen, *supra* note 229, at 628–629.
[259] *Id.* at 625–626.
[260] International Law Commission, *supra* note 227, comment on art. 3 at 16.

that a fair balancing of claims by sensible decisionmakers, is needed, who realize that both their immediate national benefit as well as their indirect interests in the common good of the whole community of nations demand restraint and tolerance if we hope to arrive at a result satisfactory to all parties concerned.

It is therefore regrettable that the Second U.N. Conference on the Law of the Sea in 1960 has not been able to arrive at a satisfactory result on the matter of the breadth of the territorial sea. Several Afro-Asian states maintained the claim of a 12-mile limit and voted against the U.S.-Canadian proposal which suggested – as a compromise – a breadth of the territorial sea of six miles, a subsequent contiguous zone of six miles where the coastal state would have exclusive fishing rights but would recognize for ten years the existing fishing rights of other nations. This proposal failed by one vote to receive the necessary 2/3 majority.[261] To Indonesia the condition of a 12-mile territorial sea was essential. She voted against the above-mentioned proposal.

(e) High seas regarded as contiguous to the claimant state

Next adjacent to the territorial sea is the area generally described as the "contiguous zone." Owing to its more remote position from the shore the authority of the coastal state is less comprehensive than in the preceding zones. Traditional practices show that in this zone exclusive claims refer to an authority of a more temporary and limited character, which is specially invoked for such purposes as customs, sanitary regulations, conservation of animal as well as mineral resources, and defensive regulations. Other states advance competing inclusive claims in defence of their inclusive interests which are usually expressed in terms of the general and broad concept of the "freedom of the seas."

To support its contention the coastal state tries to prove as a rule that the asserted authority is not unreasonable since it does not interfere with the legitimate inclusive interests of all other nations whereas in their inclusive claims opposing states maintain that the authority of the coastal state should stop at the dividing line of territorial seas and high seas.[262]

It cannot be denied, however, that traditionally many specific

[261] François, *La Deuxième Conférence Sur Le Droit de la Mer*, 7 *Neth. I. L. R.* 249–254 at 250 (1960).

[262] McDougal & Burke, *supra* note 194, at 554–563.

claims have been recognized which go beyond the limits of the territorial sea for the protection of the exclusive interest of the coastal state in various matters such as security, conservation of animal and mineral resources, customs, fiscal and anti-smuggling regulations. The increasing importance of this zone in recent times is apparently due to the extensive claims which have been put forward with respect to the continental shelf.[263] All these enumerated matters play an important part in the Indonesian decree and in fact, there are few countries which can point to such a clear example of extensive continental shelves as Indonesia.[264] Yet the principal Indonesian claims have not been made on the basis of any of these considerations but rather on the theory discussed earlier that the intermediate waters of the Indonesian Archipelago are considered internal waters and furthermore that the surrounding belt of territorial waters has a width of twelve miles measured from straight baselines connecting the outermost points of the islands.[265] Since the claims in such zones are of a more comprehensive nature than those made with respect to the contiguous high seas there is no need for Indonesia to justify her claims also in terms of the narrower contiguity. In the contiguous zone around the outer fringe of the archipelago the situation is naturally different and claims to this zone should be made in terms of the limited rights which a coastal state possesses there. There is as yet no reason to believe that Indonesia has so little sense of proportion and discrimination as to intend an exercise of authority in this contiguous zone proper which will go beyond the traditional prescriptions for the contiguous zone.

It has been pointed out that the claims which are put forward in this zone are of an occasional and provisional character; therefore, they do not warrant the establishment of a permanent exclusive authority by the coastal state.[266] This seems to be perfectly correct

[263] *Id.* at 581–582.

[264] See *supra* at 169.

[265] In the 4th Committee of the Geneva Conference of 1958 the Indonesian representative stated that his country accepted art. 67 of the ILC draft. New techniques of exploitation made restriction of such exploitation necessary in order to protect the resources of the continental shelf for the coastal state, regardless of whether this state is technically able or willing to exploit these resources or not. Indonesia then rejected the suggestion of placing the exploitation of the continental shelf under the control of an international body. Furthermore, Indonesia favoured the Philippine statement "that art. 67 could not apply to the island shelves of an archipelago forming a continuous submarine platform around the perimeter of the archipelago and linking all its islands, islets, shoals and rocks." *Summary Records, 4th Committee*, U.N. Doc. A/Conf. 13/42, at 26 (1958).

[266] McDougal & Burke, *supra* note 194, at 582.

with respect to the contiguous high seas around the archipelago as a whole. In the intermediate waters of the archipelago the situation is slightly different, though of great significance. One of the basic implications of the term "contiguity" is that it is situated further away from the shore and thus from the landbased authority which diminishes gradually in the direction of the high seas proper. In the case of an archipelago like Indonesia, a movement away from the shore is only truly in a direction away from the land-based authority of the coastal state if the starting point of that movement is taken from the outer edge of the archipelago. Within the archipelago any movement away from a land-based authority is at the same time a movement closer to another authority which has its origin on the nearest land territory of one of the innumerable islands in the neighbourhood. In view of this basic difference, it does not seem unreasonable to look at the interconnecting waters of the archipelago in terms of internal waters rather than of a contiguous zone.

The same reasoning may be used with regard to the concept of special contiguous zones for special purposes in areas beyond the territorial sea, which are preferable to the establishment of permanent zones of exclusive authority by coastal states since the latter might harm the legitimate interests of other states. Again, it is in general tenable that "to deny broad inclusive community uses in certain areas by honoring the exercise by a coastal state of the most comprehensive authority imaginable, merely to secure a single, narrow interest, whatever its specific significance to the claimant state, is comparable to cutting off a healthy arm in order to heal a pimple on the tip of a finger."[267] This general truth does not seem to be entirely applicable, however, in the case of an archipelago like Indonesia, at least if she can establish on the basis of facts, that her exclusive claims in the intermediate waters are of such essential nature as to make a comprehensive authority more efficient and effective than a number of occasional contiguous zones of varying widths. Proving this point might not be too hard for Indonesia, especially if it is taken into account that the weight of all separate interests, taken together, (e.g. security, conservation, continental shelf and others) will in the waters of a complex archipelago favour the simple comprehensive but practical authority of the coastal state if only exercised in a reasonable way. For, it cannot be denied that the efficiency of the authority exercised by the coastal state

[267] *Id.* at 580.

in an archipelago of such an enormous size and contrasting features is better served by simplicity rather than by the more difficult determination of a number of overlapping zones of varying widths. This, it is suggested here, is not "a compensatory measure to correct an injustice,"[268] but a contention inspired by practical considerations.

(f) High seas not regarded as contiguous to the claimant state

In this area most remote from the shore, the exclusive claims which an individual state is entitled to assert are least comprehensive, and reversely, the freedom of the seas as claimed by other states is most extensive and inclusive. Having reached the end of the series of zones by moving away from the shore, we find that the weight of the claims has shifted from the one extreme of almost exclusively comprehensive authority of the coastal state in its internal waters, to the other extreme of almost inclusively comprehensive authority of all states on the high seas. In this zone of non-contiguous high seas the claims of the individual state and those of all other competing claimants meet each other on the same level in the sense that – as a result of a lack of any specific authority – the coastal state may find it convenient to avail itself of the inclusive claims which it has as a regular member of the community of nations.

The controversy concerning the interpretation of the meaning and scope of the term freedom of the seas has for a long time had a negative implication. Some states considered it to mean that no one was entitled to interfere with the freedom of action of a state in the waters of the high seas.[269] Such a restrictive interpretation, however, seems to constitute a handicap rather than an asset to a progressing community of states which is forced by circumstances to develop the material resources of the world in the most intensive and efficient way for the common good of mankind.[270] It is obvious

[268] See McDougal & Burke, *supra* note 194, at 580, note 140, dealing with a claim of Mr. Escudero of Ecuador on the right of economically weak states to extend their territorial sea as a means of saving their economies. Although such a right is not entirely indefensible, the justification is here sought in a compensatory measure to correct injustice, which is apparently decided subjectively by the claimant state, and which in turn might cause other injustices. A justification should be based on firmer grounds, for it is perfectly true, as Mc Dougal & Burke remarked, that the inclusive uses of other states did not necessarily mean that the economically weaker state has always become the victim of economic development of world resources. In the case of Indonesia, however, the consideration of mutual benefit does not hold, for it cannot be seen what advantage will ever be enjoyed as a result of an establishment of various contiguous zones.

[269] *Cf.* Briggs, *supra* note 220, at 329.

[270] McDougal & Schlei, "The Hydrogen Bomb Tests in Perspective – Lawful Meas-

that such a goal can only be achieved by the greatest co-operation between the states concerned rather than by an all-out competition, each trying to secure for itself the greatest benefits, without regard for the needs and rights of neighbouring states.

As in the case of the contiguous zone, Indonesia, which considers all intermediate waters as internal waters over which she has the most comprehensive authority, views the arguments on the nature and implication of the high seas consistently as not relevant to her case, a contention which is built on the proposition that the intermediate waters of an archipelago are not high seas. This also makes a refutation of the arguments as advanced here from the viewpoint of the high seas as unnecessary as it was with regard to the contiguous zones since the most comprehensive authority which it claims to have in internal waters certainly covers the less exclusive one over the high seas.

In the sea areas which under the Indonesian decree would constitute non-contiguous high seas proper, the competing states will most probably not find any objection raised by the Indonesian state, and the inclusiveness of their claims will not be disputed at all.[271]

3. Final Observations

The Indonesian declaration of December 13, 1957 promised the elaboration of the national position on the laws of the sea at the future Geneva Conference. This was indeed done, though only with very moderate success.

The principal basis of the Indonesian claims, i.e. the special regime of an archipelago, was not adopted by any of the conventions. What is more, some deliberate attempts to include a provision to that effect had to be given up for lack of support.[272] On the other hand, no general denunciation of the archipelago concept can be

ures for Security," 64 *Yale L. J.* 657 (1955), which clearly expounds that the major policy purposes of the regime of the high seas is not only "negotiation of restrictions upon navigation and fishing, but also the promotion of the most advantageous peaceful use and development by all people of a great common resource..."

[271] With regard to fishing on the high seas the Indonesian representative stated in the Third Committee of the Geneva Conference of 1958 (*Summary Records, 3rd Committee*, Doc. A/Conf. 13/41, at 127) that Indonesia was in general satisfied with the fisheries articles as adopted by the Committee. It can be said that Indonesia supported the view that the coastal state has a special vital interest in the living resources of the sea. Agreements with neighbouring coastal states should be concluded with regard to the respective interests in the living resources of the particular maritime area, *Id.* at 9–10.

[272] *Supra* note 234.

found in the conventions either. Therefore, this question, like the breadth of the territorial sea, constitutes one of the remaining problems of international law. The fact that the Philippines are taking more or less the same position,[273] and that support was given by Yugoslavia, and in a sense also by Denmark, proves that there was at least some understanding for the Indonesian position.[274]

Another side of the Indonesian case has often been overlooked. The Indonesian declaration also contended that from time immemorial this archipelago constituted one unit. This argument had the effect of reinforcing the general trend of the Conference – in fact in the present world as a whole – towards greater awareness of historical claims. A resolution adopted by the Conference,[275] on the basis of a revised proposal of India and Panama,[276] requested the General Assembly of the United Nations to arrange for a further study of the "juridical regime of historic waters, including historic bays." Some authors apparently regard this resolution as excluding the regime of an archipelago,[277] but it is very well possible that the committee which will make a study of historic waters will have to look into the problem of archipelagos. For, the Indonesian concept of an archipelago as one historic unit implies consequently that the intermediate waters are historic waters.

The Indonesian views also give support to another tendency which could be observed at the Conferences. The "young" and underdeveloped nations favour the extension of a fisheries zone in order to protect the marine resources for their own fishermen who cannot as yet compete with the modern equipment of fishing fleets of the more advanced nations.[278] On the basis of this particular point, however, the exclusive claims of the underdeveloped states

[273] See 2 *Yearbook of the ILC* 18 (1956) or *U.N. Doc.* A/Conf. 4/99 at 28–29.

[274] *Supra* note 234, but *cf.* Mouton, *De conferentie betreffende het recht van de zee, gehouden te Geneve van 24 februari tot 29 april 1958.* (The Conference on the Law of the Sea of Geneva, from 24 February till 29 April 1958) 37 (1959).

[275] Min. v. B. Z., *op. cit. supra* note 196, at 37.

[276] U. N. Doc. No. A/Conf. 13/Cl/L. 158/Rev. 1.

[277] Mouton, *op. cit. supra* note 274, at 37.

[278] *E.g.* Statement of the Indonesian representative in the 1st Committee (A/Conf. 13/39 at 14), of the Indian representative in the 1st Committee (*Id.* at 14), and of the Indonesian representative in the 4th Committee (A/ Conf. 13/42 at 22). For other claims for preferential fishing rights, see the proposals of Brazil, Cuba and Uruguay (A/Conf. 19/L. 12) and of Iceland (A/Conf. 19/L. 13) at the 2nd Conference.
The 2nd U.N. Conference on the Law of the Sea adopted a proposal submitted by Ethiopia, Ghana and Liberia (*UN* Doc. A/Conf. 19 /L 8) with regard to technical assistance in fishing activities. However, the proposal lost much of its significance when the Canadian-American plan, which the three abovementioned sponsors assumed would be adopted, was rejected.

do not seem to be strong enough to justify the establishment of a permanent regime having an exact breadth. Unlike geographic and perhaps also strategic facts, economic considerations are of a very temporary nature. In a few decades some of these underdeveloped states might succeed (perhaps even with the aid of the more advanced nations) in competing with other nations on an equal basis. Then there will be less reason to grant them the protection of a special fisheries zone. Therefore, the solution cannot lie in the creation of a rigid legal rule for the future, but in the contemporary balancing of the exclusive national claims against the inclusive demands of a world community.

Since the laws of the sea need much adjustment, revision and even entirely new prescriptions, the case of Indonesia has greater significance as an example of contemporary claims with regard to expectations of "young" nations than as evidence of existing prescriptions. Indonesia, and many other Asian nations, are therefore somewhat resentful of what they consider, unfair criticism of their practices, especially when they are reminded by other nations that these prescriptions are "well-established rules of international law" to which they, as newly admitted members to the community of states, must subject themselves, which is, as it were, the price they have to pay for the privilege of membership.

It is, of course, true that many such concepts of international law can point to a general or even universal acceptance, and there is no reason for the new states to reject or ignore such well-established principles. This does not apply, however, to other and more controversial matters.

For instance, a new state accepts with its admission to the United Nations the obligation to honour the recognized community prescriptions, but even if such a commitment is interpreted in the narrow sense of accepting the rules of international law as interpreted by the contemporary community of states, it still remains a fact that in many matters of international law a great degree of disagreement exists. If it can, therefore, be held that newly admitted members of the world community are committed to abide by well-established and generally accepted principles of international law, no such rigid stand can be taken with respect to many highly controversial matters. This then was the case with the Geneva Conference on the law of the sea. Actually, it was perhaps the first occasion on which these newly established nations gave vent to their views on the validity of traditional international law in the presence of practically all nations of the world. The general tenor of these statements has been that the new states were not willing to accept certain rules of international law which had been created before they achieved statehood.[279] The laws of the sea, for instance, are so vague with regard to the waters of an archipelago, that Indonesia (and other archipelago-states as well) felt entitled to determine her own position on this question, taking into account existing theories. The controversial nature of the subject assured beforehand a stormy reception of these claims, but such was inevitable and should not frighten her. What is more important is that in her claims she is not only guided by her own interests but also by a respect for the legitimate claims of other members of the community of states. It is only in this process of balancing claims and counterclaims that one can hope to find a reasonable solution. It is, of course, quite easy to maintain that the standard of reasonableness is a highly subjective criterion which cannot lead to a satisfactory solution. To hold this, however, would not only deliberately ignore the influence of practical considerations like reciprocity, by which the balancing process is affected, but also the fact that history has shown that states indeed possess an accommodating ability when attempting to arrive at a decision.

In the case of the Indonesian claims the balancing process showed a remarkable fact. It is true that Indonesia advanced in support of the claims her historical rights on the waters of the Indonesian archipelago, but surprisingly Indonesia based her claims heavily on arguments of a clearly authoritative nature, thereby trying to meet her mainly Western critics on their own terms. The arguments advanced in support of her actions and intentions are, in fact, not of her own making, but have been made much earlier by Western scholars. One of the striking facts in this controversy is indeed the way in which Indonesia, and other Asian states as well, rely sometimes on legal rules which found their origin and development in a Family of Nations of essentially European character. Some may regard this as the attempt of a young state to prove its maturity by trying to make its case in the sophisticated and legalistic way applied by many advanced Western nations. Others, however, will

[279] See statement by the Philippine delegate, *Summary Records, 1st Committee, op. cit. supra* note 200, at 153.

say that it only proves that these new nations must have a long legal tradition of their own.

What then has been the attitudes of the Asian new nations at the Geneva Conferences? What has been the influence of their combined strength on the decision making process? It has been said before[280] that these states may well become a decisive factor in the solution of international issues. Have the issues at the Geneva Conference indeed been decided on the sheer weight of the number of Asian and African states voting pro and contra regardless of the real merits of the case?

To find some answer to this question it may perhaps be useful to examine the composition and results of the Geneva Conferences on the Law of the Sea.[281] At the 1st Conference of the 87 participants (86, after the merger of Egypt and Syria into the United Arab Repubic) 24 were Asian, 7 African (including here for convenience's sake the Union of South Africa), 31 European, 22 American (North and South) and further Australia and New Zealand. Since proposals on questions of substance needed a two-thirds majority in order to be accepted, the important position of the Asian-African group seems obvious. However, it should be said immediately that, on the whole, there was little resembling an Asian-African bloc. Actually, strict bloc voting did not occur, not even along the lines of the East-West blocs.[282] This does not mean, of course, that the sessions were carried on in a spirit of close harmony or even with full understanding of the practical importance of many of the issues. The propaganda battle was also inevitable here.[283] Of the Asian nations it can perhaps be said that they were not swayed by propaganda moves of any other nations but were rather guided by their own interests. That such an individualistic attitude was not very conducive to a successful conclusion of the Conference is obvious, but it is not characteristic of Asian-African states only. No spectacular results emerged from the Conference and the present results need further testing before their value and actual success can be determined.[284]

[280] *Supra* Chapter I at 16.

[281] Dean, "The Geneva Conference on the Law of the Sea. What Was Accomplished," 52 *A.J.I.L.* 607–628 (1958); Jessup, "The Geneva Conference on the Law of the Sea; a Study in International Law-Making," 52 *A.J.I.L.* 730–733 (1958); Young, "The Geneva Convention on the Continental Shelf," 52 *A.J.I.L.* 733–738 (1958).

[282] Jessup, *supra* note 281, at 731.

[283] Dean, *supra* note 281, at 608–609.

[284] For some of the reasons of partial failure see Johnson, "The Preparation of the 1950 Geneva Conference on the Law of the Sea," 8 *I.C.L.Q.* 142 (1959).

The general conclusion must therefore indeed be that there was no question of solid Asian-African voting, not even of a Southeast Asian vote for that matter. Asian states acted, in general, not differently from other states, in the sense that they voted on the merits of the case only in so far as they could be reconciled with the national interests.[285]

In considering the Asian voting pattern two further remarks must be made. In certain matters the Arab nations took a particular stand due to their disputes with Israel on rights of passage in the Gulf of Aqaba.[286] The other reservation concerns the attitude of certain states towards Japan. As has been pointed out earlier[287] the position of this country in Asia is a peculiar one.[288] Although being in many respects one of the most prominent Asian nations, she finds herself to-day in a difficult position in her relations with other Asian states.[289] Whereas most Asian nations rejected the three-mile limit rule, Japan, for understandable reasons, was the only important fishing nation in Asia which sided with those Western nations favouring the adoption of a territorial sea limit of three miles.[290] Burma, on the other hand, supported the twelve-mile rule in order to prevent Japanese fishermen from coming too close to her territory. Indonesia, which maintained her archipelago concept, could also exclude the Japanese from her waters. The other nations with which we are concerned here, India, and Ceylon, supported a rejected U.S. proposal for a territorial sea of six miles, but giving the coastal state the right to regulate fishing in an additional six-mile zone, taking into consideration also historical fishing rights of other nations.[291]

The subject matter of the 2nd U. N. Conference on the Law of the Sea (i.e. the question of the breadth of the territorial sea and fishing limits) was in contrast to the 1st Conference, of a more limited, though at the same time more controversial, nature. As a result, extreme positions were defended which could only partially be reconciled.

We must again ask the question now: What has been the position

[285] For a review of some Asian claims, see synoptical table, *infra* at 204.
[286] Dean, *supra* note 281, at 600–609.
[287] See Chapter I, *supra* at 3.
[288] For a clarification of Japan's difficult position on this matter, see Oda, "Japan and the U.N. Conference on the Law of the Sea," 3 *J.A.I.L.* 65–86 (1959).
[289] Dean, *supra* note 281, at 609, 615.
[290] Oda, *supra* note 288, at 610.
[291] *Id.* at 614.

SYNOPTICAL TABLE OF SOME ASIAN CLAIMS[1]

States	Breadth of Territorial Sea	Continental Shelf	Limits for Special Purposes					
			Customs	Security	Criminal & Civil Juris-diction	Fishing	Neutrality	Sanitary Regulations
BURMA								
CAMBODIA	5 miles (1957)	(1957) 50 metres Including sovereignty over super-jacent waters.	12 miles (1957)	12 miles (1957)		12 miles (1957)		
CEYLON	6 miles (1957)		6 miles (1952)			100 miles (1957)		
CHINA	3 miles (1930)		12 miles (1934)					
INDIA	6 miles (1956)	(1955). Seabed and subsoil only.						
INDONESIA	12 miles (1957)							
JAPAN	3 miles (1956)						3 miles (1928)	10,000 metres (1948) Pollution of Sea
KOREA Republic of		(1952) Including sovereignty over superjacent waters.				3 miles		
LAOS								
MALAYA	3 miles							
PAKISTAN	3 miles (1878)	(1950) 100 fathom line and seabed only.					3 miles (1897)	
PHILIPPINES[2]								
THAILAND	6 miles (1958)					12 miles (1958)		

[1]) From: The Society of Comparative Legislation and International Law 1958: *The Law of the Sea*, The Final Act and Annexes of the United Nations Conference on the Law of the Sea, Geneva, 1958, together with a Synoptical Table of Claims to Jurisdiction over the Territo rial Sea, the Contiguous Zone and the Continental Shelf, 36-42 (1958).

[2]) The position of the Philippines is given in Doc. A/CN.4/99 (*Yearbook of the I.L.C.*, 1956, vol. II, pp. 69-70).

of the Asian and African states at this last Conference? A cursory survey of the voting results shows again that there was nothing like a solid Asian-African stand. When the various proposals were put to the vote, Asian and African states could always be found among the states voting in favour, against, as well as those abstaining. The important joint Canadian-U.S. proposal, for instance, was supported by sixteen Afro-Asian states. On the other hand, it was rejected by eleven such states, while four other ones abstained. There is, therefore, no reason to state or imply that Afro-Asian states voted irresponsibly or that they decided the issues by sheer weight of their number. On the contrary, in the Committee of the Whole, for instance, a pure Afro-Asian proposal of 16 nations (later revised and co-sponsored by two South-American states)[292] failed to receive even a simple majority vote. Another ten-power proposal[293] (among which eight from Africa and Asia) failed similarly in the Plenary Meeting.

Moreover, as far as responsibility is concerned it is hard to say what this means at a world conference where bargaining and lobbying for votes is common practice. And it is not the small nation that has much to offer in order to make others change opinions.[294] It seems, therefore, justified to say that there is little reason to blame Afro-Asian nations for the unsatisfactory outcome of the Conferences. In fact, their attitudes at the Conferences were perhaps less controversial than could have been expected in view of the extensive claims which had been made by some of them with regard to their sea territories. On the whole, it can be said that the Indonesian delegation returned home neither particularly strengthened nor weakened by the results of the conference. A further appraisal of her claims will be greatly dependent on the way in which she will apply her archipelago concept in the future.

[292] *U.N. Doc. A*/Conf. 19/C. 1/L. 2 /Rev. 1 (1960).

[293] U.N. Doc. A/Conf. 19/L. 9 (1960).
For the result of the roll-call, see *U.N. Doc.* A/Conf. 19/SR. 13 (1960).

[294] The delegate of Saudi Arabia made severe accusations to this effect. U. N. Doc. A/Conf. 19/SR. 13. Whether they are true or not, it is common knowledge (and even understandable) that this bargaining practice exists.

PEACEFUL COEXISTENCE

1. Origin and Development

Almost all writings on peaceful coexistence will inevitably start with quotations from Lenin's speeches in 1918 or 1919, which are said to form the basis for the concept of peaceful coexistence. One such quotation reads:

> The existence of the Soviet Republic side by side with imperialist states for a long time is unthinkable. One or the other must triumph in the end. And before that end supervenes, a series of frightful collisions between the Soviet Republic and the bourgeois states will be inevitable.[295]

This statement implies apparently two things. First of all, it conceives of a period of side-by-side (i.e. peaceful) existence between the present two world systems with their conflicting social, economic, political and legal structure.[296] Secondly, it follows from the same statement that peaceful coexistence is only accepted as a transitory period, and not to be regarded as a permanent state of affairs. It represents the brief state of equilibrium after the inception of the socialist state in Russia, but before the end of the world revolution at which time communism will take full control of the entire world. The transition would be brief, for Lenin could not conceive of two such completely contrasting systems living together over a long period of time.[297]

This intermediary period had more or less imposed itself on the Soviet peoples. At the start of their existence as a socialist nation they had no choice, as they stood alone in a hostile world[298] which threatened them with a "capitalist encirclement."[299] This threat would remain so long as the Soviet Union was weaker than or about equal in force to, the capitalist powers. The inevitable clash, however, would result in a resounding victory for communism. Lenin's successors, from Stalin to Krushchev, all stood for peaceful coexistence, but basic differences of opinion and interpretation had

[295] Quoted by Chacko, "Peaceful Coexistence as a Doctrine of Current International Affairs," 4 *I.Y.I.A.* 14-15 (1955).

[296] See Tunkin, "Coexistence and International Law," 95 *Hague Recueil*, Part III, at 51 (1958).

[297] See Chacko, *supra* note 295, at 15.

[298] *Ibid.* Active propagation of this theory of coexistence was apparently not started before 1930.

[299] Alexeyev, "Peaceful Coexistence and Economic Competition of the Two Systems," *Int. Aff.* (Moscow) 19-24, at 20 (Jan. 1959).

already emerged. The reason was primarily that capitalist supremacy was more difficult to eliminate than was initially expected. The present nuclear stalemate made it even more necessary to abandon the idea that the period of transition would be brief.[300] Meanwhile the Soviet Union had already laid greater emphasis on the idea of cooperation during peaceful coexistence. All this led them to change their minds and declare with regard to the impending war that such a clash was no longer inevitable.[301] This did not mean that they abandoned all hope for an ultimate socialist victory. On the contrary; but they had become convinced that to this end war was no longer the only possible means. Instead the capitalist system with its inherent flaws would be eliminated by self-destruction.[302]

The latest views on this subject have recently been elaborated by Kruschev himself. Today, he says, it is too late for the capitalist world to "roll back" communism.[303] Peaceful coexistence is the only way out, for the alternative to such coexistence is universal destruction. But in order to make coexistence effective, not only cooperation is needed, but peaceful competition as well, for peaceful coexistence will only have a firm foundation if it allows for an increase in extensive and absolutely unrestricted international trade.[304] Nevertheless, Krushchev could not help to remind the West casually that the Soviet system will no doubt emerge victorious from this peaceful struggle, for the simple reason that its system will prove to be the more progressive and advantageous to the world.[305]

Side by side with this communist philosophy, the Soviet conception of international law underwent a new development. As usual in the Soviet system, newly created political doctrines had to be based on, and backed by, international law theories whose task it was to fit the new doctrines (i.e. peaceful coexistence) into the existing Soviet theories of international law. In fact, this became

[300] Chacko, *supra* note 295, at 27.

[301] See Krushchev in his report at the 20th Party Congress, in *New Times* (Moscow), No. 8 (suppl.), 16 February 1956.

[302] Aaron and Reynolds, "Peaceful Coexistence and Peaceful Cooperation," 4 *Pol. Studies*, 284–285 (1956). Lenin must have said that capitalist supremacy was doomed to pass away, since the economic development of these countries led to that end. See also Khvostov, "The Seven-Year Plan and Peaceful Coexistence," *Int. Aff.* (Moscow) 8 (Febr. 1959). Krushchev also stated: "The capitalist world, torn by the exacerbated general crisis, is coming nearer to its inevitable collapse." *Id.* at 10.

[303] Krushchev, "On Peaceful Coexistence," 38 *For. Aff.* 1–18 at 15 (1959).

[304] *Id.* at 4.

[305] *Id.* at 6.

about the first and only task of Soviet international law.[306] It is perhaps commendable that international lawyers in Russia try to treat law and policy as parts of one process, but in doing so their views on the law were formulated entirely *ex post facto*. Even that would perhaps be excusable if it were not that they made it a habit to switch their views completely and frequently. The basic questions as to the existence, character and scope of international law were treated in contradictory ways at different times. Official Soviet views, originated by certain Soviet jurists, were frequently reversed. The originators of these theories were reproached, forcing them to indulge publicly in self-criticism and self-accusation, though there always remained the possibility that they would be restored to prominence at some later date.[307] The doctrines on peaceful coexistence underwent similar ordeals. The elaboration of this doctrine by Soviet jurists raised the question as to the law governing the mutual relations of the two opposing systems during the transitional period.[308] Is there to be a universal international law system as a "super structure" over both the capitalist and socialist world? Or would there be different types of international law for each of these public order systems?[309] The official Soviet position oscillated between these two possibilities. At present the leading Soviet opinion is apparently that international law is universal and binding upon both systems in their relations during a period of peaceful coexistence.[310] It needs, however, no further explanation that this general international law as conceived by the Soviet Union is not necessarily the same as the Western conception of the same term. For instance, the difficult term "sovereignty" still reigns supreme in the Soviet world. Consequently, the state is primarily bound only by its commitments under international treaties. The latter attitude, which in

[306] Snyder and Bracht, "Coexistence and International Law," 7 *I.C.L.Q.* 54–71 at 55 (1958).

[307] See *id.* for praise and criticism of Korovin, Pashukanis, Sarabin and Hrabar, at 60, 63, 70.

[308] Prof. Tunkin rejects completely any state or states of intermediacy between war and peace, as suggested by Prof. Jessup ("Should International Law Recognize an Intermediate Status between Peace and War?," 48 *A.J.I.L.* 100–102 (1954)) and Prof. McDougal ("Peace and War: Factual Continuum with Multiple Legal Consequences," 49 *A.J.I.L.* 67 (1955). Prof. Tunkin bases his rejection on the fear that the acceptance "would result in legally consecrating the situation of international tension." Tunkin, *supra* note 296, at 74. It is not quite clear what he means with a "legal consecration." Apparently he chooses here not to adopt this factual situation for reasons of Soviet policy, although most Soviet theories on international law seem to be based on the idea of legally consecrating factual situations if only they fit into the Soviet philosophy.

[309] Snyder and Bracht, *supra* note 306, at 67–68.

[310] *Id.* at 70.

fact minimizes the value of international customary law,[311] is even more regrettable since the position taken can apparently easily be reversed if need be.[312] It is therefore clear that in this case an appeal to general international law does not mean much. A solution can only be reached if both parties are willing to balance their claims and counterclaims in the realization that the common interest in the preservation of peace requires such an act. The idea of peaceful coexistence, which is by itself a recognition of a factual balance, seems to point clearly to the balancing process as the only way to find a reasonable solution.

What has been the response from the other camp, from the so-called capitalist world? It appears that the Soviet Union had all the advantage of taking the initiative in propagating the concept first. It left the West with the difficult task of finding an answer to something which, by its very nature, was hard to deny, since peaceful coexistence is under present world conditions obviously the only sensible answer to the cold war. What made the Western position even more disadvantageous was that the idea caught on quickly and found enthusiastic support with the new Asian countries. Western reactions were at first hesitant and full of suspicion, and there was great aversion to accepting the idea. There was a dislike to using the term, probably for fear that it would give too much credit (and therefore propaganda material) to the Russians.[313] As a counter-move some efforts were made to win over the support of the nations of the world for the term "peaceful cooperation" which, it was contended, had more positive meaning than peaceful coexistence. The latter term, it was said, implied only a "passive condition of live and let live."[314] Although it is realized here that a problem can never be solved by a comparison of definitions, it is nevertheless worthwhile to examine the different points of view since they reveal the thoughts behind the arguments.

Looking back at the attitude of the West in the past (in so far as

[311] Krylov, "Les Nations Principales du Droit des Gens," 70 *Hague Recueil* 442 (1947).

[312] Such an attitude has a destructive and paralyzing effect on the development of international law and puts the non-communist world before grave problems in their dealings with the Soviets. Although by itself the Soviet attachment to general international law seems to create possibilities for peaceful coexistence and peaceful cooperation, their manipulation of international law as an instrument of Soviet policy only, makes the so-called commitment to general international law meaningless. See for a discussion of the Soviet attitude, McDougal and Lasswell, "The Identification and Appraisal of Diverse Systems of Public Order," 53 *A.J.I.L.* 1–29 at 4 (1959).

[313] See Chacko, *supra* note 295, at 24–28.

[314] Hazard, "Legal Research on Peaceful Coexistence," 51 *A.J.I.L.* 65 (1957).

one can speak of a general Western attitude) it seems that her reactions were badly timed and lacking in foresight, thus allowing the Soviet propaganda machine to score important successes. For, the effort to reply with a counter-suggestion of peaceful cooperation led to a fruitless battle of definitions,[315] in which, of course, that definition gained a victory which had the greatest, immediate appeal to the nations of the world. After the introduction and apparent success of the term peaceful coexistence at the Geneva Conference of 1954 (on Indo-China and Korea) and thereafter, an attempt to offset this success by introducing another term, which clearly had neither the suggestive background nor the appeal to uncommitted nations, was to invite defeat, regardless of the merits of the idea. Moreover the Russians quickly retorted that peaceful coexistence was clearly the more correct term since it was inclusive enough to include peaceful cooperation.[316]

Most of all, the Western sponsors of the cooperation idea perhaps overlooked the fact that in the present dangerous state of a cold war the world seems to clamour primarily for a commitment to peaceful coexistence, however passive the concept might be.[317] Only if this first step has been taken can one think of a succeeding, more positive step, towards cooperation. Not the truth, but the strength of this argument must have secured support for the Soviet idea among Asian nations. Perhaps it would have been wiser if the term had been accepted from the very start, not however by giving credit to the Soviet Union for a new invention, but by stating that this

[315] *Id.* at 64.

[316] Tunkin, *supra* note 296, at 53.

This does not seem to be the general view in the Soviet Union. Alexeyev, at least, seems to imply that there is a clear distinction between the two when he wrote: "... the Soviet Union and the United States can do more than just coexist. They can cooperate..." Alexeyev, *supra* note 299, at 20.

For a philosophical discussion of these two terms, see Aaron and Reynolds, *supra* note 302.

[317] At the 12th and 13th session of the General Assembly of the U.N. two resolutions were tabled by Communist countries which dealt with peaceful coexistence. However, another proposal to use instead the term "peaceful and neighbourly relations" was adopted. See Res. of 14 December 1957 (1236 (XII) and Res. of 10 December 1958 (1301) (XIII). This does not detract anything, however, from the popularity of the term "peaceful coexistence," for the new term was only adopted as a compromise in order to get support from both camps for the resolution. Even after the adoption of the new term writers and statesmen continue to use "peaceful coexistence." For instance, a joint declaration of Argentina and Chile on the peaceful settlement of outstanding frontier questions, made at Santiago de Chile on 22 March 1960, stated, *inter alia*: "... it is easier, less costly and fairer and thus more befitting to build the peace and coexistence of nations upon the permanent values of agreement, justice and right..." *I.C.J.* Communiqué 60/5 (unofficial) of 21 April 1960.

idea would gladly be accepted since it always has been a basic principle in the West. While the Soviets might have introduced the term, it is absurd to say or imply that the concept of peaceful coexistence was not invented until Lenin mentioned it. Indeed, if the Soviet concept implied a peaceful coexistence of two conflicting systems (including their cooperation and competition) then this amounted to nothing more than a restatement of principles of international law and international relations which have been applied for a long time.

Fortunately, there were other reactions in the West reflecting a greater willingness to accept the term peaceful coexistence, since "there is nothing to be ashamed of in accepting the concept of peaceful coexistence, if we understand why we do so.... There is no reason why the non-communist world should not be able to use peaceful coexistence to even better advantage than the communist."[318]

Finally, Krushchev's above-mentioned views have been answered in a competent and dignified manner by Kennan.[319] In accepting the term peaceful coexistence on its own merits, Kennan not only met the Russians on their own terms, but at the same time he stole the thunder from their idea. Kennan also protested against the historical distortion hidden in Krushchev's statement that "from the very inception (the Soviet state) proclaimed peaceful coexistence as the basic principle of its foreign policy."[320] It is very well possible, said Kennan, that the Soviet leaders are sincere in their adherence to the present principles of peaceful coexistence but it is not a very adequate way of convincing others of one's own sincerity to have such a complete disregard for the actual facts which indicate that basic to the Soviet philosophy was, certainly at its inception, the call to conquer the world.[321] Kennan then proceeds to expose other weaknesses of the Krushchev statements and points out – something

[318] 35 *Time & Tide* 908 (July 10, 1954).

Cf. Sir Roger Makins who, although preferring the term *modus vivendi* himself, accepted the fact that the use of "peaceful coexistence" is fully established.

[319] Kennan, "Peaceful Coexistence – A Western View," 38 *For Aff.* 171–190 (1960). For a Yugoslavian criticism of the Soviet view and the Soviet reply to this, see Frantsev, "The Policy of Peaceful Coexistence and its Ill-Starred Critic," *Int. Aff.* (Moscow) 78–80 (May 1959).

[320] Kennan, *supra* note 319, at 172. Soviet writers today continue to propagate this view disregarding former contradictory statements. Khvostov, for instance writes: "The policy of peaceful coexistence springs from the very nature of Soviet Socialist Society..." Khvostov, *supra* note 302, at 7. See for identical Chinese views, *infra* note 339.

[321] Kennan, *supra* note 319, at 174.

surprisingly rarely done in the West – that "there is nothing new in the prolonged peaceful residence, side by side, of ideologically antagonistic systems." [322]

Yet, although peaceful coexistence is an old concept, we have only recently seen a great upsurge of interest in this doctrine so that it has become one of the most important topics of our time. And it is to the development of this doctrine that Asian states have been able to contribute.

2. *The Asian Attitude*

It would perhaps be very helpful to examine to what extent conditions, beliefs and practices of Asian nations have influenced their favourable reactions towards the Soviet suggestion to live by the doctrine of peaceful coexistence. This would lead us, however, to a discussion of many historical and social facts of which it might be said that they were rather irrelevant here. Therefore, the discussion of the Asian attitude will center around the question of the particular form in which peaceful coexistence is practised in Asia.

This doctrine first achieved greater significance outside the Soviet Union when the settlement of the Korean and Indo-Chinese questions was discussed at the Geneva Conference in 1954.[323] There it found a willing ear among the Asian participants. It was first applied in a treaty between India and China on Tibet in April 1954. According to the Chinese Prime Minister Chou En-lai[324] this treaty gave expression to the attachment of both parties to the Five Principles of Peaceful Coexistence, comprising:[325]

(1) Mutual respect for each other's territorial integrity and sovereignty;
(2) Non-aggression;
(3) Non-interference in each other's internal affairs;
(4) Equality and mutual benefit;
(5) Peaceful coexistence.

These principles were reaffirmed during a visit of Chou En-lai to Nehru in June 1954. From then on the idea caught on quickly

[322] *Id.* at 177.
[323] *Keesings Historisch Archief* (Keesing Historical Archives) 11115–11345 (1954).
[324] A joint statement of the two Prime Ministers and two speeches by Chou En-lai speak about the spirit of co-existence and cooperation. *People's China*, July 16, 1954 (suppl.) at 4, 6 and 7 (1954).
[325] *Id.* at 4.
See also Fifield, *The Diplomacy of South East Asia* 198 (1958).

in Asia. Immediately after his visit to India, Chou En-lai went to Burma where the Prime Ministers of both countries issued a joint statement endorsing wholeheartedly the Five Principles.[326] Subsequently, many different nations, Asian as well as European, declared their attachment to the Five Principles of Peaceful Coexistence. The following nations have declared to carry on relations with other states on the basis of these principles: Afghanistan, Burma, Cambodia, Ceylon, Communist China, Indonesia, Laos, Nepal, Poland, Vietnam, Viet Minh, Soviet Union and Yugoslavia.[327]

The Asian-African Conference at Bandung in April 1955 was another milestone in the development of the doctrine of peaceful coexistence.[328] Yet, although many delegates subscribed to this concept the Conferences did not adopt the Five Principles in its final communiqué. A Declaration on the Promotion of World Peace and Cooperation[329] listed instead ten principles which included four of the five principles but refrained from stating explicitly the fifth principle (i.e. peaceful coexistence). Apparently the enthusiasm of certain Asian states for the Five Principles failed to convince other participants that the five principles, in that form, were a sound basis for mutual relations. Actually some other delegates, e.g. Pakistan, wanted to add more principles. Perhaps the Cambodian delegate made himself the spokesman of this group when he said that the countries which supported peaceful coexistence nevertheless mistrusted the communist states, and it was up to the latter to disprove these fears.[330] Ironically it was Communist China which saved the debate by showing this time that she could be an understanding and reasonable member. She suggested to use another term for peaceful coexistence if other delegates objected to it.[331] A compromise was found in the inclusion of the terms

[326] People's China, *supra* note 324, at 6.

[327] Fifield, "The Five Principles of Coexistence," 52 *A.J.I.L.* 504–510 (1958). At the 12th session of the General Assembly of the U. N. Gromyko stated that Russia had relations of peaceful existence with India, Indonesia, Afghanistan, Egypt, Syria, Finland, Switzerland and Austria. Min. v. Buitenl. Zaken, *De Twaalfde Algemene Vergadering van de V.N.* (Neth. Min. of For. Affairs, The Twelfth General Assembly of the U.N.) 145 (1958).

[328] Fifield (*supra* note 327, at 508) also mentioned as an important event the declaration of Soviet leaders and groups at the 40th Anniversary of the Bolshevik Revolution which supported the idea of peaceful coexistence.

[329] Min. of For. Affairs of the Republic of Indonesia, Bulletin of the Asian-African Conference (No. 9) at 6 (1955). Also in Kahin, *The Asian-African Conference,* 83–85 (1956).

[330] Kahin, *supra* note 329, at 22-23.

[331] *Id.* at 25.

"tolerance and live together in peace," while also "cooperation" was especially mentioned.[332] This did not prevent Chou En-lai, however, from stating after his return to China that living together in peace is identical to peaceful coexistence.[333]

Thus it appeared that the doctrine succeeded to get much support, particularly in Asia, where it is more known under the Indian name of *Panch Shila*. Fifield has given a brief but clear description of the Asian views on the significance of *Panch Shila*:

> Basically Prime Ministers Nehru and Nu believed the Five Principles would help to destroy apprehension, create confidence and establish security. Adherence to the Panch Shila would expand the "area of peace." Alliances, on the other hand, were conducive to dividing states who should be friendly neighbors. Universal acceptance of the Panch Shila would contribute to a world-wide system of collective peace. At the same time it was realized that the Five Principles did not constitute a "magic formula."[334]

If it is true that Asia contributed significantly to the popularity of the doctrine of peaceful coexistence, then it would be desirable to examine the extent of the Asian impact on a concept which was derived from a communist philosophy.

In examining this matter, one's attention is immediately drawn to the detachment of the Asian concept from the Soviet source. The application of *Panch Shila* was for Asia not directly linked to the existence of Russia and the Communist philosophy. In spite of the advances of modern education, science and technology, Asia is still too little developed in these fields to make the Asian people aware of the imminent nearness of Russian danger. Moreover, Russia's record in Asia is still fairly clean, since she has not been associated with the experiences of European colonialism, regardless of whether she at present indulges in subversive activities or not. Even the Asian-African Conference was rather mild on Russia. And when some members attacked Soviet colonialism, it was more like an attempt to put Soviet policy at the same level as that of European colonial powers. They did not directly mention the Soviet threat to Asia.[335] It is therefore correct to say that there is no feeling of an imminent danger of a Russian invasion, as there may be, for instance, in some parts of Europe. The absence of feelings of real danger and involvement in a cold war, so essential in the

[332] *Ibid.* See also Fifield, *supra* note 327, at 506–507.
[333] See *China and the Asian-African Conference*, 41 (Peking, 1955).
[334] Fifield, *supra* note 327, at 509.
[335] Kahin, *supra* note 329, at 18–19.

Russian concept, puts the *Panch Shila* on a rather different level.

It can, of course, be maintained that if the Russian threat is unlikely, that of Communist China seems fairly real. This is indeed true, for the threat of Communism, if it exists in Asia,[336] can only be expected from Communist China. If one accepts this, then it is worthwhile to examine the Asian position *vis-à-vis* the idea of peaceful coexistence as it was presented by the Communists, in order to see whether their views on peaceful coexistence have sufficient common ground.

First, it can be said that in their confrontation with the Soviet concept Asians have not made the mistake of turning into the blind alley of definition seeking. It is irrelevant here whether this was due to wisdom or simply to an aversion of too technical a concept. The very connotation of peaceful coexistence as a living together in peace was for them sufficient reason to make it the cornerstone of their international relations. This is not to say that peaceful coexistence is to them nothing more than a plea to live and let live.[337] Asian states have not been so naive as to disregard completely the ideological differences between the communist and non-communist world. For instance, Chou En-lai himself admitted that he had some difficulty in convincing non-communist delegates at the Bandung Conference of both the Chinese ability and willingness to live in peace. There were serious doubts about Chinese sincerity but Chou En-lai managed to prevent a thorough discussion of the merits of his ideology.[338] Had this been done anyhow, it might have brought about some clashes in opinions and could have faced the Conference with a grave dilemma. Not being faced with such a dilemma here, it will be attempted to go deeper into this matter in order to see what points of contact there are between the Asian and the communist concept.

What can be said is that, if China adheres to the same Marxist views as the Soviet Union on the development of socialism as the ultimate destroyer of and successor to capitalism (a belief which Marxist ideology true to itself, can never relinquish)[339] then it was

[336] Theoretically, one could perhaps also discuss the chances of a threat to Asia from the "capatalist" countries. See, however, the discussion of the Soviet accusations against capitalism in Kennan, *supra* note 319, at 174–177.

[337] See Chacko, *supra* note 295, at 35.

[338] China and the Asian-African Conference, *supra* note 333, at 36.

[339] How identical China's views can be to those of the Soviet Union appears, for instance, from an article on peaceful coexistence by a Chinese writer who repeats almost exactly Krushchev's remark (*supra* at 211) when he writes: "From the very first day of

perhaps a wise tactic of Chou En-lai to allay all fears by sidetracking a discussion on the real nature of the ideological foundation of his state. Whatever the idea of peaceful coexistence stands for in Asia, it does not, and will not stand for the communist presumption that there exist in the world today a capitalist and a communist bloc which are basically mutually incompatible, though one or both might decide that a certain period of peaceful coexistence is temporarily desirable.[340] Since it touches upon the core of the matter, this difference must clearly set the Asian example apart from its Soviet counterpart. Moreover, *Panch Shila* is not conceived as temporary, but indeed as the ultimate and permanent state of affairs.[341] Nor does it concern only two hostile camps either, but purports to cover all, friends and enemies alike. This should cause no surprise to those aware that the Asian views are an extension of the doctrine of neutralism,[342] non-commitment or non-alignment. It is indeed often forgotten that the attachment of Asia to peaceful coexistence sprang from a commitment to a policy of "active" or "positive" neutralism which means precisely a rejection of the division of the world into two hostile systems[343] and rather tries to bring the opposing groups to some measure of agreement.

Perhaps more than anyone else Chou En-lai understood this. From the viewpoint of communist statesmanship he can perhaps be commended for his success in allaying the fears of the other states. As a result other Asian states have shown their willingness to ap-

its existence the Socialist Chinese People's Republic, basing itself on the principle of peaceful coexistence, has strongly emphasized good relations with the "nationalistic" states of Asia and Africa." Yi Li-yu, People's China's Relations with Asian and African Countries," *Int. Aff.* (Moscow) 75 (1959). See also Ting Hsi-lin, "New Gains for the Principle of Peaceful Coexistence," *People's China*, No. 16 (Aug. 16, 1954) at 6 (1954).

340 See Aaron and Reynolds, *supra* note 302, at 285.

341 The flexibility (or opportunism) of the Soviet position also appears from Khvostov's article in which he states, disregarding Lenin's theory, that "the peaceful character of Soviet Foreign Policy is *not of a temporary nature* (italics added here), nor is it mere tactics or propaganda. It is a permanent and inalienable feature of Socialist foreign policy ..." Khvostov, *supra* note 302, at 7.

342 *Supra* at 2.

343 See e.g. Mahadevan, "India's Policy of Non-Alignment," 2 *I.Y.I.A.* 89–105 (1953); Morgenthau, "Neutrality and Neutralism," 11 *Y.B. W.A.* 47–75 (1957); Denis Healy, *Neutralism* (1955); Fenwick, "The Legal Aspects of Neutralism," 51 *A.J.I.L.* 71 (1957).
The relationship between *Panch Shila* and peaceful coexistence is illustrated by President Sukarno of Indonesia who stated, while discussing the Indonesian *Pantja Sila* as the guiding principles of his country's foreign policy: "A non-alignment policy in this present world of division into two antagonistic power blocs is nothing but logically consistent with our higher principles." Sukarno, "Where do we stand? – Where do we go?", 1 *Indonesia*, no. 1, at 4 (1954); see also Fifield, *op. cit. supra* note 325, at 110.

proach Communist China on the basis of "tolerance and live together in peace." The acceptance of this common ground, however vague, is in the eyes of the Asians the one positive point which has emerged from the entire discussion on peaceful coexistence.

However, Asian states should examine more closely whether such a commitment to live together in peace indeed is enough ground for real peaceful coexistence. For if they do, they will probably run into other such substantial differences of opinion as those already dealt with above. For instance, it is natural that, if differences occur in the interpretation of *Panch Shila*, states will fall back on their own interpretation of these principles. This, however, may pose new problems. To take one example, Indonesia would in such a case probably refer to her own principles of *Pantja Sila*[344] which is mentioned in the Constitution and is made the basis of the state.[345] It provides the guiding principles for all foreign relations. The Indonesian *Pantja Sila* includes: 1. Belief in God (and the rejection of atheism), 2. Humanitarianism or internationalism (but not in the sense of "cosmopolitanism" since "this denies the existence of such nations as Indonesia, Japan, Burma...")[346] 3. Nationalism, 4. Democracy, and 5. Social Justice.[347] An effort to reconcile this concept with the communist example might run into difficulties with regard to the first two principles.

After the discussion of the theoretical aspect of peaceful coexistence one might wonder what the actual practices of this concept so far has been in Asia. Unlike the Soviet Union, Asians have not felt an urge to change or alter their views of international law in order to bring it in line with this doctrine. There was no need for that for, as they see it, all five principles have already been covered by contemporary international law.[348]

[344] This Indonesian term, which is derived from Sanskrit, has been adopted by Mr. Nehru to indicate the Five Principles of Peaceful Coexistence, although now spelled in the Sanskrit way. See Fifield, *supra* note 325, at 510.

[345] Sukarno, *supra* note 343, at 2–5; Hatta, "Indonesia's Foreign Policy," 31 *For. Aff.* 450 (1953).

[346] Sukarno, "Pantja Sila – The Basic Philosophy of the Indonesian State," 1 *Indonesian Review* 15 (1951).

[347] *Id.* at 16–17; See also Human Relations Area Files, *Handbook on Indonesia,* Part II at 803 (1956); Yamin, *Proklamasi dan Konstitusi Republik Indonesia* (Proclamation and Constitution of the Republic of Indonesia) 108–117 (1951).

[348] Prof. Chacko, for instance, comes to the conclusion that all five principles of peaceful coexistence are included in the Charter of the U. N. Chacko, *supra* note 295, at 39–41. For a discussion of peaceful coexistence in the light of the Charter of the U.N. (before the time that peaceful coexistence became such a popular concept), see Berlia, "International Law and Russo-American co-existence," 79 *Journal du Droit Int.* 27–47

As far as the actual success of this doctrine in Asia is concerned, it is obviously impossible to expect a clear-cut affirmative or negative answer. As in the case of neutralism opinions differ. At first non-Asians were very sceptical, as one will remember, about the viability of such a neutralist attitude, and they even regarded it as a lack of a sense of responsibility for the future of this world.[349] Asians, however, have pointed with some pride to the present record which shows that such an attitude was not only possible but might even be commendable.[350] This significant change of world opinion on neutralism has given Asians a tremendous boost in self-confidence and convinced them at the same time that even in the contemporary world it is better to believe in one's own convictions than to succumb to outside opinions.

The same difference of opinion exists with respect to *Panch Shila*. If one were to look, for instance, at the peaceful solution of the Sino-Burman border dispute[351] one might well say that *Panch Shila* have been applied successfuly. On the other hand, if one would point to the Sino-Indian frontier conflict,[352] where military force has been used by the Chinese, arousing so much resentment in India that many were willing to react militantly, then perhaps *Panch Shila* has failed in this respect. Only the coming years will enable us to to give a more exact answer to this question.

However, there is one evident advantage of the Asian concept of peaceful coexistence. Unlike the Soviet doctrine it is not suspect in Western countries. They might, therefore, be more willing to accept the Asian *Panch Shila* as a basis for mutual international relations and thus enlarge considerably the number of states adhering to the Five Principles.

Summarizing, it can be said of the picture of the Asian attitude toward peaceful coexistence that the chances of success are not wholly non-existent. On the contrary. Aaron and Reynolds came to the conclusion in their article that peaceful coexistence is "based on false premises, its validity is denied by the facts of the present situation, and as a guide to policy it leads into the wilderness." They

(1952), and Lyon-Caen, "International Law and the Coexistence, in a State of Peace, of States with Opposing Political Systems," 79 *Journal du Droit Int.* 49–83 (1952).

[349] Fifield, *op. cit. supra* note 325, at 110.

[350] See *e.g.* President Eisenhower at a press conference on June 6, 1956 (quoted by Morgenthau, *supra* note 342, at 47), and Gaitskell, the British Labour leader in a similar statement (*N.Y. Times*, May 24, 1956, "Gaitskell departs, sees shift on India.")

[351] *Supra* Chapter III at 115.

[352] *Supra* Chapter III at 163.

arrived at this conclusion[353], however, after a careful analysis of the concept as it developed in the world of rigid and self-defeating Marxist philosophy. As has been tried to show above, the Asian concept of peaceful coexistence is not rigid, less theoretical, unsophisticated, perhaps even naive, but precisely for these reasons its chances of success are greater than the Soviet concept of peaceful coexistence.[354]

[353] Aaron and Reynolds, *supra* note 302, at 296.

[354] Recently much has been written and speculated upon an alleged difference of opinion between the Soviet Union and Communist China on the meaning and implications of peaceful coexistence. The Chinese are said to be unwilling to renounce, in the spirit of peaceful coexistence, the revolutionary wars against imperialism. "Peking on Coexistence," 38 *For. Aff.* 676–681 (1960). Whatever the truth of this statement may be, one observation can perhaps be made here in respect of Asia. Whenever the policy of peaceful coexistence runs into difficulties between the leading powers, Asian states often show an inclination to revert to an attitude of neutralism in order to stay out of the cold war.

CHAPTER IV

CONCLUSIONS

An appraisal of the above material will now be made in the light of the question whether the practices of the Asian nations dealt with above have contributed positively – or perhaps negatively – to the development of international law.[1] It is proposed here to discuss this matter under the following headings:

(1) The attitudes of the Asian states as appear from their past practices.

(2) The contributions of these states to the development of international law.

(3) Some speculations on their future attitudes.

One remark should be made first. Since the primary aim of this work is to contribute to a clarification of Asian views, it is to the claims and expectations of these nations, *as they see and state them*, that the greatest attention will be given. If ever a fair appraisal of practices can be made, it should be made with a clear understanding of the ambitions, claims and expectations of those who are the subject of observation and discussion. The important question is, therefore, *what* the Asian nations themselves think. The question as to what they *should* think can only be considered after having made oneself acquainted with the answers to the first question. It may well be that a discussion of the second question will be very critical of the outcome of the first one. So be it, if only that criticism has been arrived at after due consideration has been given to what the Asian states think themselves. Then the result can only be to the benefit of these Asian nations. On the other hand, if criticism is poured out over these countries without regard for their own attitude, nor for the compulsion of certain facts, criticism will only cause more resentment. Especailly an attitude of ill-concealed self-righteousness on the part of older states who claim that they themselves abide by "established rules of international law," implying that the new states act as irresponsible, young members of a family

[1] See *supra* at 25.

of nations, arouses angry protests from these young nations and not always without justification. If anything, these new nations have quickly discovered that international relations today are carried out primarily on the basis of hard facts, and that there is much lip service and hypocrisy. A more realistic approach to international relations is desirable in all parties concerned.

THE ATTITUDES OF THE NEW ASIAN STATES

Soon after the entry of the new nations into the world community non-Asian observers, from a tentative examination of the first practices of these Asian states, came to the conclusion that Asian attitudes toward the "established rules of international law" would be selective: they would choose whatever they thought to be useful to and compatible with their own views, but reject the remainder as not, or no longer, applicable.[2] Is there any reason for such an expectation?

In the past when wars were recognized instruments of policy, international law has frequently been used as a justification of violence and aggression once the objective was successfully achieved. To expect now of the new states, so often in the past subjected to such violence and aggression, that they should abide by "established rules of international law," often seems like telling a maltreated child, finally grown up and become stronger than the parent, that he should behave. The child may want to do so, but will not necessarily wish to accept all rules of conduct set by the once stronger adult. This point is mentioned because it touches upon two important aspects which will be discussed first, namely,

(1) the influence of historical facts, and
(2) the value of moral arguments.
Then the discussion will be continued with
(3) an appraisal of the actual practices of the Asian states, followed by
(4) some other observations.

1. Historical Considerations

The importance of historical facts for these Asian nations is

[2] See e.g. quotation of Brierly in Chapter I *supra* at 21.

evident. Their present state is the apex of a development which goes far back into history. It deals with the important place which nationalism occupies in the thoughts of Asians. Nationalism has been the starting point of their views in the years of the struggle for independence. It is still the basis of their present activities. It will remain an important consideration in the immediate future in spite of the other world trend toward greater regional and international integration. Especially in new countries – and their number is increasing steadily – there is a growing nationalistic desire to develop the indigenous community and culture to the fullest extent. This nationalistic desire is indeed not only characteristic for Asia and Africa; in the Pacific and in South America the same tendency can be perceived.

Few people today deny the existence and influence of nationalism. The significance of this development in international relations is today generally acknowledged. Too often, however, this is an acknowledgement springing from goodwill and liberal thought. Too rarely it comes from a clear realization of the meaning, power and impact of nationalism. In Chapter II it has been attempted to show how certain doctrines of traditional international law are based on distortions of historical data, the final exposure of which has a far-reaching effect on the validity of certain doctrines, e.g. with regard to the status of ancient Asian states and of colonies. For, historical distortions, whether made deliberately or not, inevitably undermine the theories which are built on them. This is not only true for Asia; it can be observed elsewhere. Kennan, in his article on peaceful coexistence,[3] severely criticizes the Soviet leaders – and rightly so – for distorting history in order to attack the capitalist position. Such an attitude makes an honest reconciliation of two opposing views, and the fair balancing of two conflicting claims, impossible since the factual basis of a conflict is all-important.

But there is a more direct reason why history occupies such an important place in the practices of international law by these new Asian states. The process of creating authoritative prescriptions took place in the past without the active participation of the new Asian states which were then only colonies. Those prescriptions, of course, may have such inherent merits that they are even acceptable to any new member of the world community. Yet, when applied to a particular case, they cannot be more than one of the relevant con-

[3] Kennan, "Peaceful Coexistence – A Western View," 38 *For. Aff.* 172 (1960).

siderations. In the process of balancing claims the position in the past must also be taken into consideration. Now, here comes the point. When it comes to the past of these Asian states, i.e. their past practices of international law, it is not the immediate past that counts, for during that time they were excluded from direct participation in the decision making process. Therefore, the past to them means often two, three or more centuries ago. It leads us nowhere to hold that that past is irrelevant and that modern international law is only three or four centuries old. Such an attitude is not only too legalistic, but it is clearly disproved by present practices which do take account of ancient history. In the Minquiers and Ecrehos dispute, for instance, the significance of historical facts came up for discussion. Although it is often still said that international law started in the 16th and 17th century, the World Court had to examine treaties and facts which go back as far as the 11th century[4].

This point is even more important for the new Asian states. Having been excluded from any decision making for the last few centuries they will now often fall back on earlier history, on a time when they did play an active role in international relations. In fact, Asian states do not regard themselves as really "new" or "young" states, but as the successors of formerly existing political entities the independence of which has been interrupted for a few centuries. Often they do not speak of the establishment of their state, but of its *re*-establishment. This is a point of some importance which frequently returns in Asian thinking, whether it is exactly true or not.[5]

In the above discussion in Chapter III of recent practices of Asian states we have repeatedly run into historical arguments. In the Burma-China border disputes China claimed to have rights going as far back as the 3rd century, while the entire matter of vassalage demands a careful scrutiny of historical records.[6] With respect to the Kashmir borderline (especially in Ladakh) arguments were heard that the boundary was "fixed from ancient times."[7] Finally, the Indonesian position with respect to the claims of sovereignty in the waters of the Indonesian archipelago rested for a large part on the argument that from time immemorial the Indonesian archipelago has formed one unit.[8]

[4] *Reports I.C.J.* 47–109 at 53 (1953).
[5] In Africa too reference is frequently made to ancient empires, *e.g.* the Mali empire.
[6] *Supra* at 121.
[7] *Supra* at 163.
[8] *Supra* at 175.

A more recent affirmation of the significance of historical facts for the development of international law can be found in a resolution of the Geneva Conference on the Law of the Sea in 1958 which recommended the study of the juridical regime of historic waters, including historic bays.[9] It is clear from these facts that there is a need for a new, less biased, and more enlightened study of history and its impact on the development of international law.

2. *The Value of Moral Arguments*

The second consideration, closely connected with the independability of the historical accounts and the occurrence of historic distortions, is the issue of morality. For the Asians they are indeed inseparably linked since they regard the entire colonial era as a period of immoral subjugation by foreign powers. Even if colonial expansion was admissible during a time when war was a legitimate instrument of policy, there still remains the matter of continuing colonial domination which in Asian eyes was morally reprehensible. This basic but difficult controversy, which also touches upon the different sense of time between the Eastern and the Western world, has been discussed by Professor Julius Stone and Justice Pal. Professor Stone rejects Justice Pal's contention that "no present war can be unjust" and that the present interest of Western powers in the Eastern hemisphere may have been formerly acquired "through armed violence" and cannot therefore be just.[10] Whatever the truth of the matter, it does not help to solve the problem by closing one's eyes to these moral arguments. Western nations cannot deny a responsibility by refusing to look at the problem with a bad conscience. Statements to that effect ignore the fact that it was not the East but the West which came to propagate the idea that colonial powers have the responsibility of developing their colonial subjects into full and equal members of their community with all concomitant rights and duties. Terms like "sacred trust" and the "white man's burden" were not coined by Eastern nations. They have for some decades been the official policy of many colonial administrations. Liberal Western thinkers have also continually told the colonial subjects that they were entitled to demand the recognition of their full rights. This is a point to the credit of

[9] U. N. Doc. No. A/Conf. 13/L. 56.
[10] Stone, *Aggression and World Order*, 143 (1958).

Western democracy, and it seems therefore rather strange that now voices are heard in the West which urge that the argument be dropped as to who must be held responsible for the present state of world affairs.[11] Such may be the attitude of an earnest and impartial scholar, but it is unrealistic to expect of the Asian leaders who have led their peoples through long years of cruel and ruthless struggle to independence that they should just drop the argument of responsibility.

Morality, therefore, still plays an important part in the considerations of Asian nations. That this applies even in their post-independence practices is illustrated by their present policies whether they concern self-determination, neutralism, non-alignment or peaceful coexistence.[12] This will probably remain so the first few years. One may disapprove of such a moralistic approach but when dealing with Asian nations one should at least be aware of the existence of such an attitude.

3. The Actual Practices of the New Asian States

What is most remarkable in these practices is the simultaneous occurrence of a legalistic as well as a non-legalistic approach. It is perhaps surprising to find Asians adopt a legalistic attitude since it is generally held that they have an aversion of legalistic theories.[13] Yet this attitude becomes more obvious if one goes a little deeper into the matter.

This point is perhaps best illustrated by the use of the term sovereignty which for the Asians has often had the connotation of an absolute authority of almost mystical quality which makes them independent of any community control. This, too, can be explained historically. In their struggle for independence the Asian nations have run into seemingly insurmountable legal barriers. In fact, the political and legal history of the Asian colonies show various examples in which the interest of the colonial ruler is upheld by the manipulation of a legal interpretation. Such an attitude, of course, is not only a feature of a colonial administration. Every institution which has established its vested interests will often depend

[11] See Kennan, *supra* note 3, at 190.
[12] Mahadevan makes the statement that "politics must be fair."
Mahadevan, "India's Policy of Non-Alignment," 2 *I.Y.I.A.* 97 (1953).
[13] *Supra* at 23.

for its defence on a dogmatic attitude. Sovereignty, dependence and recognition were legal barriers which at one time or other barred the Asian way to statehood. Consequently the resented legal barriers became the subject of their ambitions. Once statehood was achieved they applied those doctrines with all the connotations of absolute authority which they seemed to have during their struggle for independence.

There is another reason. It is true that in the closed village communities, which are still predominant in Asia, life is regulated not by rigid legal rules but by a balancing of interests of the community as well as of the individual. However, it is too naive to draw from this fact the conclusion that such an attitude will also be adopted in the handling of state affairs. The basis for a modern state – and it is a modern state that all new nations aspire to become – was inherited from the Western colonial rulers and is thus of a clearly western nature. The colonies had been run with the help of Western type political and administrative bodies. The Civil Service, for instance, though composed of mainly native officials, was a typical Western institution. Finally, the national leaders, who now fill the top functions once held only by foreigners, are mostly men with a high degree of education, often acquired at Western institutions of learning. Faced with the task of guiding their nation in an increasingly dynamic world these leaders believe they serve the interests of their country best by trying to turn it as quickly as possible into a modern state which can deal with the other members of the world community on equal terms. In view also of their Western legal education, it is understandable that in the shaping of their policies these leaders have come to adopt all Western ways in defending their claims, the legal method as well, if that can asure them greater chance of success. The clearest illustration is provided by the Kashmir dispute where the contending parties have thrown in all legal arguments which they could possibly find, including aggression, invasion, accession, non-aggression, state succession, self-defence, self-determination, domestic jurisdiction and fraudulous treaty. With respect to authority in her archipelago Indonesia also resorted partly to a legal defence of her claims in order to put her main point across to the world community. In so doing these countries have deliberately decided to walk the difficult path of legal interpretation and it seems that they have thereby fallen into some of the same traps which their Western predecessors have been unable to avoid. In their respect for the rule of law coupled with their desire to give their arguments the hall-mark of legality, Asians have often concentrated particularly on the legal aspects. This, of course, is the right of every decision maker, but in their anxiety to apply the relevant rules of law Asians too have frequently been guilty of applying such rules mechanically without giving due consideration to the context in which these rules belong. The preceding discussion in Chapter III testifies to this fact. A few other examples may be added for further clarification on the point of mechanical application and the overemphasis of legal technicalities.

In Chapter II it has been attempted to prove with regard to Burma that, on the basis of the origin and underlying principles of the laws of military occupation, the creation of an independent state by the Japanese occupant is not necessarily contrary to international law.[14] One is, of course, entitled to disagree with this contention, but then such a different viewpoint should be based on more than just a reference to a textbook rule or some cases as is sometimes done. For instance, in one of the cases decided after the war by a Burmese Court[15] it was held that the Japanese had no powers under international law to confer independence on Burma for

> Oppenheim has stated on p. 342 of his International Law, vol. II, 6th edition, Revised, 'As the right of an occupant in occupied territory is merely a right of administration, he may neither annex it, while the war continues, nor set it up as an independent state.'[16]

In the Indonesian case an identical support by textbook material has been advanced. Looking for theories in support of their archipelago-concept the Indonesian authorities give almost a verbal reproduction of the examples given by Professor François in his Manual of International Law which is the basic textbook for all those who have had their legal training in Dutch universities.

On the other hand, nobody is more aware of the causes of this insufficiency in the practices of international law than the Asians themselves. The absence of adequate teaching and training in international law is fully realized and much regretted. As long as no increase can be expected in the number of Asian lawyers who can

[14] *Supra* at 92.

[15] Krishna Chettiar v. Subbiya Chettiar, High Court of Burma, 5 April 1948, *Annual Digest* 537–548, at 544 (Case no. 178) (1948).

[16] Maung Maung, *Burma in the Family of Nations* 101 (1956).

devote themselves to the study and practices of international law, a situation will remain which has so aptly been described by an Asian writer in the following way:[17]

> With concentrated and specialist research on international law so deficient, the tendency is to rely mainly on textbooks, which are frequently cited in courts. Since the national judicial or executive organs have yet to apply their minds independently to many international law questions, no authoritative local decisions or statements on those questions are available, and the practice is to hurriedly consult textbooks when an immediate need arises. Thus the limit of territorial sea, to take an example is generally accepted as three miles from the low water mark because the text books lay down that limit .... Text-book writers therefore wield great authority in Burma and those who are most frequently consulted are, naturally, British and American jurists.

As is said above, however, there is a counterpart to the legalistic approach, for at the same time Asian states characteristically show a decided interest in non-legalistic arguments. It is today generally accepted that the binding nature of law is a less dogmatic concept in Asia than in the advanced countries of other parts of the world. This observation applies, of course, rather to the binding nature of native law than to that of Western law which has also been adopted by the legal systems of these Asian states. With regard to commercial law, for instance, European principles have been adopted and applied in the same way as in their countries of origin. Bills of lading, credit transactions and insurance regulations are as commonly used here as in the Western countries. As regards native customary law, however, the question is quite different. In civil cases, and even in criminal cases in so far as they have been left to the jurisdiction of the village authorities the object is not so much to apply relevant legal rules, but rather to bring parties together in an effort to compose their differences through a better understanding of their conflicting points of view.[18] This preference for conciliation rather than an application of the legal rule idea may be attributed to the basic principles of the village dwellers who have come to see their existence in the context of a divine harmony. Their task in this life is to conserve and prevent any disturbance of the highly regarded harmony. If such a disturbance is nevertheless brought about by a violation of the customary rules by one of the village members then the first concern of the village is to restore the divine harmony. The punishment of the violator is a secondary consideration; in

[17] *Id.* at 128.
[18] Thayer, *Southeast Asia in the Coming World*, 244 (1953).

fact, if the desired restoration can be achieved without punishing the culprit, no such action will be taken. Such a practice illustrates the relatively subordinate role which legal rules play in the lives of the people a majority of whom still live under the regime of a closed village system in spite of the modern, Western influences which have been introduced by the European rulers. Today the modernization is continued by the native governments. In their desire to lift up their people to a higher level of existence the Asian leaders themselves now try to introduce modern Western institutions. The urgency and speed with which these introductions are carried out are matters which are open to debate, and it is often maintained that the country should fall back on its own traditional values in order to develop into a healthy community. All that is intended here is to point out the basically non-legal attitude of Asian people as a result of a different attitude towards the value of legal rules.

The ambivalent nature of their attitude clearly appears from an examination of the three cases of Chapter III where legalistic and non-legalistic arguments have been applied simultaneously or alternatingly. Yet it can be said that for a peaceful settlement of these disputes there seems to be a preference for methods which have a non-binding nature, (e.g. negotiations, enquiry, mediation, conciliation) rather than those with binding force (such as arbitration and judicial settlement).[19] The latter have clearly been used less frequently. With respect to judicial settlement, for instance, it can be observed that few Asian nations have accepted the compulsory jurisdiction of the International Court of Justice and they have shown a marked reluctance to invoke the Court's assistance in settling their disputes.[20] In the case between India and Portugal on the right of passage, where India was forced to appear before the Court, she raised no less than six preliminary exceptions to contest the jurisdiction of the Court in this particular case.[21]

Under these circumstances it is obvious that the most adequate means of settlement are those which leave the parties free to balance and adjust their claims during the process of decision making, i.e. the diplomatic instrument of policy. In all three cases of Chapter III parties, after rejecting judicial settlement, have ultimately shown

[19] See Nehru's rejection of arbitration in the Kashmir case, *supra* at 166.
[20] See *infra* at 233.
[21] Thomas, *The Right of Passage over Indian Territory*, 6–24 and 46–55 (1959).

their willingness and even their preference to discuss the claims and counterclaims by way of negotiations. That such a policy can indeed lead to a successful result is proved by the peaceful settlement of the Burma-Yunnan border disputes. That it is not perfect appears from the experiences in the two other examples (i.e. Kashmir and the Indonesian territorial waters).

4. Other Observations

After the above analysis of the practices of the new Asian states a direct answer must be given to the basic question which has become one of the leading topics today, namely, the impact of the emergence of so many new states on the authority of traditional international law, and possible resentments towards that system.[22]

There are indeed good reasons for Asian states to resent traditional international law. It has often been an obstacle rather than a help for their national aspirations. The position of a colony under international law was minimized and the transition of such a territory into an independent state met with great barriers of doctrines of international law. Traditional international law has not given enough attention to the creation of ways to peaceful change. Asian states have never accepted the idea that the creation of colonial empires must ultimately be accepted as a legitimate act. The subsequent sanctioning by international law of such acts must have given them the impression, especially before the second World War, that international law could be used to justify such acts once successfully accomplished.

A second consideration is whether the deep-rooted changes in the structure of the present world which involve the rejection of hitherto generally accepted and basic ideologies,[23] warrant an attitude of upholding the sanctity of traditional international law as a system applying to all peoples in all circumstances. One cannot deny that there is at least some justification in a contention that a colonial revolution by a population which differs racially, ethnically, religiously and culturally from the legitimate rulers must be distinguished from an overthrow of the legitimate government of, for instance, a West-European country whose government is produced and chosen by the same population. Although there is a

[22] Brierly, *The Law of Nations* 44 (1949).
[23] See Chapter I, *supra* at 17.

similarity with the Russian revolution,[24] the colonial uprising has, in a way, even a more outspoken revolutionary character, for the new Soviet leaders emerged in fact from the same people as the former rulers.

It is perhaps best to let the facts speak for themselves by examining the three above mentioned cases of Chapter III. Does such an examination prove the truth of the view that the new Asian states choose rather arbitrarily from traditional international law what they are willing to accept and then reject the remainder? It certainly does not appear so from the Burma-China border dispute, nor from the Kashmir conflict. The former is not concerned with any resentment towards traditional international law since it is essentially a question as to whose claims to the border area are substantiated by strongest evidence. As for the Kashmir case, it is the outstanding example showing that new Asian states do not always reject international law. As we have seen parties have advanced an amazing array of doctrines of international law, relevant as well as irrelevant, in order to build up their case.

On the other hand, the third example of Indonesia and the Law of the Sea does bring an Asian state into conflict with Western views and then there is indeed more reason to expect a rejection of certain parts of international law. What then has been the actual reaction in this instance?

International conferences, like the Geneva Conference on the Law of the Sea, have this great merit that they force participating states to give a clear explanation of their country's position. This is of particular importance when many new states participate which have seldom before made a clear statement of their position. At the Geneva Conference we find indeed that Asian representatives have come out with statements which clearly emphasize that they did not regard themselves bound by certain prescriptions which were made at a time when they could not participate in the decision making process.[25] This attitude has been sharply criticized, among others by Mr. Loftus Becker,[26] Legal Adviser to the State Department, who stated:

[24] Lyon-Caen, "International Law and the Coexistence, in a State of Peace, of States with Opposing Political Systems," 79 *Journal du Droit Int.* 53 (1952).

[25] See *supra* at 201.

[26] Becker, in an address made before the Am. Soc. Int. Law, Washington 26 April 1958, 38 *Dept. of State Bull.* 835 (1958).

> In large measure at the Conference such (new) states made no serious effort to weigh the advantages they might retain by maintaining the freedom of the seas.... They opposed the three-mile limit on the ground that it had been adopted by the major maritime powers before they had come into existence. For that reason alone the pre-existing rule had to be changed. That was regarded as progress.

Is this a fair criticism? Though it might hold true for certain incidental cases, in its generality it is too sweeping and therefore unfair.[27] This is proved by several facts.

Firstly, it is unfair to accuse of ill-will countries which do not agree with the three-mile limit if that so-called rule has never been fully accepted as authoritative, not even by the pre-war family of nations which was predominantly Western. Secondly, the new states in Asia themselves disagree with each other on the width of the territorial sea.[28] Moreover, Indonesia and the Philippines did not receive much support for their archipelago concept from their immediate Asian neighbours either. This proves that the youth of a state is only coincidental with its opposition to certain parts of traditional international law. Thirdly, though related to the preceding point, it is hard to deny that the new Asian states who support the more-than-three-mile proposition do that for the simple reason that their interests seem to demand that. Those states which, equally new and Asian, do not claim more than a three-mile limit, act in this way because they have no interest in a broader limit. It is therefore incorrect to imply, as Mr. Becker's statement seems to do, that the partial failure of the conference is due to the irresponsible and egoistic attitude of "new states." Their deviating attitude mostly concerned matters which have never been universally accepted (such as the three-mile limit of territorial sea, and the protection of interests of underdeveloped countries in the living resources of the high seas). The record of the Geneva Conference, as well as the discussion in Chapter III, shows that there is *no* arbitrary rejection of international law as being a product created before they became independent. There is only a resentment towards certain parts of international law if they are felt to lead to unfair practices or if they give too little attention to the particular

[27] Fortunately, Mr. Becker's statement does not seem to be very representative of U.S. opinion. Mr. Dean, the Head of the American delegation said in his closing statement that "Every country must be the judge of its own position and needs, and, while we are disappointed, we have nothing to say about the decision made here." 38 *Dept. of State Bull.* 1110 (1958). See also Jessup, "The Geneva Conference on the Law of the Sea," 52 *A.J.I.L* 731 (1958).

[28] See the Synoptical Table of Some Asian Claims, *supra* at 204.

claims and interests. Such an attitude cannot be said to be arbitrary. It is perhaps the universal attitude of all participants in the world power process. On the other hand, it might be said that if the claims of these new states are approached not only with the yardstick of so-called established international law, but also with a willingness to balance their exclusive claims against the inclusive claims of other nations and the world community as a whole, some reasonable solution might be arrived at which gives due consideration to all parties.

Actually it is surprising that in certain quarters the influx of so many new states is immediately received with fears for a decline of the system of international law. History gives examples to the contrary. New states (especially if not very powerful) are only too keen on declaring their adherence to the prescriptions of the established public order system. They sense very clearly that in the beginning of their existence an arbitrary behaviour might not win them the recognition and sympathy which they certainly need during their first steps in the world arena.[29] Of course, it does not mean that a statement at the beginning of their existence as a state, to the effect that they recognize the full force of traditional international law, is evidence of a complete adherence to that system. But the initial attitude is a willingness to accept international law, though perhaps with reservations, and not an arbitrary selection of what they regard as useful or not. There is a significant difference between the two positions.

Finally, the connection between "new state" and a rejection of international law is disproved by the acceptance of the compulsory jurisdiction of the World Court by some of these nations. Of the 39 countries which in 1960 had deposited their declarations accepting the jurisdiction of the Court, 12 were European countries, 12 American, 4 African, Australia, New Zealand and 9 Asian (Cambodia, Nationalist China, India, Japan, Pakistan, the Philippines, Thailand, and further Israel and Turkey).[30] The acceptance of the compulsory jurisdiction means (unless rigid reservations are made) that the new states are willing to subject themselves to the authority of traditional international law as applied by the World Court. It is true that the number of Asian states accepting the

[29] See for a similar attitude of Russia after the Revolution, Snyder and Bracht, "Coexistence and International Law," 7 *I.C.L.Q.* 55 (1958).

[30] *Yearbook I.C.J.* 233–256 (1959-1960).

Court's jurisdiction has been small but "older" states show an equal hesitancy to do so. Therefore, it can be said that complaints of arbitrary practice by new states are exaggerated and incorrect.

THE CONTRIBUTION OF THE NEW ASIAN STATES TO THE DEVELOPMENT OF INTERNATIONAL LAW

From the discussion in the preceding chapters it appears that the main contributions of the Asian states have been in four particular fields:

(1) The process of transition of colonies into independent states.
(2) Self-determination.
(3) Neutralism.
(4) Peaceful coexistence.

1. The Colonial Issue

The colonial development has now come to a climax. In the quest for final recognition as independent states those territories which may be regarded in all respects as standing upon the threshold of independence are joined by dependent areas which according to traditional standards will not be ready for it for a long time to come. Since the facts cannot be ignored it is worthwhile to examine the significance of this issue.

Firstly, such an examination might enrich the law of nations with more adequate historical material on the law and diplomacy of these new states in the time that they existed as independent entities in the past. In fact, scholars of Asia are doing such spade work now[31] and in the short time that these studies have been carried out they have already been able to expose certain incorrect premises on which some doctrines of traditional international law have been built.

But the attitude is not only restricted to a historical review and research. For the first time Asian states themselves are testing the established doctrines of international law on their own views and practices thereby stating approval as well as criticism. In doing so they contribute positively to the development of international law.

[31] See *e.g.* Chapter II *supra* note 3.

Still another aspect of the colonial issue can be seen in the new forms of association which are established by former colonies with the metropolitan countries. Under the impact of new ideas of colonial relationship all countries administering such colonial territories have either voluntarily or involuntarily found new forms of integration or association with their dependencies.

Finally the impact on international organizations is undeniable. One of the most amazing developments in this field is perhaps that under the influence of the rapid growth of the number of states the principle of equality, which so far has often been treated as sacrosanct is now being attacked for various reasons.[32] The folly of a war today and the consequent greater significance of peaceful and democratic procedures increase the significance of the vote of every state, even the smallest one. Here again two views are expressed. The first one, frequently heard today, condemns the atomization of the world community which is said to lead to sheer chaos as a result of the manipulation of and bargaining with votes. Another more hopeful voice states quite the opposite view that practices of international organizations show the remarkable picture, not of atomization but regionalization in the voting patterns, and those regions, often called blocs, do in fact contribute to the stability and efficiency of the international organization.[33]

2. *Self-determination*

The question of self-determination, an inseparable part of the colonial issue, has now become the logical outcome of the accelerated development of dependent peoples toward a greater participation in the shaping and sharing of values. This idea of self-determination is now generally recognized and justified. Its implementation, however, often leads to great difficulties. Therefore the Asian states, which have contributed so much to this field, are not yet released from their responsibility to develop this doctrine further. Moreover, although they are themselves the pioneers and defenders of this doctrine they have not been very successful in reconciling this doctrine with the aspirations of minority groups in their own national communities.[34]

[32] The principle of "weighted voting" has become more popular now.
[33] Goodwin, "The expanding U. N.," 36 *Int. Aff.* 182–185 (1960).
[34] Fifield, *The Diplomacy of Southeast Asia*, 164, 213–214 (1958).

3. Neutralism

For a while the term neutralism was widely used, not the least in the Asian world. Today its popularity has been bypassed by the doctrine of peaceful coexistence.[35] The loss of popularity can easily be explained. Neutralism sprang from the idea that the two great power blocs were inevitably headed for a war. In the event of such a disaster the new Asian nations which have hardly started their existence and felt no close links to either bloc, reserved for themselves the right to play a neutralist role, be it passive or active. More recently, however, the prevailing policy has become that neither bloc would have any advantage in a war since that would result in total destruction of all parties. The alternative became therefore a policy of peaceful coexistence which was broader in concept than neutralism since it was meant to include all states, Western, Communist and neutralist. However, if the policy of peaceful coenistence fails, the idea of neutralism may gain popularity again.

4. Peaceful Coexistence

This is today a leading policy concept. Because of their clearly neutralist attitudes Asian states have been among the staunchest supporters of this concept. Yet if looked upon with some detachment the picture is less encouraging. While their contributions have certainly been substantial, they have themselves found it difficult at times to apply this doctrine consistently and successfully. International conflicts among themselves remain, e.g. as regards Tibet.

Moreover, countries in Africa have not shown themselves very enthusiastic of peaceful coexistence. This may have several reasons. An important one is perhaps that the African continent today is in a process of ferment. Unlike Asia, Africa is still very much in a spirit of revolution which conflicts with the concept of peaceful coexistence since revolutions mean in the first place war, violence and destruction. For these African nations peaceful coexistence is not enough, not even in the propagated form of peaceful cooperation and peaceful competition. These terms may be attractive to already independent states but to those who are still struggling for independence they mean very little. Something else is needed in addition to the attractive ideology of peaceful coexistence: the possibility of peaceful change. To find the ways and means by which

[35] *Id.* at 110, 175–176, 498.

the possibility may be realized will, therefore, remain the task of all African and Asian countries. The search might help to bring the colonial issue to a quiet close.

FURTHER DEVELOPMENTS

It is a rather hazardous undertaking to speculate on the future international law practices of these new states since, as we have seen, even their present practices are still very much in a state of flux. The thing to do, therefore, is to study carefully all available information about the modes of operation of these new states in order to be able to make some estimates for the future.

When Asian states explain their own views they often use such general terms that their real perspectives and expectations remain vague. The first important occasion on which their views did attain some measure of clarity was at the Asian-African Conference at Bandung in 1955. The objectives of the Conference were more or less a reflection of those ideas which had been the subject of their constant attention and to the development of which they had contributed most. The four issues mentioned in the preceding section[36] thus occupied an important place on the agenda of the Bandung Conference. Besides the promotion of the mutual and common interests of the participants, it was the objective of the Conference to consider problems of special interests such as "problems affecting national sovereignty and of racialism and colonialism," as well as "the contribution they can make to the promotion of world peace and cooperation."[37] If one were to judge the Bandung Conference on the basis of concrete results then the success has perhaps been moderate. The significance of this Conference lies, however, in the meeting of minds which led to a statement of principles. For, general as these principles were, nevertheless they are the driving power of their exponents. It is in this respect that the Conference is indeed a basis for speculation and prediction on the future practices of the participating nations.[38]

It was at the Geneva Conference on the Law of the Sea of 1958

[36] *Supra* at 234.

[37] Min. of Foreign Affairs of the Rep. of Indonesia, *Bulletin of the Asian-African Conference* (no. 1) at 3 (1955).

[38] See Kahin, *The Asian-African Conference*, 32–33 and 36–38 (1956).

that more distinct Asian voices were heard expressing their expectations as to the nature of future prescriptions of international law. As explained above[39] they have to a large extent voiced agreement with existing prescriptions, while at the same time the views of some Asian nations on certain controversial matters have added even more uncertainty to the over-all confusion. It does not seem justified to expect that these nations will in the near future give up their claims which they regard as being of vital importance to their national interest. In the future difficulties are to be expected in the attempts to balance the exclusive national claims on these matters against the inclusive community claims.

Since Asian states express concern over the lack of attention paid to their claims it is understandable that they have a keen interest in the prospects of international law. Already before the Bandung Conference of 1955 India had suggested an Asian collaboration in the field of international law. This led in 1954 to an International Legal Conference where the view was advanced that a permanent organ should be established as the sounding board for traditional Asian views.[40] In 1956 an Asian Legal Consultative Committee was established which had as one of its main purposes the exchange of views on legal matters of common concern,[41] for it was regretted that the views of the International Law Commission were not sufficiently representative of Asian nations.[42] In his opening speech at this Conference Prime Minister Nehru made himself the interpreter of these feelings by stating that, though international law should be uniform, the views of Asian nations should be represented more positively in the course of its development.[43] The Consultative Committee prepared itself along these lines to review the work of the International Law Commission "with particular reference to the interests of the Asian states."

These facts all show an Asian belief in the existence, or at least the desirability, of Asian views, implying at the same time that they might differ from prevailing prescriptions of international law. Two remarks should supplement this point.

[39] *Supra* at 232.

[40] Hafez Ghanem, "The Asian-African Legal Consultative Committee," 14 *Revue Egypt. de Droit Int.* 63 (1958).

[41] Takayanagi and Tanaka, "The First Session of the Asian Legal Consultative Committee," 2 *J.A.I.L.* 110–124 at 110. (1958).

[42] Such views were also heard at the Geneva Conference on the Law of the Sea, among others by the Ceylonese delegate.

[43] Takayanagi and Tanaka, *supra* note 41, at 111.

First of all, the Asian Legal Consultative Committee acted wisely in limiting itself in its first session to a review of less controversial matters, such as legal aid, divorce laws, diplomatic immunities, extradition, state immunity, while other subjects were referred to a next session.[44] These issues, though undoubtedly very important, fall mainly within an area of international law which does not yet show particular Asian views. On the contrary, the similarity with traditional international law is often striking. In contrast, the Committee did not take up the suggestion of Prime Minister Nehru to examine the question of the legality of atomic weapons and their tests, a subject which in Asian public opinion is clearly of the greatest importance.

The second point is, that there should be some caution in referring to *the* Asian view. Participation to this conference was limited to Burma, Ceylon, India, Indonesia, Iraq, Japan and Syria. Though they are clearly representative of Asia and therefore certainly representing Asian views, the composition of the Committee is still too limited to regard this body as the spokesman for *the* Asian view. Important, and even controversial views, can be expected from such leading countries as Communist China and Pakistan.

The trend towards greater coordination in the field of international law in this part of the world received a further boost when African states joined the Committee and in 1958 the Asian-African Legal Consultative Committee convened in Cairo. The number of participants had increased considerably. Besides Burma, Ceylon, India, Indonesia, Iraq, Japan, Sudan, United Arab Republic, the following states or organizations sent observers: Cambodia, the Philippines, Thailand and the League of Arab Nations.[45] As can be seen, some important Asian nations have not yet joined the Committee. As at the first session of the Asian Legal Consultative Committee, the subjects discussed were of a general nature.

One can say of this Asian-African Legal Consultative Committee, therefore, that it revealed a great awareness among its members of the importance of further development of international law, as well as of their right and responsibility to contribute to that development. There was no tendency to disregard arbitrarily certain existing prescriptions simply because they have once been adopted without their participation or consent.

[44] *Id.* at 113–123.
[45] Hafez Ghanem, *supra* note 40, at 65.

In dealing with the subject of this book it has become clear that the new Asian states are partly guided by feelings of resentment towards the Western world. They have good reasons for that. But there is also another side to the problem. No state in Asia, under whatever colonial rule it has lived, can truthfully say that it has not in some way or other benefited or will benefit from the achievements of Western culture. One is inclined to think in this respect only in terms of the technological achievements of the West. Yet it is not only in her adoption of such a technology that Asia has benefited from the West, but also in the intellectual and spiritual contact. The greatest factor, however, which should link these two worlds today is the realization that they have a common interest in the establishment of a legal system which would provide them with prescriptions for their continual and renewed interactions. To arrive ultimately at such a legal system more information should be supplied and processed in order to find prescriptions which do not only represent common expectations, but are considered authoritative as well as deserving application.

It is here that Asians in general, and Asian jurists in particular, can be of great value in providing information and clarification of Asian attitudes. Nobody but the Asian himself knows the feelings and aspirations of his people better; no one but he is able to see, feel and understand all the facts and implications of his country's position. If, therefore, Asians invoke these facts to justify their resentments towards authoritative prescriptions, it is also up to them not only to prove how these facts affect their case, but also to work out alternatives. In doing so they would contribute to the development of international law.

INDEX

T